evangelical awakenings

in AFRICA

evangelical awakenings

in AFRICA

J. EDWIN ORR

BETHANY FELLOWSHIP, INC.
Minneapolis, Minnesota

This edition is a revision and expansion of the book, *Evangelical Awakenings in South Africa*, copyright©1970 by J. Edwin Orr.

Published by Bethany Fellowship, Inc.
6820 Auto Club Road, Minneapolis, Minnesota 55438

Printed in the United States of America

Library of Congress Cataloging in Publication Data:

Orr, James Edwin, 1912-
    Evangelical awakenings in Africa.

    Published in 1970 under title: Evangelical awakenings in South Africa.
    Bibliography: p.
    Includes index.
    1. Revivals—Africa, Sub-Saharan—History.
I. Title.
BV3777.A4077   1975   269'.2'0967   74-32018
ISBN 0-87123-128-X

BV
3711
A258
O 75
1975

TABLE OF CONTENTS

5478

Introduction

EVANGELICAL AWAKENINGS

An Evangelical Awakening is a movement of the Holy Spirit bringing about a revival of New Testament Christianity in the Church of Christ and in its related community. Such an awakening may change in a significant way an individual only; or it may affect a larger group of believers; or it may move a congregation, or the churches of a city or district, or the whole body of believers throughout a country or a continent; or indeed the larger body of believers throughout the world. The outpouring of the Spirit effects the reviving of the Church, the awakening of the masses, and the movement of uninstructed peoples towards the Christian faith; the revived Church, by many or by few, is moved to engage in evangelism, in teaching, and in social action.

Such an awakening may run its course briefly, or it may last a lifetime. It may come about in various ways, though there seems to be a pattern common to all such movements throughout history.

The major marks of an Evangelical Awakening are always some repetition of the phenomena of the Acts of the Apostles, followed by the revitalizing of nominal Christians and by bringing outsiders into vital touch with the Divine Dynamic causing all such Awakenings—the Spirit of God. The surest evidence of the Divine origin of any such quickening is its presentation of the evangelical message declared in the New Testament and its re-enactment of the phenomena therein in the empowering of saints and conversion of sinners.

It is more than interesting to compare the characteristics of the Awakenings of various decades with the prototype of evangelical revivals in the Acts of the Apostles, a perennial textbook for such movements.

Our Lord told His disciples: 'It is not for you to know the times or seasons which the Father has fixed by His own authority. But you shall receive power when the Holy Spirit has come upon you; and you shall be My witnesses . . . to the end of the earth.' Thus was an outpouring of the Spirit predicted, and soon fulfilled.

Then began extraordinary praying among the disciples in the upper room. Who knows what self-judgment and confession and reconciliation went on? There were occasions for such. But, when they were all together in one place, there suddenly came from heaven a sound like the rush of a mighty wind and it filled all the house. The filling of the Holy Spirit was followed by xenolalic evangelism, not repeated in the times of the Apostles nor authenticated satisfactorily since.

The Apostle Peter averred that the outpouring fulfilled the prophecy of Joel, which predicted the prophesying of young men and maidens, the seeing of visions and dreams by young and old. He preached the death and resurrection of Jesus Christ. What was the response? The hearers were pierced, stabbed, stung, stunned, smitten— these are the synonyms of a rare verb which Homer used to signify being drummed to earth. It was no ordinary feeling; nor was the response a mild request for advice. It was more likely an uproar of entreaty, the agonizing cry of a multitude.

Those who responded to the Apostle's call for repentance confessed their faith publicly in the apostolic way. About three thousand were added to the church. Then followed apostolic teaching, fellowship, communion and prayers.

What kind of fellowship? Doubtless the words of Scripture were often used liturgically, but it is certain that the koinonia was open. What kind of prayers? There are instances of individual petitions of power and beauty, but there are also suggestions of simultaneous, audible prayer in which the main thrust of petition is recorded, as in the prophet's day.

The Apostles continued to urge their hearers to change and turn to God, which they did by the thousands. And no hostile power seemed for the moment able to hinder them. Persecution followed, but the work of God advanced.

The events recorded in the Acts have been repeated in full or lesser degree in the Awakenings of past centuries. From the study of Evangelical Revivals or Awakenings in cities and districts, countries and continents, generations and centuries, it is possible to trace a pattern of action and discover a progression of achievement that establish in the minds of those who accept the New Testament as recorded history an undoubted conclusion that the same Spirit of God Who moved the apostles has wrought His mighty works in the centuries preceding our own with the same results but with wider effects than those of which the apostles dreamed in their days of power.

Although the records are scarce, there were Evangelical Awakenings in the centuries before the rise of John Wycliffe, the Oxford reformer. But such movements in medieval times seemed very limited in their scope or abortive in their effect. What was achieved in the days of John Wycliffe—the dissemination of the Scriptures in the language of the people —has never been lost, nor has the doctrine of Scriptural authority. Thus the Lollard Revival led to the Reformation, which would have been unlikely without it; and the principle of appeal to the Word of God in the matter of reform has not been lost either. The Reformation thus led to the Puritan movement in which the essentials of evangelical theology were refined; and the Puritan movement prepared the way for the eighteenth, nineteenth and twentieth century Awakenings occurring in more rapid succession.

A student of church history in general and of the Great Awakenings in particular must surely be impressed by the remarkable continuity of doctrine as well as the continuity of action. Anyone could begin reading the story of the Gospels, continue on into the narrative of the Acts of the Apostles, then without any sense of interruption begin reading the story of the poor preachers of John Wycliffe, the itinerants of the Scottish Covenant, the circuit riders of John Wesley, the readers of Hans Nielsen Hauge in Norway, or the Disciples of the Lord in Madagascar.

Not only so, but the student of such movements would find in the preaching of the Awakenings and Revivals the same message preached and the same doctrines taught in the days of the Apostles. But non-evangelical Christianity, with its accretions of dogma and use of worldly power, would seem a system utterly alien to that of the Church of the Apostles, resembling much more the forces both ecclesiastical and secular that had opposed New Testament Christianity.

The reader of the Acts of the Apostles must surely notice that the Church began to spread by extraordinary praying and preaching. So too the 'upper room' type of praying and the pentecostal sort of preaching together with the irrepressible kind of personal witness find their place in Great Awakenings rather than in the less evangelical ecclesiastical patterns.

The first three centuries of progress were followed by a millenium of changed direction when the Church was united with the State and political force compelled the consciences of men. These centuries are rightly called the Dark Ages, though they were not entirely without light.

Before the fifteenth century, a change began, commencing a progression of awakenings that moved the Church by degrees back to the apostolic pattern and extended it all over the world. Not only were theological dogmas affected and missionary passion created, but society itself was changed.

From the times of the Lollards onward, the impact of the Evangelical Revivals or Awakenings was felt in the realm of personal liberty— knowing the truth made men free, and made them covet freedom for all. Thus the Social Rising of 1381 championed a charter of freedom based on evangelical conviction. Its daughter movement in Bohemia defended its freedom against the forces of tyranny for a century.

The consequent Reformation that soon began in Germany caused such a ferment in men's minds that a rising became inevitable— but it was crushed, only because some of those responsible for the hunger for freedom betrayed it. The hunger for righteousness of the early Puritans brought about another attempt to establish freedom under the law, but, like various ventures before it, the Commonwealth failed because it relied more upon secular force than persuasion.

In the eighteenth, nineteenth and twentieth centuries, the revived Evangelicals re-learned an earlier method. New Testament counsel began to prevail, helping persuade freethinkers and Christians, traditionalists and Evangelicals, that freedom was God's intent for every man, everywhere. Thus the nineteenth century became in itself the century of Christian action, taking Good News to every quarter of the earth, to every phase of life. Those whose hearts the Spirit had touched became the great initiators of reform and welfare and tuned even the conscience of unregenerate men to a sense of Divine harmony in society.

Yet Christians believed that the horizontal relationship of man to men was dependent upon the vertical relationship of man to God, that social reform was not meant to take the place of evangelism, 'so to present Christ in the power of the Spirit that men may come to put their trust in Him as Saviour and to serve Him as Lord in the fellowship of His Church and in the vocations of the common life.'

What may be called the General Awakenings began in the second quarter of the eighteenth century, among settlers in New Jersey and refugees from Moravia about the same time. The First Awakening ran its course in fifty years, and was followed by the Second Awakening in 1792, the Third in 1830, the Fourth in 1858-59, the Fifth in 1905.

1

THE SECOND GENERAL AWAKENING

The infidelity of the French Revolution represented the greatest challenge to Christianity since the time preceding the Emperor Constantine.[1] Christians had endured the threat of the northern barbarians, the assault of the armies of the crescent, the terror of the hordes from the steppes, and an eastern schism and a western reformation. But, until 1789, there had never been such a threat against the very foundations of the Faith, against believing in the God revealed in the Scriptures. Voltaire made no idle boast when he said that Christianity would be forgotten within thirty years.

In France, even the Huguenots apostasized.[2] Deism rode high in every country in Europe, and so-called Christian leaders either capitulated to infidelity or compromised with rationalism. The infant but sturdy nation on the American continent was swept by unbelief, so that the faithful trembled. Between the mailed fist of French military power and the insidious undermining of faith, there seemed no escape.

The spiritual preparation for a worldwide awakening began in Great Britain seven years before the outpouring of the Spirit there.[3] Believers of one denomination after the other, including the evangelical minorities in the Church of England and the Church of Scotland, devoted the first Monday evening of each month to pray for a revival of religion and an extension of Christ's kingdom overseas. This widespread union of prayer spread to the United States within ten years and to many other countries, and the concert of prayer remained the significant factor in the recurring revivals of religion and the extraordinary out-thrust of missions for a full fifty years, so commonplace it was taken for granted by the Churches.

The outbreak of the Revolution in France at first encouraged lovers of liberty in the English-speaking world to hope that liberty had truly dawned in France.[4] When the Terror began, and when military despotism rose, they were fearfully alarmed. The British people decided to fight. In the second year of the Revolution, John Wesley died.

The revival of religion, the second great awakening, began in Britain in late 1791, cresting in power among the Methodists who seemed unafraid of the phenomena of mass awakening.[5] It was also effective among the Baptists and the Congregationalists, though manifested in quieter forms. It accelerated the evangelical revival going on among clergy and laity of the Church of England, strengthening the hands of Simeon and his Eclectic Club and those of Wilberforce in his Clapham Sect—an Evangelical party in the Anglican Establishment which soon became dominant in influence.

At the same time, the principality of Wales was overrun by another movement of revival, packing the churches of the various denominations and gathering unusual crowds of many thousands in the open-air.[6] The revival accelerated the growth of the Baptists and Congregationalists, increased the number of Wesleyan Methodists, and caused the birth of a new denomination, the Calvinistic Methodist Church of Wales, now the Welsh Presbyterians, who separated from the Church of Wales because of its failure to provide either ministers or sacraments for its societies.

Phenomenal awakenings also swept many parts of the kingdom of Scotland, raising up such evangelists as the Haldanes,[7] and such pastoral evangelists as Chalmers in Glasgow and MacDonald in the North. The Scottish revivals began in the teeth of majority opposition in the Church of Scotland but within a generation had evangelized the auld Kirk. The coverage of the Scottish Revival was patchwork, its occurrence sporadic, because of the desperate state of the country. The light prevailed over the darkness.

Not for the first time, nor the last, the unhappy kingdom of Ireland, a majority of whose inhabitants were disfranchized, was rent asunder by turmoil that boiled over into the Rebellion of 1798. In the midst of strife, local awakenings occurred among the Methodists,[8] affecting the evangelical clergy of the Church of Ireland. The Presbyterians of the North were fully occupied contending for orthodoxy against a Unitarian insurgency. Revival brought forth societies for the evangelization of Ulster and the renewal of church life.

This period of revival in the United Kingdom brought forth the British and Foreign Bible Society, the Religious Tract Society, the Baptist Missionary Society, the London Missionary Society, the Church Missionary Society, and a host of auxiliary agencies for evangelism.[9] It produced also some significant social reform, even in wartime.

Before and after 1800, an awakening began in Scandinavia, resembling more the earlier British movements of the days of Wesley and Whitefield, though borrowing from the later British awakening in adopting its home and foreign mission projects, its Bible societies, and the like. In Norway, the revival was advanced by a layman, Hans Nielsen Hauge, who made a lasting impact upon Norway as a nation.[10] Another layman, Paavo Ruotsalainen, expedited the movement in Finland.[11] There were several national revivalists operating then in Sweden, but the influence of George Scott, a British Methodist, later exceeded them all.[12] In Denmark, the revival seemed less potent and was sooner overtaken by a Lutheran confessional reaction, which inhibited the renewal of revival in the 1830s—unlike Norway, Sweden, and Finland, which experienced extensive movements up until the mid-century, Gisle Johnson and Carl Olof Rosenius being the outstanding leaders in Norway and Sweden respectively.

In Switzerland, France, and the Netherlands, the general awakening was delayed until the defeat of Napoleon.[13] A visit to Geneva by Robert Haldane triggered a chain reaction of revival throughout the Reformed Churches of the countries named, raising up outstanding evangelists and missionary agencies. In Holland, the movement was somewhat delayed, and was sooner cramped by confessional reaction among the Dutch Reformed, some of whom objected to state control as well as evangelical ecumenism.

In the German States, the general awakening followed the defeat of Napoleon, and raised up scores of effective German evangelists, such as the Krummachers, Hofacker, Helferich, von Kottwitz, and the von Belows; German theologians, such as Neander and Tholuck; social reformers, such as Fliedner; and noteworthy home and foreign missionary agencies.[14] As in other European countries, the complication of state-church relationships provoked confessional reaction among Lutherans who repudiated the evangelical ecumenism of the revivalists in general. Next to British evangelical pioneers, the German revivalists achieved the most lasting social reforms. Close collaboration between British and German revivalists existed in home and foreign mission projects.

Confessionalism in Europe, whether Anglo-Catholic in England, Lutheran in Germany and Denmark, or Reformed in Holland and Switzerland, inhibited the renewal of revival in the 'thirties, unlike the United States, where the free church system accelerated it.

In the United States and in British North America, there were preparatory movements of revival in the 1780s that raised up leaders for the wider movement in the following decade. Conditions in the United States following the French Revolution were deplorable, emptying churches, increasing ungodliness and crime in society, infidelity among students. Sporadic revivals began in 1792. Then Isaac Backus and his friends in New England adopted the British plan for a general Concert of Prayer for the revival of religion and extension of Christ's kingdom abroad. Prayer meetings multiplied as church members devoted the first Monday of each month to fervent intercession.[15]

In 1798, the awakening became general. Congregations were crowded and conviction was deep, leading to numerous thoroughgoing conversions. Every state in New England was affected, and every evangelical denomination.[16] There were no records of emotional extravagance, and none among the churches of the Middle Atlantic States, where extraordinary revivals broke out in the cities of New York and Philadelphia as well as in smaller towns. In the western parts of New York and Pennsylvania, there were more startling displays of excitement.[17] The population of these eastern States was three million, and the extent of the revival therein was three times more considerable than in the frontier territories, with three hundred thousand people.

In 1800, extraordinary revival began in Kentucky, long after its manifestation east of the Alleghenies. Among the rough and lawless and illiterate frontiersmen, there were extremes of conviction and response, such as trembling and shaking—described as 'the jerks,'—weeping for sorrow and shouting for joy, fainting. Extravagances occurred among a comparative few, but were exaggerated by critics out of all proportion, so that twentieth century historians have stressed the odd performances and ignored the major thrust of the awakening in the United States, even pontificating that the awakening actually began, extravagantly, on the frontier— an obvious misreading of history. It cannot be denied that the revival transformed Kentucky and Tennessee from an utterly lawless community into a God-fearing one.[18]

On the frontier, there were minor schisms following the awakening, due largely to defects inherent in denominational organization than to the revival, which raised up voluntary evangelists among the laity. Reaction against evangelical ecumenism and lay evangelism forced some people out.

The awakening spread southwards into Virginia, North and South Carolina, and Georgia, again—as in Kentucky and Tennessee—attracting crowds so huge that no churches could possibly accommodate them, hence five, ten or fifteen thousand would gather in the forest clearings. The Negroes were moved equally with the whites.

In the Maritime Provinces of British North America, the revival of the 1780s was renewed among the Baptist and New Light Congregationalist churches. In Upper Canada— now Ontario—the Methodists promoted revival meetings and grew very rapidly, as did some Presbyterians and (later) the Baptists. American itinerants were most active in the movement, anti-American Churchmen and secular leaders most opposed to it. The war of 1812 interrupted the work, which resumed with the coming of peace, though still discouraged by conservative British leaders.[19]

As the influence of infidelity had been so strongly felt in the American colleges, so the blessing of revival overflowed in collegiate awakenings. Timothy Dwight, erudite president of Yale, proved to be the greatest champion of intelligent evangelical Christianity on campus, but the movement among students soon became a spontaneous, inter-collegiate union. The revived and converted students provided the majority of recruits for the home ministry, educational expansion, and foreign missionary effort.[20]

Revived Americans duplicated the formation of various evangelical societies in Britain, founding the American Bible Society, the American Tract Society, the American Board of Commissioners for Foreign Missions, the Foreign Mission of the American Baptists, and society after society. The order and extent of missionary organization reflected in some measure the degree of involvement of denominations in the Awakening.[21]

The Dutch colony of 30,000 at Cape Town experienced an awakening under the ministry of Dr. Helperus Ritzema van Lier, and thrust out local missionaries to evangelize the Khoisan (Hottentot and Bushmen) in the Cape hinterland.[22] A revival broke out in British army regiments in 1809, the Methodist soldier-evangelists gaining a hearing after an earthquake of great severity had shaken the Cape. There was little in the way of a free constituency to be revived in Australia, but the first chaplains to the settlements were Anglican Evangelicals, and revived congregations in Great Britain sent out evangelistically-minded laymen as settlers.

There is no doubt that the general awakening of the 1790s and 1800s, with its antecedents, was the prime factor in the extraordinary burst of missionary enthusiasm and social service, first in Britain, then in Europe and North America. Thomas Charles, whose zeal for God provoked the formation of the British and Foreign Bible Society, was a revivalist of first rank in Wales.[23] George Burder, who urged the founding of the Religious Tract Society, was a leader in the prayer union for revival. William Carey, a founder and pioneer of the Baptist Missionary Society, was one of a group who first set up in England the simultaneous prayer union that spread throughout evangelical Christendom and achieved its avowed purpose in the revival of religion and the extension of the kingdom of Christ overseas. The London Missionary Society and the Church Missionary Society grew out of the prayers of other Free Church and Church of England Evangelicals in the awakening. Methodist missions came from the same source, as did other Scottish societies and the Church of Scotland missions. The revival provided dynamic.[24]

The participation of Germans and Dutch in the Church Missionary Society and the London Missionary Society had its origin in the revival prayer groups in those countries, as did the proliferation of national missionary societies. A student prayer meeting in Williams College, the Haystack Compact, led to the foundation of the American Board and the American Baptist Missionary Union. The origins of the other denominational societies lay in the general revival.

It is all the more amazing to realise that these unique developments took place in Britain while that country was engaged in a titanic struggle with Napoleon, supported by ten times as many people. And the eager readiness of revived believers in Europe and North America transcended the political divisions and upheavals between them and Britain. The coming of peace in 1815 brought about a renewal of the revival in Britain, the rise of the Primitive Methodists to undertake an outreach to the masses somewhat neglected by Wesleyans.[25] In the Church of England, Charles Simeon was at the height of his influence, and the Church Building Society with government help was building hundreds of parish churches. The Baptists and Congregationalists were active in revival in England, and in Wales there were local revivals in many places. In Scotland, local awakenings and pastoral evangelism and social service built up the Church of Scotland Evangelicals. Revivals occurred in Ireland.

2

QUICKENING AT THE CAPE

The spiritual life of the Hollanders at Table Bay continued quietly through the eighteenth century, theirs a religion that was 'severely unemotional and chiefly a matter of form' that 'exercised but little vital influence over the everyday life of the congregation,' to quote a South African authority, Prof. J. du Plessis.[1]

In the last quarter of the eighteenth century, there were signs all over Protestant Christendom of disquiet with the deadly deism of the period, and this showed itself in Cape Colony also. In 1786, a brilliant young Hollander, Helperus Ritzema van Lier, arrived at Table Bay to become minister of the Groote Kerk.[2] He was as evangelistic as he was precociously scholastic,[3] a teenage Doctor of Philosophy who became an ardent evangelist in his twenties.[4]

Van Lier exercised an effective ministry in Cape Town, winning many burghers to a vital faith in Jesus Christ, some of whom became pioneer missionaries to the heathen near at hand and far away. Van Lier burned out in seven years, but left an abiding memory of purity and power.[5] He was one of the great men of the Groote Kerk.

That he was not a voice crying in the wilderness was made clear by the arrival of Michiel Christiaan Vos,[6] a graduate of the University of Utrecht, who returned home to minister in the parish of Tulbagh.

Converts of Van Lier's preaching sought to reach the Hottentots with the Gospel,[7] Jan Jakob van Zulch working in Wagonmakers' Valley, while others worked among the people of mixed blood around Cape Town, as did Mrs. Machteld Smith,[8] a truly remarkable self-appointed missionary who helped extend the work far and wide.[9] These pioneers laid the foundation of missions sustained by the Dutch Reformed Churches of South Africa in the nineteenth century, more particularly extended by later Awakenings. Said Latourette: 'The tide of religious life which was so evidently rising in Europe and the United States was also having its effect in the Dutch churches of South Africa . . .'[10]

Meanwhile, events were transpiring in Europe which were to change the face of South Africa. France had emerged as a revolutionary power, and, in view of the threat, the Stadholder of the Netherlands arranged in 1788 with the British to occupy the Cape to prevent its falling into the hands of the French.[11] When French armies overran Holland in the winter of 1794-95, the British occupied the Cape for about eight years, returning it to the Netherlands at the Treaty of Amiens. The second British occupation came in 1806, again as a war measure against France.

These vicissitudes of war had no untoward effect upon the preaching of the Gospel in the Cape Colony, whether among the burghers in Cape Town and its satellite communities or on the widening frontier among the Hottentots and other heathen tribespeople.

Garrisoning the Cape was a strong British force, comprising the 72nd and 83rd Regiments, among whom were a few active Methodists who suffered petty persecution for the faith. For four years, John Kendrick (a soldier-Methodist preacher) had failed to find one serious person among a thousand men of the regiment,[12] a judgment that seemingly ignored the likelihood of believers grown indifferent or lukewarm because of the temptations of army life.

But, late in 1809, an earthquake shook the Cape Peninsula and neighbourhood, rocking the settlements for eight days and putting fear into the inhabitants.[13] George Middlemiss in the 72nd Regiment found that this godly fear had led to a seriousness about the more important things of life and a thirsting after salvation, followed by an outpouring of Divine grace,[14] and John Kendrick noted the same with 'unspeakable satisfaction' concerning the 83rd Regiment at Saldanha Bay, north of Cape Town:[15]

> The spark of grace soon began to catch from soul to soul. Prayer meetings now commenced among them and such a cry for mercy followed as is most wonderful. The room frequently has been so crowded that many have been unable to approach the door.

As the Spirit was outpoured, soldiers sought the Lord with cries and tears, notorious sinners pleading for pardon. Soon there were fifty men in the Methodist Society. The number of English-speaking Evangelicals at the Cape grew into the hundreds, but there came an amicable parting of the ways into Arminian and Calvinist gatherings, the two parties soon taking permanent denominational form.

Arriving in 1816, the first Methodist minister encountered much opposition, his chapel being burned by a regimental colonel.[16] Presbyterians entering with Scottish troops met with less difficulty, thanks to establishment.

In 1820, more than five thousand British folk came out to South Africa and settled on the frontier between the Boers and the Bantu, founding Grahamstown and Port Elizabeth and creating the Eastern Province.[17] As picked artisans and fine settlers, they overcame initial hardships—such as crop failures, frontier forays and official bumbling—to prosper gratifyingly.

The official sponsors of British colonization were tardy indeed in providing official Anglican churches and clergy. The High Church S. P. G. and S. P. C. K. which followed the Church of England communicants and adherents into South Africa helped build Anglo-Catholic predominance, while by default (due to Anglican comity arrangements)[18] Evangelical churches remained weak in the country.

The early beginnings of the Baptist, Congregational and Methodist work as well as Scots Presbyterian in the Eastern Province demonstrated a measure of home-bred piety and evangelical fervour among the British settlers, who were all voluntary immigrants.

It was among the Methodists that the first sign of revival was reported. The Reverend William Shaw,[19] converted in Glasgow in 1812, came out as an immigrant pastor and began to preach the Gospel in the new settlements and, travelling on horseback, organized a local preachers' band, dedicated to building churches in various places.

Shaw had found conditions among the troops and settlers and hangers-on deplorably bad, the people often given over to drunkenness and debauchery. There was no ministry of any kind, Anglican or otherwise, for a thousand souls. Soon Shaw's powerful preaching and the kind of praying it provoked resulted in an awakening which cleaned up the community and began its civic reputation for a vigorous church and academic life. The Grahamstown Awakening of 1822 came not from special efforts but followed the usual means of grace in church life, its unusual impact on the community producing many converts.[20]

With almost unanimous support, the Methodists erected a chapel in the centre of Grahamstown,[21] generously allowing the Baptists to use it for services, and even granting the Anglicans its use while their parish church was being planned and built—though the parish priest protested the Methodists ringing their own church bell for Methodist services as they did willingly for the services of their Anglican guests.

Nine years later, in 1831, a second season of revival was enjoyed in Grahamstown and district.[22] It began in the local Wesleyan Church and spread to other towns and farms.[23] Many young people were converted to God, and a number entered into the Christian ministry.[24]

Minutes of the District Meeting of Methodist ministers and local preachers in Albany (Grahamstown) District noted:[25]

> Throughout the past year, the English congregations have been large, and from want of room in the chapel, great inconvenience has been experienced . . .[26]
> It has pleased the Head of the Church to grant us a gracious revival of religion in our Grahamstown congregation, in the early part of last year, principally among our young people. . . we have a clear increase of fifty-six members.

As among the Dutch-speaking congregations, the revival of the European Christians produced a vital interest in the evangelization of the heathen. Demonstrating the essential oneness of the work of God, whether among European South Africans or Hottentot or Bantu, there were outbreaks of the fervour of revival in mission station after mission station. The movement was inter-racial and interdenominational.

In the first quarter of the nineteenth century, the Dutch Reformed folk in South Africa were suffering from a dearth of clergy. The Awakenings had already moved Scotland, but not the Netherlands, so a Governor of the Cape succeeded in persuading a number of Scottish ministers to emigrate to the colony to minister to its Dutch-speaking people in dorp and veld. The experience proved a happy one, giving broad Scots names to some of South Africa's best-known Afrikaner families.[27]

Among these Scots came the elder Andrew Murray,[28] who not only quickly identified himself with his adopted people but prayed earnestly for an evangelical awakening in South African churches similar to the movement stirring Scotland, a habit which he continued until his death.[29]

This Andrew Murray sent his sons John and Andrew to study in Scotland, where they were deeply moved by the awakening begun with W. C. Burns, whose preaching had moved Dundee.[30] Both young men decided to enter the ministry, and went on to Utrecht for their theological studies.

The Awakening provoked by the visit of Robert Haldane to Geneva was already spreading since 1820 from France into the Netherlands.[31] Their involvement in the Revival both in Holland and Scotland had lasting results in South Africa, yet another example of the interplay of Evangelical Awakenings across time and space.

Not only was Evangelicalism the major influence in the Dutch Reformed Church, but it predominated in the English-speaking Churches also, in the Baptist, Congregationalist, Lutheran, Methodist and Presbyterian, and others. This is confirmed in standard histories of South Africa, as in the writings of Walker, Cambridge historian,[32] and Latourette, missions historian at Yale, who said:

> The main recruitment of the clergy came through the missionary societies. The Wesleyan movement, the Evangelical revival in Great Britain, and the Lutheran revival in Germany had put new life into Protestantism ... had even affected the far-distant Cape ... welcome support to the incoming evangelical missionaries.

Evangelicalism had its own distinctive type of ecumenism, one which began at the grass-roots between individuals who shared the same spirit of brotherhood, concern and cooperation. The ministers of the Dutch Reformed Church in the days preceding the quickening at the Cape were often jealous of Moravian, Lutheran, Anglican and other workers in the vineyard. What a vital difference of attitudes in the early nineteenth century when the Church of England clergy held their services in the Groote Kerk,[33] Wesleyan and Lutheran congregations happily sharing the Cape Town constituency with Reformed parishes. This evangelical ecumenism was reflected in the founding of the Cape of Good Hope Church Missionary Society, in a meeting presided over by the good Sir Benjamin D'Urban. It came to an end with the arrival of Churchmen with a non-Evangelical view of the Church.

In the vast area of western South Africa, the Bantu were unknown, its sparse inhabitants being a nomadic, pastoral people called Hottentots by Europeans. These Hottentots, and their more primitive racial cousins, the Bushmen, were a people of parchment-coloured skin, not negro.[34]

The country, partly arid, was very lightly occupied by the Hottentot clans, which maintained their simple life by keeping cattle and sheep, and by hunting. The Bushmen, one of the most primitive of aboriginal peoples, were nomads who maintained a more precarious existence by hunting and collecting.

The Bushmen were able to survive, even in the arid Kalahari Desert, by natural peculiarities—including steatopygia (or accumulation of fatty tissue on the rump) of the womenfolk.

As early as 1662, a first Hottentot convert had been baptized at the Cape settlement. She married a Danish surgeon. Little more was done for a hundred years. Georg Schmidt, a Moravian of German birth, came to South Africa in 1737 and founded the still-flourishing mission station known as Genadendal.[35] He baptized five Hottentots, but a dispute with the officially appointed ministers at the Cape forced his withdrawal in 1743.

When the Moravians reopened their mission in 1792, they were happy to find an aged survivor of the work of Schmidt with her worn copy of the New Testament in Dutch. Fifty years had passed since Schmidt's departure.[36]

Within a couple of years of their return, the Moravians witnessed a spiritual awakening at Genadendal:[37]

> A veritable hunger for the Word of God was apparent. The emotional Hottentots were moved to tears by the preaching of the Gospel... Those colonists who from time to time were witnesses of the work of God's Spirit in ignorant heathen, were moved to confess that they could hardly believe that such results were possible.

The preaching and teaching of the missionaries Marsveld, Schwinn and Kühnel bore fruit in the lives of the Hottentots. Mrs. Machteld Smith, convert of Van Lier, visited the work at Genadendal a few years later and rejoiced in the fervour of the three hundred Christians she found there.

Thanks to the rising tide of spirituality, Dutch-speaking burghers even before the British annexation had begun to evangelize the Hottentots and other non-Europeans in their vicinity, in a master-servant relationship.

Van Zulch, another convert of Dr. Van Lier, proved so successful in his work among slaves and Hottentots near Wellington that he was able to build them a meeting-hall. M. C. Vos, an ardent evangelist, laboured for the conversion of Hottentots not only by his own labours, but through teaching farmers to teach their slaves and labourers the Word of God daily in their own quarters.

At the turn of the century, Jan Theodor van der Kemp arrived at the Cape to serve the London Missionary Society. He and his friends founded a mission for the Hottentots in the eastern Cape Colony.[38] His first wife having died in the Netherlands in a tragic accident, he married—not happily—

a girl of mixed-blood, as did some of the other missionaries of the London Society.

After reviving their mission to Hottentots, the Moravians commenced in 1818 to evangelize the Bantu in eastern Cape Colony.[39] A Swede, Hans Peter Hallbeck, became bishop of the Moravians, and the work went forward steadily.[40]

In 1820, a vigorous Scottish minister, John Philip, was appointed superintendent of London Missionary Society work in South Africa. For a full generation he directed the work, embracing the viewpoint of the natives and exasperating the Afrikaner farmers by his advocacy of the rights of the non-Europeans. He lived a stormy life.[41]

But the work of the Christian missions went forward in the disintegrating society. The people were transformed. On one occasion, a visiting judge, John Thomas Bigge, and an officer, Major W. M. C. Colebrooke, asked a humble but grateful worker—Jantjies Spielman by name—what the local missionaries at Bethelsdorp had done for their Hottentot charges and their children.

Through his interpreter, the Hottentot replied that when the missionaries came among them, they had no clothing but filthy sheep-skins; now they were clothed in British cloth. They were without letters; now they could read their Bibles or hear them read to them. They were without any religion; now they worshipped God in their families. They were without morals; now every man had his own wife. They were given up to licentiousness and drunkenness; now they were sober and industrious. They were without property; now Hottentots at Bethelsdorp alone possessed fifty wagons and the cattle with them. They were liable to be shot like wild animals; and the missionaries stood between them and the bullets of their enemies.[42]

That was the impact of English-speaking missionaries at Bethelsdorp upon Hottentots. The same was true of those who spoke Dutch. The town of Philippolis, founded in 1823 on the recommendation of Ds. Abraham Faure of Graaff-Reinet to evangelize the Hottentots, was visited by Adam Kok, chief of the Griqua mixed-bloods who settled there. The Griquas then possessed 35,000 sheep, 3000 oxen, and 500 horses, and Griqua country was as Christian as the Cape itself.[43] The Griquas persisted in Christian civilization.

In 1813 and 1814, awakenings were reported from many of the stations of the London Mission. Many Hottentots repented of their sins and turned to God at Bethelsdorp, near

14 QUICKENING AT THE CAPE

Algoa Bay where the future Port Elizabeth was built. The movement was marked by strong conviction of sin and by tears, and it arose through strong preaching.[44]

Far away, at Griquatown beyond the Orange River, a great awakening began in June of 1813. Many awakened settlers and mixed-bloods began to confess their sins and to evangelize the unreached tribesmen among the heathen. One of the missionaries, William Anderson, described the movement as 'life from the dead.'[45]

The news of one awakening provoked many another. At Hooge Kraal, near George in the Cape Province, there was such conviction that crying and sobbing drowned out the message of the missionary.[46] The populace was transformed into a godly community commended by colonial inspectors.

In Namaqaland occurred similar happenings. News of the awakening at Griquatown stirred the people at Pella.[47] There were many baptisms of heathen from the hovels around and a lasting work was accomplished.[48]

The London Missionary Society workers assembled in Graaff-Reinet in August of 1814. They rejoiced to report hundreds of conversions.[49] The burghers of Graaff-Reinet were impressed by the good tidings of the workings of God among the heathen, and in high enthusiasm founded there an auxiliary missionary society.[50] Andries Waterboer, later to become a military leader and chief of the Griquas, himself preached in the meeting house.[51]

It is of more than passing interest to note that a revival-awakening occurred in Sierra Leone about the same time as these ingatherings far to the south and east. Sierra Leone was being settled by liberated slaves, almost five hundred from London's slums and twelve hundred from Nova Scotia being landed before 1800, sundry other companies seized by the Royal Navy from slave ships after 1807.[52] Conditions in the Sierra Leone settlements were deplorable, cargoes of freedmen being dumped on shore to forage like swine.

In March 1816, the Church Missionary Society sent out to Freetown a missionary team, chiefly Germans, among them William Augustine Bernard Johnson, a Hanoverian subject of George III.[53] Johnson was stationed at Hogbrook, as aptly named for its wild hogs as for pigsty-like conditions; there he found fifteen hundred poor Negroes, spiritually degraded, some starving, all in misery. His ministry thus combined famine relief and monitorial schooling with an elementary evangelism.[54]

Johnson preached on simple themes: 'Who is Jesus Christ? What has Jesus Christ done? What is He doing today? And what is He going to do?' As early as midsummer, the response became encouraging. The crowds overflowed his vocal range.[55] He preached at 6 a.m., 10 a.m., 3 p.m. and 7 p.m., and these Sunday services were preceded by Saturday prayer meetings. All the while the school was increasing in size, and Johnson managed masons, bricklayers, carpenters, blacksmiths and other craftsmen.

Many were the signs of an imminent outpouring of the Spirit. On 31st March 1817, weeping and praying in the congregation became so general that Johnson stopped his preaching.[56] The awakening deepened and spread all year. In 1818, the church was densely thronged, vestry, stairs, tower and windows filled, seats collapsing under the load. Even children were holding their own spontaneous meetings. A missionary society was formed to carry the Good News elsewhere. All the while, Johnson was baptizing believers by the scores and hundreds. The Governor put pressure on Johnson to baptize more people, but he refused to baptize any whose hearts had not been changed.

In Regent's Town, as Hogbrook was renamed, honesty and purity and love replaced pilfering, uncleanness and incessant quarrels. The movement affected the whole Colony, for only six were held for trial in a population of six thousand in 1822 compared with forty out of four thousand in 1812.[57]

Ill-health, of which there was plenty in West Africa, sent the Johnsons home to England for a while in 1819, during which the work in the settlements somewhat declined. The Johnsons returned in 1820, and began a rehabilitation of the ministry. In 1823, according to Johnson's last report, there were more than six hundred African communicants in Sierra Leone, two-thirds at Regent's Town; and there were more than three thousand pupils in school, about a thousand under Johnson's care. But Johnson's health was undermined, and he died on board ship returning to England.[58]

The British Wesleyans also opened a work in Sierra Leone, carrying revival-evangelism with them.[59] As in all parts of West Africa, the heavy death-rate among residents of European stock was their worst handicap.

The revival impulse had much to do with the resettling of Negroes in Liberia, to which project Samuel J. Mills of Connecticut gave his life.[60] In 1821, Lott Carey, a Negro Baptist in Virginia, commenced work in Liberia.

3

ORGANIZING FOR ADVANCE

It has been noted that there were sporadic movements of revival in Great Britain and the United States during the decade preceding the French Revolution, but that a general awakening began in the 1790s. The same pattern is seen in the formation of the evangelical societies founded to advance the work of evangelization, for most of them had their roots in the 1780s, but reached their organizational form between the dates of the Bastille and Waterloo in Great Britain, but after Waterloo in many other countries.

Latourette, in his consideration of the Great Century and the movements within Christianity through which the expansion of the faith had been chiefly accomplished, first noted the 'revivals' which were particularly effective in the United Kingdom and the United States; second, the organizations in large part growing out of them.[1] The European countries also shared fully in the movement.

It was in Great Britain that the first of these organizations had their beginning.[2] Reasons for prior British leadership included the effects of the Evangelical Revival on the thinking of Christians and the effects of the industrial revolution on the income of the people. With their desire to serve, the people were given the wherewithal to serve, an over-ruling of Providence later seen in other countries and in other centuries.

The rekindling of evangelical revival in Britain during the decade before the outbreak of revolution in France had caused a stirring in the hearts of dedicated Christians, and when the awakening became more general, their ideas were taken up and their burdens shared in a remarkable burst of organizing enthusiasm, all the more remarkable in wartime. In nearly every case, the initiative came from men who had been involved in local evangelical revivals, whether of the staider type within the Church of England, or the more dynamic kind occurring in companies of believers outside. Some of these founding fathers have been remembered for their works, the source of their dynamic forgotten.

To meet the demands of a population increasing in wealth
and literacy, whose appetite for the printed Word was being
whetted by the Awakening, spontaneous efforts were made.
George Burder, a Congregationalist minister at Coventry,
who had been influenced by George Whitefield and William
Romaine, continued active as a pastoral evangelist. In 1799,
he urged the formation of the Religious Tract Society to
promote the diffusion of evangelical literature.[3] It was
supported by both Church of England and Free Church folk,
and its example was followed elsewhere, the foundation of
the American Tract Society taking place a quarter of a century later, its avowed objective the providing of suitable
Christian literature to the religiously destitute.[4]

The awakenings in Wales in the late 1780s had produced
a hunger for the reading of Scripture among the common
people. In 1787, an appeal was made from Wales for more
Bibles in the Cymric tongue. The extraordinary revivals
of 1791 onward catapulted Thomas Charles of Bala to the
place of leadership in spiritual affairs in the principality.
Thomas Charles continued active in these startling movements. When little Mary Jones tramped fifty miles over
the Welsh hills with her six years' savings, only to find
that the last copy of the Welsh Scriptures had been sold,
she returned in tears to her home. Thomas Charles of
Bala took up the matter with the Society for Promoting
Christian Knowledge and, failing to persuade them, made a
suggestion to the Religious Tract Society that a Bible Society
be formed.[5] He returned to his work in the Awakening. The
outcome was the foundation of the British and Foreign Bible
Society in 1804. It was interdenominational in character,
dedicated to the dissemination of the Scriptures without note
or comment, at home or abroad. Its first officers largely
were members of the 'Clapham Sect,' another expression
of the awakening of Napoleonic times.[6] It is very clear that
this history-making event resulted from the Awakening of
1791 onward in Britain. After the Battle of Waterloo, the
American Bible Society[7] was formed to combine the efforts
of several state-wide associations begun as a result of the
American Awakening, and following the example in Britain.
Bible Societies were formed in other European countries,
generally after the coming of peace.

The Bible became the chief text-book of the Sunday School
movement in Great Britain and the United States and elsewhere in the Protestant countries.

During the eighteenth century, many isolated attempts were made to evangelize children. Griffith Jones in Wales had concentrated upon teaching the young as well as adults to read. Hannah More, a godly Anglican woman committed to supporting the Establishment, circulated cheap tracts, and became concerned about the illiteracy of the rural folk in the Mendip Hills. While sharing a contemporary Anglican notion of full education for only the governing elite, Hannah More set out to provide elementary education for children in the rural countryside.[8] As her concern arose from her evangelical convictions, she too was interested in the Bible as a text-book. Just before the outbreak of the Revolution in France, she settled down in a country home near Bristol, and became wholly absorbed in the work of teaching the children. She was an intimate friend of Wilberforce and the Clapham Sect of Evangelical reformers encouraged her.

Joseph Lancaster, an evangelical Quaker, was likewise concerned about the hordes of illiterate and lawless children roaming the streets of London.[9] He devised a method of teaching a class of boys, then using them to teach a younger set while he taught them a second year, thus developing a school based upon the monitorial principle. In 1805, George III learned of the remarkable experiment whereby a single teacher kept order among hundreds of boys. The King asked how it could be done. 'By the same principle,' replied the Quaker, 'that thy Majesty's Army is kept in order!' So impressed was the King that he lent his support, and these monitorial schools fast multiplied. The Royal Lancasterian Society was formally constituted in 1810, becoming in 1815 the British and Foreign School Society. This monitorial school was a necessary development on the way to the public school system. It had its birth in the Revival.

In 1780, a social reformer named Robert Raikes stood among the unruly children of Gloucester's working class and asked himself: 'Can anything be done?' A Voice answered: 'Try.' And he tried.[10] He gathered the illiterate children on Sundays and taught them to read, using the Bible as the inevitable text-book. In 1803, the interdenominational Sunday School Union was formed, as much a product of evangelical revival as Raikes himself. One of the early promoters in London professed a desire to teach everyone in the world to read the Bible. Before the end of the second decade of the new century, the Sunday School movement in England and Wales had a half a million scholars enrolled.

It was in 1784 that John Sutcliffe called upon the Baptist Association of Northampton and Leicester Counties to set aside the first Monday of each month to pray for a general outpouring of the Holy Spirit and a spread of religion. John Sutcliffe had been challenged indirectly by Jonathan Edwards whose 'humble attempt to promote explicit agreement and visible union of God's people in extraordinary prayer for the revival of religion' included the advancement of Christ's Kingdom on earth pursuant to Scripture promises and the prophecies concerning the last time.[11]

Jonathan Edwards's writings helped Sutcliffe and others of Calvinistic conviction to reconcile their doctrine of Divine sovereignty with their notion of human responsibility. It is noteworthy that Sutcliffe served as pastor to William Carey and was an affectionate colleague of Andrew Fuller, the one becoming a pioneer of missions abroad and the other an advocate of missions at home.

Divine sovereignty and human responsibility were fused in the fire of the revival prayer meetings. It was natural that British intercessors were most concerned about the need of revival in Britain, but, when their prayers were happily answered, it was easy to direct the intercession into missionary enterprise, aimed at winning the whole wide world. Dr. R. Pierce Beaver, writing for an ecumenical readership, recognized the dynamic of prayer, affirming that 'the Concert of Prayer undoubtedly helped produce a climate favorable to the use of the missionary societies in the last decade of the eighteenth century.'[12] Another high authority, Dr. Ernest A. Payne, declared:[13]

> . . . It was probably these prayer meetings, as much as any other single influence, which prepared the little group of ministers to venture on the formation of a missionary society.

The noted Anglican mission director, Dr. Eugene Stock, looking back after a century's success, picked the year 1786 as the 'wonderful year' in the development of missionary passion.[14] In that year, William Wilberforce resolved to live for God's glory and for the good of his fellow-men. It was in 1786 that William Carey first suggested to the group of Baptist ministers at Northampton that they must consider their responsibility to the heathen.[15] It was in 1786 that Dr. Thomas Coke initiated a Methodist mission to the people of the West Indies.[16] Many were the intercessors burdened for revival at home and missions abroad that year.

The answer to these prayers did not come until the last decade of the century. On 30th May 1792, William Carey at Nottingham preached a missionary sermon to assembled Baptist associates, urging them to 'expect great things from God: attempt great things for God.' Within six months, at a specially convened meeting of the association, what was soon to be called the Baptist Missionary Society was formed and Carey sailed for India in 1793.[17]

The founding of the Baptist Missionary Society is usually regarded as the inception of modern Protestant missionary enterprise. There had been several efforts to evangelize the non-Christian world before 1792, but they were limited in scope or in objective. The Northamptonshire shoemaker appears in retrospect to have been the first Anglo-Saxon of evangelical faith in either Britain or America to propose that Christians undertake to carry the Gospel to the world's unevangelized millions. A real enthusiast for geography and linguistics, he cobbled shoes, taught school, and preached the Good News.[18] Carey not only promoted but pioneered in missions; and he urged not only Baptists, but all Christians to share in the evangelization of every creature.[19]

Thomas Haweis, an Anglican Evangelical who had served the Countess of Huntington as a chaplain and who had been rebuked for so doing by an Anglican court, found himself superintending ministry in the revival years following 1791, when the Countess died. Still in Anglican orders, Haweis proposed the formation of the London Missionary Society, as an interdenominational organization, in 1795.[20] In 1796, the missionary ship 'Duff' sailed for the South Seas and so began the ministry of this remarkable society, which drew its support at first from Anglican and Free Church people revived in the Awakening, but later more and more from the churches of British Congregationalism.

In 1795, the Eclectic Society of Evangelical clergymen sponsored by Charles Simeon discussed a suggestion that a mission to the non-Christian world be initiated by members of the Church of England. From Simeon's prompting came the Church Missionary Society, founded in 1799 as a society for missions to Africa and the East. Strange to relate, the first missionaries of the Church Missionary Society were Germans trained at a missionary school in Berlin. The sponsoring Eclectic Society, of course, was comprised of ordained leaders of the Awakening among Anglicans in the revival times following 1791.[21]

In the year following the French Revolution, the British Methodist Conference set up a committee of management for the West Indian venture, and in successive steps finally committed its resources to the formation of the Wesleyan Methodist Missionary Society in 1817-18.[22]

In 1796, the Scottish Missionary Society and the Glasgow Missionary Society were formed by the leaders of the 1791 Awakening in the Lowlands of Scotland; but that year the General Assembly of the Church of Scotland rejected a proposal to begin a missionary enterprise. The opposition was spearheaded by the anti-Evangelicals, just as support was forthcoming from leading Evangelicals.[23] It was not until 1824 that General Assembly reversed its decision and sent missionaries out to India—including Alexander Duff, nurtured in the afterglow of the Scottish Revival.

Prior to the American Revolution, missionary-minded British Christians had sent support to missionaries on the American frontier engaged in evangelizing the Indians. It was natural that this interest should flag, and that loyal subjects of the King would be only too ready to turn over that responsibility to his former American subjects so very determined to be independent.

With the loss of the American Colonies, the fortunes of war and the blessings of naval supremacy made possible the building of a Second Empire, retaining Canada in North America but opening up India in Asia and Cape Colony in Africa. To these new fields, the main stream of pioneers made their way, but among the first enterprises was the mission to the South Seas, a no-man's-land of islands in the far Pacific. William Carey himself had thought of going to Tahiti, for he was an avid reader of Captain Cook's travels. There was no lack of opportunity for British folk.

At the end of the Revolution, American missionary work was in a sorry state. Christian Indians, whose missionaries had largely supported the Mother Country, found their tepee villages overrun by American forces, their congregations scattered, with some in flight to Canada.[24] The Scottish S.P.C.K. showed some interest in reviving their work, and the Congregational Establishment in New England decided to revive theirs.[25] In 1787, a Society for Propagating the Gospel among Indians and Others in North America was founded. Thanks to the revival in Virginia in 1787, the Presbyterians there recovered a missionary vision, and there was a measure of interest among the Reformed.[26]

The early nineteenth century awakening had immediate
effects upon the Negro inhabitants of the United States.   In
the North, Negro Baptist churches sprang up in Boston,
New York, Philadelphia and other big cities.   In 1800, the
black members of a New York Methodist Episcopal Church
withdrew quite amicably and formed Zion Church, which in
1821 took the lead in founding the African Methodist Episcopal
Church, Zion.[27] Several years earlier, the Bethel Methodist
Episcopal Church in Philadelphia, founded about 1792, had
initiated the formation of the African Methodist Episcopal
Church, with support from Bishop Asbury.[28] The two Negro
denominations maintained their separate identity.   In the
South, Negro Baptists and Methodists continued to worship
largely in white congregations, occupying humbler space.

Before long, the greatest work in evangelizing the Negro
population was being done by black Christians themselves,
but often with white encouragement.   White Christians gave
freely to Negro educational enterprises.[29] The standard of
education among black ministers was inevitably low, and
their churches were handicapped by the evil effects of slave
relationships which often broke up families, leading to a
laxity in marriage which persisted till modern times.[30]

*   *   *   *

Heman Humphrey, president of historic Amherst College,
reviewing the Second Great Awakening during the progress
of the Fourth, delivered himself of an opinion which was
formed close to the events themselves: [31]

> The organization of these institutions ... the Religious
> Tract Society ... the British and Foreign Bible Society
> the Baptist Missionary Society, the London Missionary
> Society, the Church Missionary Society, and kindred
> evangelical movements in the mother country, far
> spreading the gospel ... all are fruits of this blessed
> work of the Spirit graciously poured out about 1792, in
> a period of darkness when the hearts of Christians
> were failing them for fear.

Heman Humphrey lived through the Second Awakening, a
young Christian; he became a leader in the Third, first in
a Massachusetts pastorate, and then in successive revivals,
generation after generation, in a collegiate community. His
testimony confirmed what so few folk have realised that the
great organizations of mission at home and abroad arose in
the Second Great Awakening worldwide, not merely from a
productive aftermath of the First Great Awakening.

The American Awakening of 1791 onwards had seemingly reached a climax in the New England and Middle Atlantic States within seven years, in the West and South within ten. Almost immediately, a missionary passion began to develop. In 1802, John M. Mason, Reformed divine, declared:[32]

> Let us not overlook as an unimportant matter the very existence of that missionary spirit . . . which has already awakened Christians . . . and bids fair to produce in due season a general movement of the Church upon earth.

The Concert of Prayer begun in 1795 had already moved believers to surrender to God for an outpouring of the Holy Spirit upon the whole country. As in Great Britain, it was not difficult to direct the prayers of intercessors towards missionary objectives. It was still a major problem to find new channels for the streams of intercession and sacrifical giving. American Baptists had begun to support the Carey project in India, but they and other Christians were looking for American-based agencies of enterprise.

In the autumn of 1796, a public meeting was held in New York to discuss the news of the foundation and progress of the interdenominational London Missionary Society, and, as a result, the New York Missionary Society was formed on similar interdenominational lines.[33] A missionary was sent to the Chickasaws of Georgia and another to the Tuscaroras in western New York State.[34] John Blair Smith, a revivalist, formerly president of Hampden-Sydney College, had become president of Union College in Schenectady, and in 1797 helped form a missionary society with Reformed backing, tackling the needs of the Oneidas.[35] In 1798, a missionary society was formed in Pennsylvania, and another in Connecticut.[36] In 1799, a society was formed in Massachusetts.[37] Each year brought forth new enterprises, dedicated in the main to a trans-cultural missionary evangelism in North America.

Meanwhile, associations of Baptist churches were taking on responsibilities for Indian missions as well as frontier evangelism, and other denominations were undertaking the same kind of work in their respective ways. Haweis of the London Missionary Society was quoted by his Connecticut Evangelical correspondents as declaring with his confreres that 'It revives our inmost souls to see the spreading of the sacred flame in America,' adding 'I trust that the sound will spread . . . till it shall reach . . . from the east to the west.' To Haweis,[38] Indian evangelism was foreign missionary work. It was still domestic to the Americans.

The catalyst needed to convert such apostolic energy from home to foreign missions was supplied by the Awakening also, arising from the widespread revival of student Christianity, more particularly prayer meetings at Williams College.

One summer afternoon in 1806, five students at Williams College were driven from a maple grove where they were accustomed to meet for prayer.[39] They sheltered from the thunderstorm under a haystack, and there prayed about the need of reaching the unevangelized heathen for Christ.

The thunderstorm was of short duration, for the sun soon broke through the clouds as the light of a clear purpose broke upon their souls. Samuel J. Mills, impressed in the revival in Connecticut but fully committed at Williams College, gave the decisive word: 'We can do it, if we will!'

The students organized a society, youthful in spirit and habit, for they met in secret and in cipher recorded their minutes. They found no less than a score of students who sincerely shared their burden.

One among them, Adoniram Judson, was prepared to go out under the auspices of the London Missionary Society, but his friend Mills discouraged him, saying that it was not right that British friends should support their own mission and American volunteers also. In 1810, while completing final studies at Andover Theological Seminary, Mills and his friends went to the home of an interested professor to meet with a number of ministers of their denomination, the state establishment in Massachusetts.

The counsel of their senior brethren was divided. Some thought the proposition a premature one; others felt that it smacked of infatuation; others that it would be too expensive; but after one minister observed that they had better not try to hinder God, a majority supported their younger brethren. Soon the American Board of Commissioners for Foreign Missions was formed; hence out of the Haystack Compact there came the initiation of overseas missionary enterprise, and American foreign missions began their enlistment of the best-educated class in society in the United States.[40]

In 1812, a party of eight A. B. C. F. M. volunteers sailed for India. Before the ship reached Indian ports, war had been declared between the United Kingdom and the United States, and the officials of the East India Company, already prejudiced against British missionaries, were doubly hostile to the American project of evangelizing British subjects, of Hindu faith.

On the voyage to India, Judson and his bride, knowing that they would encounter William Carey, began to re-study the subject of believers' baptism. The Judsons and Luther Rice decided to embrace the Baptist viewpoint, and Rice returned to ask support of American Baptists, who in 1814 founded a general missionary convention of the denomination, later the American Baptist Foreign Mission Society. Forced out of India by an antagonistic British East India Company, the Judsons went on to Burma and wrought there a mighty work for God.[41]

In 1819, the Methodist Episcopal Church of the United States of America formed its missionary society.[42] The overseas missionary project of the Protestant Episcopal Church was begun two years later.[43] Presbyterians, divided by schism, took longer to establish an official missionary society, their Board of Foreign Missions being created in 1837.[44] In that same year, the missionary society of the Evangelical Lutheran Church in the United States took form and commenced operations.[45]

When, at the height of the 1798 Revival in the Eastern States, the New York Missionary Society was formed by the ministers of four denominations, the work was launched by redirecting the Concert of Prayer into missionary prayer sessions every second Wednesday of the month at candlelight, to entreat the outpouring of the Spirit with the proclamation of the Gospel to all nations.[46]

War was raging in January 1815 when the intercessors of the Concert of Prayer were asked to redouble their zeal and pray for a return of peace, a reformation of morals, and a general revival of religion. It was suggested that a return to the first Monday of every month would re-align the prayers of believers throughout Europe, America and the mission stations on other continents and islands. The response was gratifying, a large number of churches fully supporting the union of prayer.[47]

The Concert of Prayer for revival in the 1780s in Great Britain and in the 1790s in United States, and the renewed Concert of Prayer in both countries in 1815 and in several European realms besides, was clearly demonstrated to be the prime factor in motivating and equipping Christians for service in a worldwide movement which totally eclipsed the military might of the nations at the Battle of Waterloo. A century of comparative peace among nations made the great century of pioneer evangelization possible.

4

THE THIRD GENERAL AWAKENING

As in Great Britain, revival was renewed in the United States and Canada after 1815, and for fifteen years there were revivals reported here and there.[1] This renewal saw the emergence of outstanding evangelists, such as Asahel Nettleton in New England, Daniel Baker in the South, and Charles Finney in the 'burnt-over' area of western New York State.[2] Local revivals continued in Great Britain, and a new surge of Methodism took denominational form.[3]

On the mission fields, the pioneers encountered three types of response to their evangelistic outreach and prayer: folk movements of unindoctrinated people, awakenings of instructed communities, and revivals of believers, in such places as South India, South Africa, Indonesia and Polynesia which were open to the Good news.

It seemed almost too good to be true that another general awakening of phenomenal power swept the United States in 1830-1831.[4] Whether in the eastern, western or southern States, it was without reported extravagance. The movement began in Boston and New York and other cities in summertime, 1830.[5] It began in Rochester, New York, during the autumn in Finney's ministry, and reached its peak in midwinter 1830-31, winning a thousand inquirers at the same time that a hundred thousand others were being enrolled in other parts from Maine to the borders of Texas.[6] Finney, as a national evangelist, was made by the revival of 1830-31, not vice versa. In these years, several smaller bodies of evangelistic folk unchurched by their denominations united in the virile Disciples of Christ movement.

Bishop Asbury told his Methodist preachers:[7] 'We must attend to camp-meetings; they make our harvest time.' The harvest was followed by as much work as that which preceded sowing. The Methodist Episcopal Church thrived in the 1830s, and doubled its numbers around 1840.[8] Likewise, the Baptists, carrying on their ministry by means of their 'farmer-preachers,' covered the country with a network of Baptist associations, founding a Home Mission in 1832.[9]

The revival of the 1830s was effective in Great Britain also, provoking local movements of great intensity among the various Methodist bodies in England, strengthening the Anglican Evangelicals and Free Churches.[10] It was inhibited somewhat by a confessional reaction, the Tractarian movement, which stressed a sacramental-sacerdotal churchmanship and opposed the evangelism of the awakenings.[11] James Caughey, an American evangelist, won many thousands in a series of campaigns in England—including William Booth, who commenced open air preaching.[12]

First South Wales and then North Wales were moved in awakenings in the 1830s.[13] Another general revival stirred Wales in the 'forties, influenced by Finney's philosophy of revival. In Scotland, revivals increased in number in the 1830s, culminating in an extraordinary outburst at Kilsyth under the ministry of William C. Burns, who witnessed a like revival in Dundee, then in various parts of Scotland, as spontaneous revivals broke out in the Highlands from 1839 onwards.[14] This Scottish Awakening prepared the way for the Disruption and the formation of the Free Church of Scotland, a protest against lay patronage and government interference. So great was the revival in Ireland that the bishops of the Church of Ireland were talking about 'a second reformation,' somewhat prematurely, for the converts of the time were lost to Ireland by emigration following the potato famine. In the North, Evangelicalism triumphed over Arianism among Presbyterians, who multiplied their congregations.[15]

The evangelical ecumenism of the times produced an interesting development. Dublin Evangelicals formed a group for 'the breaking of bread,' attracting many who were bewildered by denominationalism.[16] From this gathering came the Christian Brethren, miscalled Plymouth Brethren. John Darby became the leader of the Exclusive Brethren, George Muller of the Open Brethren, who promoted evangelism and missionary enterprise.

The ministry of George Scott in the 1830s precipitated a lasting revival in Sweden, Carl Olof Rosenius taking up his work after his expulsion, awakenings general in the 1840s, when revival was renewed in Norway, all Scandinavia being moved in the 1850s, despite a confessional reaction under Grundtvig.[17] There was confessional reaction in Germany also, although revivals continued. The continuing Reveil in France and Switzerland reached the Netherlands in 1830, provoking awakenings as well as a confessional reaction.

The 1830s were marked by some extraordinary revival-awakenings in Polynesia. In 1834, a phenomenal movement began in the kingdom of Tonga, described by the Wesleyan missionaries as a 'baptism from above.'[18] In 1837, a similar movement began in the kingdom of Hawaii, Titus Coan taking in 1705 tested converts in one day at Hilo, 7557 in one church during the movement.[19] Revivals were felt in other parts of Polynesia, and a movement in Tonga in the 1840s paralleled a great ingathering in the Fiji Islands, among a Melanesian fearfully addicted to cannibalism.[20] In 1822, missionaries of the Netherlands Missionary Society had entered Sulawesi in Indonesia.[21] While revival was moving the Netherlands, a folk movement of great proportions swept Minahassa, the northeastern peninsula, making that field Christian within a couple of generations.

In the 1830s, there were renewed revivals in Grahamstown in South Africa, and an overflow to the Bantu folk round about. Robert Moffat witnessed an ingathering in Botswanaland. At the same time, pioneers were pouring into southern Africa from missionary societies renewed or founded in the movements going on in the sending countries.[22] Pioneers were at the same time entering the Gold Coast and Nigeria, while freed slaves settled Sierra Leone and Liberia.

Missions of help to the Oriental Churches in the Near and Middle East resulted in revivals and awakenings, sometimes in disruption and reformation.[23] The pioneers coming from revived churches in Britain, Europe, and North America gained barely a foothold in China, where resistance to the foreign faith was strong. Japan and Korea remained closed to all missionary enterprise.

There were folk movements in various parts of India. Missionaries flocked to India after 1833 and accelerated the work of evangelism and social reform in the sub-continent. There were local revivals, among them a striking movement sparked by the ministry of Samuel Hebich.[24] A folk movement of the Karens of Burma to Christ followed the conversion of Ko Tha Byu through Baptist evangelism.[25] There was 'a time of revival' in Ceylon.

The work of James Thomson, who pioneered education and Bible distribution in the Latin American republics, was systematically destroyed in the political and religious reaction throughout the continent. In the West Indies, newly-liberated slaves flocked to the churches of the missionaries who had defended them against oppression.

After Finney became a national figure, he was invited to campaign in Boston, New York, Philadelphia and the larger cities.[26] His 'new measures' aroused opposition, and his theology moved away from the Presbyterian-Congregational brand of Calvinism to a middle course between Calvin and Arminius. He later espoused a perfectionism.

Finney's career proved most unusual in the history of evangelism. Reacting against a kind of fatalism in his own denomination, he deplored the notion that sinners should continue under conviction of sin until God should deign to grant them repentance; rather he felt that they should, by an act of the will, surrender to God. His preaching of this 'whosoever will' message achieved a powerful effect.

As a gospel tactician, Finney was second to none. As a strategist, his practice was better than his theory. Finney went to the extreme of stating that revivals of religion were nothing more or less than a result of the right use of the appropriate means.[27] His own expectancy of revival seemed justified by the results almost everywhere reported in his services. His theories, based on the assumption that times of refreshing were automatically assured, have not always applied during serious declines in community religion.

Unfortunately, besides encouraging many a local pastor or evangelist to expect revival, Finney's theory encouraged a brash school of evangelists who thought that they could promote genuine revival by means chosen by themselves in times chosen by themselves. The use of means was often blessed with Spirit-filled men, but with less-spiritual agents it gave rise to a brand of promotional evangelism, full of sensationalism and commercialism.

Neither the 1792 Awakening, at Finney's birth, nor the 1830 movement, nor the 1858-59 Awakening, nor the 1905 Revival after his death, was planned, programmed or promoted. It must be concluded that Finney's theory applied to evangelism, not outpourings of the Spirit.

One among many influenced by the writings of Finney, George Williams, converted in his 'teens, commenced in London in the 1840s the Young Men's Christian Association, at first as thoroughly evangelistic as it was social.[28] The formation of the Y.W.C.A. followed in the 'fifties. These movements experienced a remarkable expansion during the mid-century awakening in the United States and Great Britain and other countries. They were two of a host of voluntary organizations assisting the Churches.

There was nothing new in the theology of the 1830 Revival.
All of its teachings were derived from the New Testament,
its strong points the ,doctrines recovered in the Reformation
and re-emphasized in the Evangelical Awakenings of the
early and later eighteenth century.

Out of the evangelical ecumenism of the 1830s and 1840s
came the Evangelical Alliance, founded in 1846 by leaders
of the movement on both sides the Atlantic. Its doctrinal
basis reflected the views of a majority of Protestants between 1810 and 1910 before broad church and high church
partisans entered the cooperative movement.[29]

I. The Divine inspiration, authority and sufficiency
of the Holy Scriptures, and the right and duty of private
judgment in the interpretation thereof.
II. The Unity of the Godhead, and the Trinity of
Persons therein.
III. The utter depravity of human nature, in con-
sequence of the Fall.
IV. The incarnation of the Son of God, His work
of atonement for sinners of mankind, and His media-
torial intercession and reign.
V. The justification of the sinner by faith alone.
VI. The work of the Holy Spirit in the conversion
and sanctification of the sinner.
VII. The resurrection of the body, the judgment
of the world by the Lord Jesus Christ, the eternal
blessedness of the righteous, and the eternal punish-
ment of the wicked.

The Evangelical Alliance had adopted a final statement of
faith—that of the Divine institution of the Christian ministry
and obligation and perpetuity of the ordinances of baptism
and the Lord's Supper. The records of the Awakenings reveal no departure from the points listed above, but they do
indicate the participation of preachers and teachers, such as
Brethren and Quakers, whose view of Christian ministry and
ordinances differed from the other denominations.

In those times, the Roman Catholic and Greek Orthodox
Churches offered no cooperation, but often persecuted the
Evangelicals. Apart from the Anglican, Lutheran, Reformed
and other neo-confessionalists, Protestants used the Alliance
idea of Christian unity so widely that it led to a practice of
fraternal fellowship having the force of a major doctrine.
The revivalists, evangelists, pastors and missionaries at
home and abroad worked together in evangelical comity.

Meanwhile, the revivalists of the Third Awakening continued the drive for social betterment.[30] They achieved an emancipation of slaves, the protection of prisoners, the care of the sick, the improvement of working conditions, the safeguarding of women and children, and the extension of popular education, the founding of hospitals, asylums, orphanages, schools, high schools and colleges. The outstanding work of Wilberforce was followed by that of Fowell Buxton and Ashley Cooper, Earl of Shaftesbury. In Germany, Theodor Fliedner performed extraordinary social service. The more evangelistic Methodists in England provided leadership in the trade unions. In the United States, organized good works flourished as never before, promoted by societies that rose in the Awakening. On the mission fields, wherever permitted, missionaries became social activists in education, medicine, and other humanitarian projects.

The Third Great Awakening came to an end about 1842 in the United States. The unfulfilled predictions of William Miller regarding the Second Coming, the affluence of society in an expanding economy, and the divisive effect of chattel slavery tended to hinder further expansion of the Churches. In 1848, political turmoil affecting most countries brought it to an end in Great Britain and other parts of Europe. But after a decline which lasted about fifteen years, there came another great awakening, surpassing previous movements in its extent, wholesomeness, effects, and lasting impact, while sharing their theology and objectives.

5

SOCIAL IMPACT OF REVIVAL

To practise a selfish Christian faith seems impossible. 'Christianity,' said Wesley[1] 'is essentially a social religion; to turn it into a solitary religion is indeed to destroy it.'

The sowing of the seed of social reform was carried out in the eighteenth century in Britain, just as was that of political liberty in America.[2] There were two main periods of harvest in the century that followed, coinciding in their beginnings with the early and the mid-century awakenings.[3]

Europe and America were convulsed by war in the days of Napoleon, hence it was to be expected that the flowering of social reform would follow the coming of peace after the battle of Waterloo. Peace made possible a way for social improvement not only in Great Britain and parts of Europe but also in the United States. The first period of impact came to an end about the time of the abortive revolutions of 1848 and the Crimean and American Civil Wars, and the second one commenced in the 1860s.

The first social impact was felt in the emancipation of slaves, in the protection of prisoners, in the care of the sick and wounded, in the betterment of the standards of workers, in the defence of women and children and of helpless animals, and in the establishment of systems of education.

By far, the greatest social evil was that of human slavery. Inter-tribal wars provided opportunities for slavery, which was the lot of the captured, not only in Africa but in many other parts of the world. The Arabs first introduced war for the capture of slaves for the Near Eastern market as a way of life in Africa, Europeans introducing the same objective (directly and indirectly) into West Africa for the overseas, rather than the overland trade. There is no escaping the responsibility for the active promotion of inter-tribal war, although (of course) such a state of affairs could not have occurred in the nominally Christian homelands, even then. The feudal system, with its institution of serfdom, a form of slavery, had passed away in most European countries, though persisting in the most backward.

The slave trade was a diabolical affair.[4] African chiefs often raided nearby villages at night and set fire to the huts, slaughtering the very old and very young and dragging the survivors in shackles to the coast. In the overseas trade, it was estimated that one in eight died during the voyage in which they were packed like logs in stinking holds, and that another one in twenty died in the port before reaching the auctioneer's block, twenty per cent dying within ten weeks of embarking, with no more than fifty per cent reaching the plantations. Likewise, in the overland trade, ten lives were lost for every slave who reached the coast and fifty per cent never reached a slave market,[5] according to Livingstone.

Thirteen years before the formation of the Committee for the Abolition of Slavery, John Wesley published his thoughts on slavery in a direct and penetrating argument against the inhuman traffic in human beings. 'Can human law turn darkness into light or evil into good? Notwithstanding ten thousand laws, right is right and wrong is wrong still.' [6]

Wesley declared all slave-holding absolutely inconsistent with any kind of natural justice, let alone Christian ethics. He declaimed that the whole business was hypocritically greedy, that slavery bred other vices. Men-buyers, he said, were no better than men-stealers. He denounced the wealthy slave-merchants as the mainspring that put into motion the slave-captains, slave-owners, kidnappers and murderers. They were all guilty.

These were strong words to use in 1774, when plantation slavery was protected by law, when philosophers of old and statesmen of the time were quoted eagerly to justify the outrageous institution. Wesley followed the example of the Quakers, who had spoken against slavery in the seventeenth century. George Whitefield declared less opposition. But the anti-slavery advocates were only a small, enlightened minority in both Britain and the American Colonies. Their voices were scarcely heard at first.

Slavery, though not practised in Europe, was prevalent in European colonies in the New World as well as in most Asian and African countries. In the nineteenth century, slavery was practised mainly in the plantation communities of the South in the United States and in the West Indies, as well as in the Ibero-American colonies. Yet the control of the machinery of slavery lay in the efficient shipping organizations of England, Old and New. And naval police power lay in the hands of the British Admiralty.

The pioneer advocates and engineers of the abolition of slavery within the British Empire were almost all products of the Evangelical Revivals. William Wilberforce and his colleagues were Evangelicals,[7] many of them the pillars of the then-derided, now-extolled Clapham Sect, a group of Church of England Evangelicals with Free Church adherents holding greater concern for the souls and bodies of men than for current ecclesiastical strife. As the abolition movement gained strength by spiritual persuasion, great men such as William Pitt, Edmund Burke and Charles James Fox, and others of like rank, joined the Evangelicals in their grand objective,[8] as did liberals with ethics inherited from their own Christian forebears.

From the time that Lord Mansfield declared in a famous case in 1772 that any slave brought to England was automatically free, anti-slavery agitation made progress; and the slave trade was abolished in 1807.[9]

That abolition of the slave trade had been achieved in Britain was of utmost importance. Had another country so decided, only a good example at the least would have been forthcoming. After Trafalgar, however, Great Britain's naval might was unchallenged for a century, and it was used to dissuade other nations from slave-trading. The nations at the Congress of Vienna agreed that the slave trade should be abolished, and country after country took legislative action until it was internationally outlawed by the civilized nations, and by some less-civilized countries as well.[10]

At first, the patrol action of the British navy against the slave-ships in the Atlantic and Indian Oceans had the effect of worsening conditions on the voyage to slave-markets, for up to two-thirds of the human cargoes were lost, some being thrown overboard to avoid detection and capture. And thus the dwindling supply of slaves caused much overwork in the West Indian plantations.[11]

Sir William Fowell Buxton led the agitation, until in 1834 Emancipation of the Slaves came into law throughout the British Empire.[12] No less than 750,000 in the West Indies alone were proclaimed free men, their chapels being crowded at midnight July 31, while the day of liberation, far from being one of bloodshed as predicted, became a day of order, reverence and rejoicing, the Negro having been prepared for his liberty through the influence of evangelical missions. Parliament cheerfully paid twenty million pounds sterling to recompense the slave-owners.

It took another thirty years to bring about the emancipation of the slaves in the United States. The successes in the early nineteenth century of the British Emancipation had dealt a staggering blow to the American institution of slavery, but it took more agitation by tender-conscienced Christians and yet another Evangelical Awakening, before a majority of the people were ready to abolish slavery. The Finneyan Revivals had a powerful effect on anti-slavery agitation in the North, not always appreciated.[13]

In the first encounter of Europeans with African people at Table Bay, there was mutual friendship; and generations passed before anything like a 'colour bar' was erected.[14] The spread of slavery in the Cape Colony bred contempt for race which in turn poisoned the master-servant relationship, whether in Brazil, Jamaica, Alabama or Cape Colony. In some places, the prejudice lasted longer than in others, due to factors of history.

Unlike West Africa, Southern Africa had not become a slave-raiding territory. The slaves of the burghers in Cape Town were (more often than not) imported from countries overseas, across the Indian Ocean, in race chiefly of Malay stock which included Malagasy, with some Hottentot or kindred folk, a minority Bantu-speaking blacks.

Ships coming south-southwest from East-Indian or intermediate ports unloaded their slaves at the Cape, where a good slave cost $800.[15] From one quarter to one third of the human cargoes never reached Cape Town,[16] but once landed, the slaves 'enjoyed' a better treatment than was common in the West Indies.

The trekking farmers usually possessed their quota of Hottentot slaves as household property. The cultural gap between Hottentot and European was so great that menial service was the inevitable relationship of the former to the latter. Slavery was an accepted institution all over the world, and slavery at the Cape was far from being the worst. When emancipation came, the menial service continued in altered form. The life of the Hottentot, unorganized compared with that of the tribal Bantu, was doomed. Out of the submergence of Hottentots and half-castes into European society arose the Cape Coloured folk, largely Afrikaans-speaking, predominantly Christian, Islamic remnants surviving only in the community of the Cape Malays. Doubtless, were it not for the presence of the mass of black people to the north, the Cape Coloured would have been absorbed by the whites.

Afrikaners had inherited their slaves as personal property
(as in the Southern States), and it was the exception rather
than the rule for household slaves to be ill-treated. Owners
had begun to interest themselves in the evangelization of
both their household slaves and the Hottentots nearby. The
imperial rulers seated overseas at Westminster were much
of the same mind. In 1822, William Wilberforce rose in the
House of Commons to insist that 'the communication of
Christian instruction to the slaves and Hottentots is a para-
mount act of duty.' [17]

As the agitation for the emancipation of the slaves overcame opposition, the Cape was ready. When in 1834, the
British Government decreed slavery abolished, both burgher
and boer readily accepted emancipation, with its promise of
fair compensation for the loss of property.[18]

But management was hopelessly bungled in the first place,
for the compensation was payable in London in cash and bonds
—and the poorer Cape farmers were unable to get to any
colonial bank. They were thus compelled to sell their interest
next-to-nothing to good-for-nothing middlemen.

In the second place, chaos in labour markets (much resembling the disorganization of labour in the American South
after the Civil War) left farmers without help and labourers
starving. In this also, British idealism became greatly mis-
understood and distrusted.

There were now four major forces involved in the northward civilizing of Africa, the expansion of the Afrikaner
folk, the settlement of British and other colonists, the evangelism and social ministry of the missionaries among the
native races, and the imperialism of Victorian Britain. The
first two, destined to create the modern South African nation,
had renounced slavery and shunned involvement in it in their
relationship with primitive peoples, and the last two opposed
slavery and slave-trading in British territory and beyond.

South Africa was a trading, agricultural and pastoral community at that time, without any of the gross injustices which
marked an industrialized society. Yet every victory won in
advanced societies had its effects in South Africa.

Already in the eighteenth century significant prison reform
was under way.[19] The conditions of life in prisons were at
that time indescribably foul. Old, decrepit buildings were
commonly used as prisons; strait-jackets, irons and chains
were added for security on the slightest excuse. The prisons
were dens of despair with disease, drunkenness, indecency

and debauchery forced on their inmates. Not only were the vicious criminals so incarcerated but also first offenders, and even persons already declared not guilty of any crime. An Evangelical, John Howard, took up the challenge and gave his life as well as his private fortune.[20] John Howard received the official thanks of Britain's House of Commons, and was recognized[21] as the father of modern prison reform, inspiring others to take up the task only barely begun in his lifetime.[22] Evangelicals took the lead, followed by the free-thinkers, who tackled the reform of the penal code.[23]

A young Quaker mother, raising eleven children, became burdened for the women, desperate and depraved, whom she found in the notorious Newgate prison that Wesley had called the earthly equivalent of hell. Elizabeth Fry not only read the Scriptures and prayed with these unfortunates, but also opened successful prison schools for them.[24] In 1817, Mrs. Fry founded a society for prison reform, dedicated to those principles now taken as elementary; separation of the sexes, classification of all criminals, useful employment, secular education, and religious instruction with a view to restoring the prisoners to society.

One of those directly influenced was Theodor Fliedner, born in the first month of the year 1800, son of a Lutheran pastor.[25] Unconverted, he had attended the Universities of Giessen and Göttingen, but his faith was deepened elsewhere. A greater influence on his life was the evangelical impact of Halle,[26] the university where August Francke had served.

In due course, Fliedner was called to the cure of Kaisers-werth, a Protestant parish in the midst of a Roman Catholic population.[27] A threat of foreclosure of a mortgage sent him off to Holland and England to collect funds. It was in London that the effect of the Revival dispelled finally any trace of rationalism in Fliedner's mind.[28] In 1823, Theodor Fliedner met Elizabeth Fry in the British capital.

> I learned to know a whole host of institutions that minister to the bodies and souls of men. I inspected their schools and prisons. I observed their homes for the poor and the sick and the orphaned. I studied their missionary societies and Bible societies and their societies for the improvement of prisons and so forth. And I particularly noted that practically all of these institutions and organizations were called into being by a living faith in Jesus Christ and that nothing but this vital faith sustains them.[29]

On his return to Germany, Fliedner requested voluntary imprisonment, but was refused. In 1826, he organized a prison society, the first of a series of philanthropic ventures. He built a home for discharged women prisoners, another for men, another for orphans, a hospital for the sick, an asylum for the insane. He urgently needed nurses to help, but in those days an educated woman would not stoop to empty a bucket. Fliedner decided that, if a farmer's daughter could be trained to look after helpless animals, she could be trained to look after sick people. He put girls in uniform and called them deaconesses.

Florence Nightingale, an English gentlewoman, was much intrigued by a report of the ministry of Theodor Fliedner at Kaiserswerth where the sick were lovingly cared for by the German deaconesses, all of them of peasant stock, as were Elizabeth Fry's, nursing being regarded as too low for ladies. Soon she took her training in nursing at the obscure village on the Rhine.[30] Looking back years later, she deplored the backwardness of the hospital but commended its tone as 'excellent.' She recalled that she never had met with a higher tone, or a purer devotion. She returned to London to apply the lessons she had learned in the same evangelical way.

Before she died at the age of ninety, the lady with the lamp had revolutionized the life of the private soldier. She became generally regarded as the founder of modern nursing. And historians have conceded not only her training at a school born of evangelical revival but her debt to Evangelicals for her lifelong simplicity of purpose.

Secularists have contended that Florence Nightingale betrayed an anti-evangelical spirit by deriding prayer for the sick. This was a strange misrepresentation of fact. The attitude of the famous nurse was that of the modern Christian doctor. What was the good, she asked, to pray for deliverance from plague and pestilence as long as sewers ran into the River Thames?[31]

The greatest Evangelical reformer of all was Shaftesbury. At the base of the Shaftesbury Memorial in the heart of Piccadilly Circus in London is carved a striking inscription composed by W. E. Gladstone: 'During a public life of half a century, Lord Shaftesbury devoted the influence of his station, the strong sympathy of his heart and the great power of his mind to honouring God by serving his fellow-men— an example to his order, a blessing to his people, and a name to be by them ever gratefully remembered.'[32]

Great Britain was the first of the countries of the world to become industrialized. The Industrial Revolution brought about a sorry exploitation of the toiling masses, for whom Deism had done little.[33]

Shaftesbury described himself as 'an Evangelical of the Evangelicals,'[34] and this called him into a crusade for the betterment of humanity and gave an unparalleled demonstration of Christian love, rather than of class hatred, love harnessed to the improvement of the lot of the working poor.

Before Lord Shaftesbury's reforms, the workers were caught in a treadmill of competitive toil which served to keep them straining for sixteen hours a day. Shaftesbury and his friends put an end to that by legislation limiting operation of factories to ten hours a day, introducing a Saturday half-holiday, and abolishing all unnecessary Sunday duties.[35]

Shaftesbury's Mines and Collieries Act made impossible any further exploitation of women or children in coal mines where they had been used to drag coal in heavy wagons along darksome tunnels. His Chimney Sweep Acts prohibited the use of little boys to clean narrow factory chimneys of soot— many a child had suffocated in the task and others had been maimed therein. He also delivered children in the country from an agricultural exploitation as terrible as that of the factories. Shaftesbury, by his Lunacy Acts, transformed the lot of the insane from abused prisoners to patients.[36]

Shaftesbury promoted public parks, playing fields, gymnasia, garden allotments, working-men's institutes, public libraries, night schools, choral and debating societies, and other opportunities of self-help.[37]

Even Kenneth Scott Latourette in his weighty volumes has confessed that there was not enough space to list more than a few of the reformers and reforms impelled by evangelical motivation.[38] Nine out of ten of Lord Shaftesbury's colleagues in social and industrial reform were as much the products of Evangelicalism as the Earl himself.[39] A cotton-mill owner, John Wood, provided most of the money needed for the Ten Hours' Crusade. Richard Oastler, who did so much for the factory children, was a Methodist lay preacher. Others in the crusade were active in the lay preaching of the gospel. The Ten Hours' Act proved to be the Magna Carta of the liberty of industrial workers, closing factories at 6 p.m., keeping them closed for twelve hours, preventing toilers from being robbed of evening and Sunday leisure.[40] After so many years of exploitation, it was a great deliverance.

It is significant that trade unionism grew during this period of the social impact of the gospel. British trade unionism owed much to the six Dorchester labourers who were transported to the Australian penal colonies for seven years of servitude.[41] Their crime was that of forming an agricultural union to resist further depression of their wages as farm hands, wages already cut to a below-subsistence level of a shilling a day.[42] These labourers were guilty of no violence and no intimidation, not even a strike. In 1834, all six were dragged from their homes and condemned, then shipped off to Tasmania.

These Dorchester labourers, often called the 'Tolpuddle martyrs,' included three Methodist local preachers and two others active in the Tolpuddle Methodist Chapel.[43] A sixth man professed no religious convictions, but was so impressed with the religious life of one of his companions, who slaved with him in a convict gang, that he became a Christian and a Sunday School superintendent in later life. An aroused public opinion forced the early pardon of these working-men and their transportation home. The trade union cause had won a round in its battle for working men's elementary rights. Christian leadership continued for a hundred years in British trade unions. The Liberal Prime Minister, David Lloyd George, paid an unusual tribute to evangelical influence in the trade unions in these careful paragraphs:[44]

> The movement which improved the condition of the working classes, in wages, hours of labour, and otherwise, found most of its best officers and non-commissioned officers in men trained in institutions which were the result of Methodism ... John Wesley inaugurated a movement which gripped the soul of England, that deepened its spiritual instincts, trained them and uplifted them; the result is that when a great appeal is made to either England or America, there is always the response ... and it is due to the great religious revival of the eighteenth century.

Thus it was in the nineteenth century largely that the great Wesley-Whitefield Revival bore the fruit cultivated by converts of later awakenings, in Britain and the United States.

It cannot be denied that the influence of Great Britain on the United States of America was a powerful force, especially in the realm of social progress. As Great Britain was first industrialized, the hitherto unknown problems of industrial life were therein first encountered and overcome.

The decades following 1830 in American life have been called by historians[45] 'The Sentimental Years,' for it was a time when organized good works flourished as never before. There was scarcely an object of benevolence that lacked a dedicated society or institution,[46] and all of the organizations (whether church-related or not) were directly indebted to the Evangelical Awakening of the times.[47]

In the United States, there were societies to promote education, to reform prisons, to stop prostitution, to colonize Africa with freed slaves, to advance the cause of peace, to provide social and spiritual amenities for sailors in port— not to mention the multitude of home and foreign missionary societies, Bible and tract societies, Sunday School associations and temperance clubs.[48]

Out of the Revival in Britain came the monitorial school system of Lancaster and Bell, a prelude to mass education. Schools and high schools and colleges were founded in the United States as a result of the Awakenings of 1800 onward in many churches and colleges, awakenings which provided not only founders but teaching staffs. Most of the denominational schools and high schools gave way to free public school systems in turn. Latourette declared:[49]

> Even more important, the initiative and the early leadership in the creation of the system of free public schools supported by the state came largely from those who seem to have caught their inspiration from the Protestant wing of Christianity.

Much the same was true of Great Britain and the parts of Europe influenced by the Evangelical Awakenings. A Royal Society for the Prevention of Cruelty to Animals was founded in London in 1824, and became the largest as well as the oldest society of its kind in the world. Not only did it seek to stamp out cruelty, but it offered free veterinary service to as many as a quarter of a million mute creatures annually. It is not surprising to learn that the founder of the Society was an Anglican Evangelical clergyman, Arthur Broome, and that Sir Thomas Fowell Buxton, the evangelical emancipator, chaired the first meeting assisted by his friends Wilberforce and Mackintosh.[50] This was a fitting climax to a campaign by Evangelicals against cruel sports, bull-baiting, cock-fighting and other matches that caused pain to animals. In the United States, the spread of camp-meeting evangelism repressed brutal sports, and in Britain (in Trevelyan's word) it was 'humanitarianism and religiosity' likewise.[51]

6

ENCOUNTER WITH THE BANTU

The Bantu tribes,[1] of Negro-Hamitic origins, already had crossed the Limpopo when the first European settlers arrived at the Cape of Good Hope, a thousand miles south. Between Bantu and European habitations lay a wide tract of territory that provided sparse subsistence for the nomadic Bushmen and pastoral Hottentots, neither of them related to the Bantu tribes who warred upon them.

An attractive people with a musical language, the Bantu were possessed of a tribal organization capable of withstanding the impact of European colonists. It must be recognized that they lacked some elements of civilization, whether of the West or the East. Their bravery, even their chivalry in battle was unquestioned, but many of their tribal customs were considered barbaric by European and Asian observers.

The first quarter of the nineteenth century produced a military genius among the Zulus who attacked and decimated three hundred tribes, butchering and burning so that it was said that not a single square mile of what is now Natal was left unsodden by the blood of his victims. Shaka and his impis (including runaway rebels against his tyranny) desolated a wide swathe of territory that lay as comparatively empty as the southwestern veld where the Bantu folk were unknown.[2]

Among his own people, Shaka killed as the notion took him, not only individuals to whom he took a dislike but masses of people—on one occasion four hundred women were stabbed to death for entertainment. When his royal mother died, Shaka killed ten of her women servants, ordered all milk to be spilt on the ground for a year, all calves to be separated from their mothers, and all husbands and wives to be slain if pregnancy occurred to prove their cohabitation. Fynn, an English pioneer, counted 7000 corpses of those massacred in one afternoon in mourning for Shaka's mother.[3]

British traders tried to obtain a concession of land in the denuded territory south of the Zulu homeland, in what was called Natal. A British naval officer, Allen Gardiner,[4] who later laid down his life for the Gospel in Tierra del Fuego, tried to gain an entrance for Church Missionary Society workers to reach the Zulus; and Francis Owen, an Anglican clergyman, actually lived at the savage court of Shaka's successor, before giving up in sheer horror.[5] It was Shaka's policy to keep the territory to the south of Zulu country denuded of inhabitants. His terror drove the weaker Bantu tribes before him, hence pressure mounted on a line drawn by Europeans as 'the Kaffir boundary.' A series of Kaffir wars ensued. Fear covered the whole of southeastern Africa like a blanket of fog, Xhosa fear of the Zulu, European fear of the Bantu.

Joseph Williams of the London Missionary Society carried the message to the Xhosa-speaking folk who represented the first great wave of Bantu advance to the southwest.[6] His converts survived his premature death, and were gathered into a continuing congregation by John Brownlee.

The 1822 and '31 Revivals among British settlers, chiefly Wesleyan in character, moved Christians to evangelize the heathen Bantu and Hottentots. Near the Buffalo river, the Rev. Samuel Young was preaching in the Wesleyville station when a man began to cry aloud until the whole congregation was affected. 'Every soul seemed to feel much of the presence of God.' A score of inquirers were registered.[7]

These local awakenings often continued for months on end. The Methodist missionaries were delighted to win so many of various racial and tribal origins, and the British military commander was pleased with their advancement in civilization.[8] One of many chiefs converted was Kama, the first fruit of Bantu chiefs who embraced Christianity.

Among the converts of the Awakening stirring the 1820 Settlers was Joseph Warner, who went forth as evangelist among the Tembu, and who gave two sons to the Methodist ministry. Another was Henry H. Dugmore, who became a superintendent, ministering to Europeans and Bantu.[9]

Robert Moffat, another Scot, devoted himself to evangelizing Bantu tribes in Botswanaland.[10] When he and his wife Mary arrived at Kuruman, they found 'not a ray of light' in the darkness of local social and spiritual conditions.[11] A spiritual awakening began in 1829. Within five years, the population of the station had risen to 727, with 115 scholars being taught in the school; the attendances at worship on Sundays rose to 340, weekdays to 130, and 29 were regular communicants.[12] Robert Moffat—unbelievably to some—won the notorious chief, Africander, to a vital Christian faith.

The awakening in Botswanaland continued. A report of 1832 from the Plaatberg Circuit claimed that the average attendance for many months was five hundred and sometimes rose to a thousand in Christian worship.[13]

There was similar blessing in the Transkei, where the inhabitants were Xhosa-speaking. At Butterworth, the local Methodist missionary read a letter from Wesleyville:

> Cries at this time became general throughout the chapel so that my voice and the voices of those who prayed were drowned; and when we were compelled to break up the meeting, many went away from the chapel sobbing.[14]

Most of the Wesleyan stations in the Transkei and other Bantu areas experienced a visitation. The manifestations of the awakenings in homelands were being seen in Africa.

Before the end of 1834, the Sixth Kaffir War had broken out; within a few days, many settlers had been murdered and hundreds of homesteads destroyed by invading Amaxhosa impis, mission stations destroyed, the missionaries fled.[15]

Another extraordinary awakening began in 1837, again in Grahamstown, the large chapel being crowded for prayer night after night, many professing to find faith, more than two hundred in number.[16] In its membership, the European Circuit increased from 315 to 609 in a single year. The awakening spread to the Bantu congregations, taxing every bit of space. Probationers increased in number rapidly, accredited members more slowly.

In the same quarter of the century, another product of the Awakening in Scotland arrived in South Africa, a significant event. David Livingstone married Moffat's daughter, Mary. At first he took his wife and children on his long, dangerous journeys, but after losing his youngest child and almost losing the others, he sent them home and pursued his extraordinary explorations alone. His heroic exploits pointed a way to the evangelization and civilization of Africa.[17]

Scotsmen were not only well represented in the London Missionary Society, but also in national societies. Scottish Presbyterians contributed a major benefaction to the education of Bantu folk by founding, along with other schools, the Lovedale Institution in 1841.[18]

Anglicans were somewhat tardy in their outreach to the Bantu, their belated ministry chiefly to English settlers and officials absorbing their energies until the coming of Bishop Gray, a dynamic churchman, in 1847.[19]

In 1835,[20] the American Board (Congregationalist) entered Natal to evangelize the Zulus. In 1829, the Paris Evangelical Missionary Society—a product of the Revival in France—sent its first missionaries to South Africa; and in 1833 they entered Lesotho and founded a lasting work. Their greatest pioneer was François Coillard,[21] himself a revivalist whose heart had been stirred by Haldane's ministry in France.

Another Revival-sparked society, the Rhenish Mission, sent out its first missionaries to South African Hottentots and Bantu in 1829. They were followed by the alike Berlin Missionary Society workers in 1834.[22] Yet another mission thrust of the Revival in Europe began through an awakening in 1848 in Hanover, the Hermannsburg Mission.[23]

The Awakening in Norway under Hans Nielsen Hauge led to the sending of Hans Schreuder and a Norwegian Mission to the Zulus of Natal in the years following 1843.[24] Schreuder led the way for several Scandinavian missions pioneering in Southern Africa.

Missionary records from the first half of the nineteenth century have shown that the most rapid advance of the Faith was achieved in Southern Africa, undoubtedly due to a couple of factors, the extension of European interest there and the occurrence of evangelical awakenings among the people.

What of the remainder of Africa, south of the Sahara? It was indeed a Dark Continent. First European contacts with Black Africa had come through the nefarious slave trade in which the professedly Christian nations followed the Arab example in abetting raids on innocent tribes.

In the early nineteenth century, the slave trade was suppressed, but settlements around the coast begun for trading purposes continued. Explorers and missionaries began to traverse the continent. Later followed the 'scramble for Africa' in which European nations carved up the continent's mass. In many instances, missionaries preceded the flag; in others, they followed it.

Johann Ludwig Krapf of Württemberg was obviously a product of the post-Napoleonic Revival in Germany. After his training at Basel, he entered the service of the Church Missionary Society. Several attempts to enter closed doors failing, he moved southward in the 1840s to Zanzibar and Mombasa to preach, becoming proficient in Swahili.[25] Krapf dreamed of a chain of mission stations across the waist of Africa. The fulfillment of such a dream awaited the coming of recruits from the next series of evangelical awakenings.

East Africa remained largely unpenetrated. And apart from the English-speaking enclaves on the coast, so also did West Africa. Pioneering was the main activity in all of tropical Africa.

The inhabitants of the vast territory quaintly called the Cameroon were partly Bantu, partly Negro and other stock. The Baptist Missionary Society of Britain opened a work in the country in the 1840s,[26] Alfred Saker its noted pioneer.

The Church Missionary Society effected an entrance to Nigeria in 1844, thanks to efforts of liberated Yoruba slaves in Sierra Leone searching out their kinsfolk in Abeokuta. One such freedman, Samuel Adjai Crowther, later Anglican bishop of the Niger territories, began his lifelong service as an evangelist by winning his mother and sisters there.[27]

Sierra Leone Wesleyans sent a remarkable mulatto to Abeokuta, Thomas Birch Freeman, who first pioneered in Ghana in the late 1830s, then opened up a very successful work in Nigeria—like Crowther, living to a great age.[28]

Presbyterians in Jamaica, associated with the United Presbyterian Church of Scotland, took the initiative in the sending out of Scottish and Jamaican Negro missionaries to the Calabar coast in Nigeria in the late 1840s.[29] They pioneered among the Efik people.

Southern Baptists also pioneered in Nigeria in the 1850s, utilizing missionaries of white and Negro blood at first to begin a work among the Yorubas.[30] They survived many vicissitudes to build a lasting Church.

The Basel Mission entered the Gold Coast, now Ghana, in 1828. Theirs also was a pioneering ministry, many a setback overcome.[31] Thomas Birch Freeman in the 1830s developed a model farm in Ghana, and the Wesleyans soon reaped a spiritual harvest by friendly evangelism.[32]

The Baptist and Methodist enterprises in Liberia grew during the 1830s and 1840s, but the scope of their ministry was restricted to the English-speaking freedmen and their descendants. Much the same was true of Sierra Leone, where the Church Missionary Society and other missions worked among the liberated settlers.

The rest of West Africa remained closed to the Gospel message for many a decade. In the 1830s, missionaries sought to follow French immigrants to Algeria and Tunisia; efforts were made to win the Jews also; but the majority of Muslims remained untouched.[33] A Mission of Help from the Church Missionary Society arrived in Egypt in 1825.[34]

7

THE FOURTH GENERAL AWAKENING

The Evangelical Awakening which began in the United States before the end of 1857 and in the United Kingdom in early 1859 spread all over the world and remained effective for at least forty years.[1]

The preliminary prayer meetings were commenced in New York City before the sudden bank panic of October in 1857, and the extraordinary conviction of sin in evangelism was first manifested in Canada, which was not immediately affected by the bank panic.[2] (That bank panics do not cause religious revivals may be seen in the results of the crash of the stock market in 1929 and on earlier occasions.)

How did this great Awakening manifest itself? In the autumn of 1857 came the first signs of an awakening—great success in revival and evangelism in Canada, and an extraordinary movement of men to prayer in New York City which spread from city to city throughout the United States and over the world. Churches, halls, and theatres were filled at noon for prayer, and the overflow filled churches of all denominations at night in a truly remarkable turning of a whole nation toward God.[3]

The Awakening of 1858 was received with enthusiasm by the secular press, which testified gladly of the changes for good in every place.[4] With few exceptions, chiefly among doctrinaire anti-Evangelicals, the Awakening was supported by all the Protestant denominations, including the formalist Anglicans and Lutherans as well as informal Baptists and Methodists. The movement was singularly free of sectarian spirit. Its primary emphasis on prayer did not overshadow its augmented preaching of the Word. The meetings were commended for their quietness and restraint, and won the respect of citizens everywhere, enlisting some of the most mature minds of the community for Christ.[5]

In addition to uncounted multitudes of nominal church members transformed by the power of God, more than a million converts were added to the membership of major denominations during the height of the movement.[6] Beyond

all else, it was a layman's movement, in which the laymen
of all denominations gladly undertook both normal and extraordinary responsibilities in the service of God and humanity.
Despite the outbreak of the most devastating and bloody
war in all the world between the Napoleonic wars and World
War I, the awakening continued effective in the armies of
both North and South and in the civil population at home,
and the coming of peace brought about a renewal of zeal.[7]

The social influence of the Awakening was felt in wartime services, but much impetus was held in suspense until
the cessation of hostilities, after which the social conscience
asserted itself, reinforced by the social achievements of the
same Awakening across the Atlantic.[8]

The same movement also affected the United Kingdom,
beginning in 1859 in Ulster, the most northerly province in
Ireland. Approximately ten per cent of the population there
professed conversion, the same in Wales and Scotland, and
a great awakening continued in England for years, another
million being added to the Churches.[9] Repercussions were
felt in many other European countries, and in South Africa
and Australia and elsewhere among European settlers.

The phenomena of Revival were reported in parts of
India, South Africa, and the East and West Indies among non-
European peoples. Any mission field that possessed an in-
doctrinated body of believers enjoyed the same reviving. In
many countries, the reviving was followed by extraordinary
evangelism and by folk movements of tribes and castes.

Out of the 1859 Awakening in Britain arose a phalanx of
famous evangelists—aristocrats and working men. Spurgeon
built his Tabernacle on the crest of this movement.[10] The
intervention of the War between the States (in which there
was extraordinary evangelism and revival in every theatre
of operations) delayed the emergence of great American
evangelists from the 1858 Awakening. Yet the greatest of
world evangelists emerged in America in due course.[11]

There was not so much unanimity of approval in Great
Britain as in the United States. While the established Church
of Scotland and other Presbyterian bodies overwhelmingly
endorsed the Revival, there was lukewarmness or opposition
in the broad-church and high-church sections of the Church
of England. The British Free Churches fully supported the
Awakening.[12] Many of its supporters questioned the value of
the physical prostrations which marked the outset of the
movement, but these died away under sober direction.

The 1858-59 Awakenings extended the working forces of evangelical Christendom. Not only were a million converted in both the United States and the United Kingdom, but existing evangelistic and philanthropic organizations were revived and new vehicles of enterprise created—Bible Societies flourished as never before, Home Missions and the Salvation Army were founded to extend thus the evangelistic-social ministry of the Awakening in worldwide projects. The impact on the youthful Y.M.C.A. organization was noteworthy.[13]

The mid-century Awakenings revived all the existing missionary societies and enabled them to enter other fields. The practical evangelical ecumenism of the Revival was embodied in the China Inland Mission founded by Hudson Taylor in the aftermath of the British Awakening, the first of the interdenominational 'faith missions.' As in the first half of the century, practically every missionary invasion was launched by men revived or converted in the Awakenings of the Churches in the sending countries.[14]

For example, the first permanent missions in Brazil followed the 1858-59 Awakenings. In Indonesia and India, folk movements to Christianity followed. China was penetrated by the converts of the Revival from many countries. The missionary occupation of Africa was rapid, and the liberated Negro in the Anglo-American territories was hopefully evangelized.

In the 1870s, D. L. Moody rose to fame as a world evangelist. Beginning modestly in York in 1873, Moody progressed through Sunderland, Newcastle, Edinburgh, Dundee, Glasgow, Belfast, Dublin, Manchester, Sheffield, Birmingham and Liverpool, using the methods of the 1858 Revival in prayer and preaching. About 2,500,000 people aggregate heard him in twenty weeks in London.[15]

In 1875, Moody returned to his native land a national figure, campaigning equally successfully in Brooklyn, Philadelphia, New York, Chicago, Boston and other cities. From then onwards, he ministered in cities on both sides of the Atlantic. A flock of successful evangelists was associated with him. Perhaps his greatest campaign was conducted at the World's Exposition in Chicago in 1893. Moody died in action in 1899.

In the Moody period, another awakening began in Sweden, extending the work of the National Evangelical Foundation (EFS)[16] and an offshoot, the Evangelical Mission Covenant (SMF). Revivals continued in Norway, Denmark and Finland.

As a result of the impact of Anglo-American Revivalists —including D. L. Moody—a Thirty Years' Revival began in Germany, from 1880 until 1910. Outstanding leaders were Theodor Christlieb (who founded the German Committee for Evangelism and Gemeinschaftsbewegung), Elijah Schrenk and Samuel Keller.[17]

In the same period, there was revival among the Ukrainian peasantry and evangelism among the Russian upper classes, the latter done by British gentlemen, Radstock and Baedeker. I. S. Prokhanov, converted in 1886, founded the All-Russian Evangelical Union which in the next century united in denominational organization with the Baptists.[18]

It is curious to notice that Charles Darwin's most significant publication (1859) occurred at the time of the Awakening in Great Britain and the United States, heralding a clash between sceptics who interpreted many new scientific conclusions as anti-theistic and traditional theologians who too readily agreed with such a faulty interpretation.

Yet far from antagonizing the academic world, the Awakening resulted in the most extraordinary invasion of the universities and colleges by the Christian message and the most successful recruitment of university-trained personnel in the history of higher education and evangelism.

In the 1858 Awakening in the United States, revivals among students resulted in the formation of the College Y.M.C.A.s, and in the following year, prayer meetings at Oxford and Cambridge gave rise to Christian Unions which later united to form the Inter-Varsity Fellowship. In the local student fellowship at Princeton in 1875 were several outstanding young men—Robert Mateer, who became leader of the Inter-Seminary Missionary Alliance; T. W. Wilson, who became president of Princeton University and later (as T. Woodrow Wilson) President of the United States, and Luther Wishard, who as organizer and evangelist of the Inter-Collegiate Y.M.C.A., pleaded with a reluctant Moody to minister to a sincerely interested student constituency.[19]

In 1882, Moody was persuaded to campaign in Cambridge University, where at first he stirred up scornful opposition. Out of the awakening, the Cambridge Seven (C.T. Studd and other first-rank varsity men) stirred the student world and proceeded to China as missionaries.

Thus encouraged, Moody acceded to Wishard's promptings to arrange a conference for students at Mount Hermon, in his home state. A youthful delegate, Robert Wilder, presented the claims of the mission fields and a hundred of the 250 present responded—within an academic year, two thousand from American universities and colleges. Thus was born the Student Volunteer Movement, with their watchword—to 'evangelize the world in this generation.' Under the direction of men like John R. Mott, Volunteers multiplied on every continent, as recruits or as emissaries.

Out of the 1859 Awakening arose the Keswick Movement for the Deepening of the Spiritual Life (1875). In the eastern hemisphere, it became a unifying force in Evangelicalism, a missionary recruitment rally of the highest quality. Out of the same agitation in America, the organization of the Holiness Movement resulted in splintering, giving birth to vigorous denominations in the Wesleyan tradition.[20]

Christian Endeavor, a movement for training young people in church-related activity, began in a local revival in Maine in 1881, under Francis E. Clark. Within fifteen years, there were more than two million members in forty thousand local societies: they were ecumenical and evangelical. A number of the denominations promoted comparable young people's organizations on the same plan.[21]

Toward the end of the century, an Anglican, George Grubb, excelled as evangelist in the British Empire countries, as did Gipsy Smith, Hay Aitken, John McNeill and Andrew Murray.

Singular advances were made in Africa. Charles Pamla continued preaching as the leading Bantu evangelist; Spencer Walton began a new missionary enterprise; an extraordinary awakening began in Uganda, Christianizing the country.[22]

The 1880s witnessed advances in the evangelization of China, as well as a remarkable seven years' revival in Japan, but the years of rapid growth in the island empire were followed by a decline caused by an onslaught of rationalist theology among national pastors.[23]

The awakenings in sending countries caused an extension of missionary enterprise on every continent. Albert B. Simpson, a convert of the 1858 Revival in Canada, founded the Christian and Missionary Alliance in 1886, at first as an interdenominational organization but later itself becoming a denomination as missionary minded as the Moravians.

In the social impact of mid-century Revivals, greater effects were realized in the industrialized United Kingdom. Lord Shaftesbury continued his extraordinary parliamentary projects for the betterment of humanity. Great orphanages were begun. A Society was formed for the Prevention of

Cruelty to Children (1889), while Josephine Butler rallied evangelical opinion to abolish the licensing of prostitution in Great Britain (1886).[24] Aroused evangelical interests motivated much of the agitation for the betterment of conditions for working people, many leaders in the Labour Party itself being avowed evangelical Christians. In the United States, there also was a growing concern with purely social issues such as rights of the working man, poverty, the liquor trade, slum housing and racial bitterness.[25] Overseas, social action excelled in missionary education and medical services.[26]

To achieve this reform, the crusaders of the Evangelical Awakenings did not stoop to engage in class warfare. Rather, under the guidance of the Spirit, they enlisted the privileged to serve the poor. The Seventh Earl of Shaftesbury single-handed accomplished as much in his lifetime as had been achieved by any parliamentarian, yet remained an aristocrat.

Out of this evangelical concern grew a liberal social gospel whose advocates became indifferent by degrees to the dynamic of the Christian gospel, the transforming of individual lives by the power of Jesus Christ.

Some effects of the 1858-59 Awakening were not immediately apparent—the relationship of the conversion of hundreds of thousands who soon developed an insatiable desire for education to the transformation of the public school systems; or the evangelical conversion of Keir Hardie under Moody's ministry and the introduction of that evangelical spirit into the Labour Movement in contrast to the atheism of Continental socialism. This evangelical leadership among British workers continued for three generations.[27]

Unlike the Reformation, Puritanism and the Evangelical Revival, the Awakening of 1858-1859 onwards produced no cleavage among the Christian denominations, rather sewing together the rent patches of Evangelical Christianity with the thread of spiritual, if not organic, unity. The Anglo-Scottish Reformation rent the major part of British Christianity from the body of Roman Christianity.[28] Puritanism led to the expulsion of the Baptists and Congregationalists from the Anglican Established Church, and the Evangelical Revival resulted in the separation of a considerable part of the religious population from the Church of England. But the Evangelical Awakening of the mid-nineteenth century produced no further divisions and rather indicated that the tide in inter-church relationship had begun to flow in the opposite direction.[29]

8

REVIVAL IN SOUTH AFRICA, I

In Graaff-Reinet, Ds. Andrew Murray, senior, had prayed for many years for an outpouring of the Holy Spirit upon the churches of his adopted country. The younger Murrays never forgot that their father's study door was closed on Friday evenings as the faithful intercessor spent long hours in a time of fervent prayer for revival.[1]

In Cape Town, the organ of the Dutch Reformed Church carried regular news of the extraordinary 1858 Awakening in the United States of America,[2] news relayed by returning Americans or by an occasional visitor or news received by dispatch. Persistently, the details of that great awakening were carried into the homes of Christians far and wide in South Africa.

In August 1859, three ministers issued a call to servants of God in every sphere of service to pray for an awakening throughout South Africa.[3] And, in August also, the editor gave a detailed report of the Ulster Revival— 'eene groote godsdienstige opwekking in het Noorden van Ierland'— describing the revival in Ballymena, Belfast, Coleraine and Londonderry.

A further report on Irish Revivals was given, accompanied by a letter addressed to all South African Christians, calling them to prayer for a visitation of God's Spirit in the country. It was signed by A. Fourie, G. Morgan, P. E. Faure, G. W. A. van der Lingen, R. Shand, A. Fraser, A. Murray, Senior, J. Pears, G. W. Stegmann, W. R. Thomson, Alexander Smith, W. F. Heugh, W. Robertson and P. K. Albertyn.[4]

An item, 'De Kracht van het Vereenigd Gebed,' appeared in the same organ of the Nederduits Gereformeerde Kerk on 30th July 1859.[5] Later, a little book of eighty-five pages was published, entitled 'The Power of Prayer.'[6]

There is no hint in any of the South African reports that an awakening had already begun in the mission stations of the Zulu and Tswana territories, where the missionaries had relayed the blessings of the American 1858 Awakening directly to their charges.

In 1860, reports continued to feature the Irish Revival, noting its spread throughout Great Britain. English-speaking Christians also were kept informed of its progress.[7]

In response to the invitation to prayer sent out by Ludhiana missionaries, union prayer meetings were held in several churches in Cape Town every evening during the second week in January. Numerously attended, they produced no unusual results among churchgoers:[8]

> ... though profitable to many of God's people, they were not distinguished by any remarkable outpouring of the Holy Ghost . . . The appointed week ended, we all too readily sank down into our former state of comparative indifference.

In 1860,[9] church attendance in the Cape Town Methodist churches increased by five per cent over 1859, and this increase was maintained in 1861. It could not be said, however, that there had been any significant awakening among either English or Dutch-speaking churches there until later.

The South African Evangelical Alliance instituted monthly prayer meetings in Congregational, Methodist, Presbyterian and Dutch Reformed and other places of worship,[10] but the attendance was small and 'the exercises too formal and dull.'

Up country, the burden of prayer rapidly increased, more especially among the Dutch Reformed congregations and their ministers. Cautious ministers had been sceptical about the movement in the United States, but a number of careful men, including Faure, Hofmeyr, and Murray of Stellenbosch, and Neethling and Van der Lingen stood up to declare that they were convinced that it was a veritable work of God.[11]

For instance, Ds. Abraham Faure was first of all sceptical but became convinced in mind and heart. By the time that he was ready to urge his congregation to prepare, he was able to pass on details of the Ulster Revival of 1859.[12]

In far off Calvinia, Nicholas Hofmeyr studied the promises of Scripture concerning Revival, but was discouraged by the apathy and indifference of his congregation. He was encouraged to find a like-minded prayer companion, young Van der Rijst, who spent each passing Saturday night in prayer with him, and continued to pray alone after Ds. Hofmeyr long had removed to the Stellenbosch Seminary.[13]

Ds. Neethling of Stellenbosch spoke to his own elders about the matter, and addressed the congregation, using the book on the power of prayer. This prepared the local Stellenbosch congregation for the work that followed.[14]

Van der Lingen of Paarl was at first sceptical regarding the phenomenon of revival. But he was willing to study the matter in Scripture, and soon became convinced not only of the reality of revival but of the certainty of its coming to South Africa. He addressed his church council on the subject and encouraged his flock to pray.[15]

In Worcester, up country from Cape Town, there were other faithful intercessors with God for an awakening, including one who oft repaired to a nearby hilltop to pray for the town spread out before him.[16]

Interest was building up among Dutch and English folk, so a conference of missionaries and ministers was held at Worcester, 18th April 1860, to hear first-hand accounts of the Awakening in the United States and the United Kingdom given by South African ministers or overseas missionaries. It was called by Profs. John Murray and Nicholas Hofmeyr and their associate in Stellenbosch, Ds. Neethling, and was open to ministers and others of all denominations.[17]

Three hundred and seventy-four attended this conference, coming from as far away as Fauresmith and Bloemfontein in the Orange Free State.[18] Twenty congregations were represented by some sixteen Dutch Reformed ministers and Methodist and Presbyterian leaders attended. Missions and education and other topics of interest were discussed in the sessions, before presenting the main issue.

The topic of Revival was introduced by the Swellendam minister, Dr. Robertson. Adamson, the Scots Presbyterian minister at Cape Town, recounted the story of the American Revival of 1858, from its beginnings in a Dutch Reformed congregation in New York until the most recent word of its continued progress throughout 1859, vividly illustrating from his experiences therein. He spoke first in English, then in Dutch, and was able to answer questions. His hearers were very deeply moved.[19]

Andrew Murray, Senior, attempted to speak during the discussion following, but was reduced to weeping.[20] There was a profound humbling of the ministers attending the conference, and each of them returned to his work full of great expectations. It is significant that the congregations first moved in the subsequent Awakening were those that had sent delegates or observers to the conference.

A pentecost of days followed the Worcester Conference, approximately seven weeks of waiting between the breathing of the Spirit and the outpouring of the Divine power.

Andrew Murray, Junior,[21] took part in the Worcester conference by leading in prayer, a prayer so powerful that some considered its utterance the beginning of the Revival of 1860. His preaching ministry was also powerful in his new charge at Worcester,[22] where he was installed in May of that year, and great expectations were kindled in the hearts of all his hearers.[23] Like Frelinghuysen of the Raritan Valley in New Jersey (the Dutch Reformed dominie with whom began the eighteenth century Revival in the English-speaking world), Andrew Murray used a kind of 'eucharistic evangelism,' preaching at Nagmaal on such texts as 'Friend, how camest thou in hither, not having a wedding garment?' causing much searching of heart among the more careless communicants. Andrew Murray was a severe minister of the word of rebuke, both in preaching and in personal counsel. At the close of a prayer meeting, he was known to deal with each individual present. Yet he himself proved to be unprepared for the Revival when it broke out in his own congregation.[24]

The deputation from Montagu attending the conference at Worcester returned and instituted prayer meetings in their dorp. There was a Wesleyan Methodist congregation in the town, as well as the great Dutch Reformed gemeente, and a movement began in both. A Wesleyan missionary reported:

> O, Sir, what can I write! The Lord is doing wonders here. The Spirit is amongst us . . . prayer meetings every day and every night in the week. People who never prayed publicly before are opening their mouth widely. Last Sunday evening, I spoke from 'Behold, he prayeth.' I asked the people to come up to the school room on Monday, Wednesday and Friday mornings early to pray the Lord for a spiritual blessing. They came in large numbers very early, three o'clock. . . On Thursday evening, at our prayer meeting, I felt downcast when we commenced, but soon had cause for rejoicing. A poor girl began for the first time to pray. What language! It was her mouth, but the words were of the Spirit. I cried out, 'Pray, my child. Pray to the Lord. He is here!' and glory to His name, it was so! Young and old commenced crying for mercy, and I was kept till about twelve o'clock. The congregation of the Dutch Reformed Church came out of their prayer meeting; the place was crowded, while a great number had to remain outside.[25]

The Methodist report did not specify whether their local congregation was English-speaking or Dutch-speaking— or whether European or Cape Coloured in membership.

The meetings thus begun in the Montagu Dutch Reformed
Church[26] following the Worcester conference were led by a
layman who continued to direct the movement until it became
general.[27] It is significant that the first outbreak of Revival
among the Dutch Reformed occurred where the pastorie was
temporarily vacant.[28]

In July, two ministers visited Montagu for Nagmaal, and
conducted a prayer meeting that Sunday evening. A year
before, prayer meetings were unknown in that district, yet
in the first full tide of revival, the people complained that
the meetings ended too soon.[29]

For many weeks, the awakening at Montagu was marked
by intense conviction of sin, strong men crying out in anguish,
as in Ireland and Scotland. Montagu underwent a complete
transformation, a community noted for its indifference becoming one committed to serious religion; and weeks later,
the new minister——who was not installed in the Montagu
congregation until September 1860—found a revived constituency, with six prayer meetings going on in the dorp.[30]

Montagu is within easy reach of Worcester, along a valley,
and lay people in the latter dorp began to engage in fervent
intercession for revival. So, within the limits of the parish,
cottage prayer meetings were commenced and continued till
Pentecost. In the Breede River ward, a prayer meeting was
started with only a handful of people but began to increase
in size. Whole families, European and Coloured, attended
and a spirit of conviction of sin humbled them as preliminary
evidences of revival. The preaching of the local dominie
helped forward the phase of heart-searching. But it was in
the youth fellowship that the awakening really began.

The new minister at Worcester was Andrew Murray. One
Sunday evening, sixty young people were gathered in a hall,
led in intercession by J. C. de Vries, an assistant of Andrew
Murray.[31] Several had risen to announce the singing of a hymn
and to offer prayer, when a Fingo girl in the employ of a
farmer asked if she might do the same. Permission granted
after hesitation, the girl poured out a moving prayer.[32]

De Vries reported that while she was praying, a roll of
noise like that of approaching thunder was heard, coming
closer and closer until it enveloped the hall, shaking the
place. The company burst into prayer, a majority audibly, a
minority in murmuring tones. An unusual outpouring of the
Holy Spirit appeared to be taking place.[33] Long afterwards,
J. C. de Vries recalled his emotions:

A feeling that I cannot describe took possession of me. Even now, forty-three years after these occurrences, the events of that never-to-be-forgotten night pass before my mind's eye like a soul-stirring panorama. I feel again, as then I felt, I cannot refrain from pushing my chair backwards and thanking the Lord fervently for His mighty deeds.

Meanwhile the Worcester congregation had engaged in its regular Sunday evening exercises, Andrew Murray having preached. Notified, the minister hurried over to the hall and found the whole company still engaged in the simultaneous prayer, with de Vries kneeling at a table instead of trying to control the unusual manifestation.[34]

Asked for an explanation of the extraordinary conduct of the people, de Vries explained— if explanation it could be called. Andrew Murray was far from satisfied, and walked among the distressed people calling for silence, 'Mense, bly stil! Mense, bly stil!'

No one took the slightest notice of their new and revered minister, and even de Vries kneeled at the table in holy awe of the Divine visitation. In a loud voice, Andrew Murray called again: 'I am your minister, sent from God. Silence!' Again, no one responded and the prayer continued.[35] Each seemed more concerned with calling on God for forgiveness of an intolerable weight of sin and shame.

Andrew Murray went back to his assistant and requested him to start singing the hymn in Dutch,[36] 'Help the soul that helpless cries!' but the simultaneous intercession continued. So the bewildered Andrew Murray departed, exclaiming 'God is a God of order, and here everything is in confusion!' It was some time before Andrew Murray was convinced of the Divine nature of the visitation.[37] De Vries, who had experienced the phenomena from the beginning, was not only convinced but wholly overwhelmed. He remained in prayer, as did the sixty young people.

Prayer meetings were held in the little hall, evening by evening; each meeting generally began in a period of profound silence, but, as soon as several prayers had arisen, the place was shaken as before and the whole company of people engaged in simultaneous petition of the throne of Grace. The meetings often went on until three in the morning, and even then the people were reluctant to disperse, singing their praises on the way home through the sleeping streets. Worcester was stirred, meetings multiplying in the valley.

Crowded attendances moved the meetings to the larger school building, which soon filled up. On the first Saturday evening in the school, Andrew Murray took a lead by reading a passage of Scripture and giving his pastoral commentary. Then he engaged in prayer and invited others so to do. Again the mysterious roll of approaching thunder was heard in the distance, coming nearer and nearer, until it enveloped the building, and all were engaged in prayer again.[38] Andrew Murray tried to quieten the people, walking up and down among them, but a stranger tiptoed to him and whispered: 'I think that you are minister of this congregation. Be careful what you do, for it is the Spirit of God that is at work here.' He said that he had recently arrived from America.[39]

There is nothing quite like contemporary and unedited writing to convey impressions of actual happenings. Mrs. Andrew Murray wrote to her mother at the time:[40]

. . . We are having many visitors from the surrounding places who come to see us on account of the revival meetings, and they go away blessed, saying that the half has never been told. It is a solemn thing to live in such a congregation at such a time. I feel sure that the Lord is going to bless us even more, and yet there are heavy trials before us; the work is deeply interesting and yet some things are painful.

In the midst of an earnest address, a man drove a dog into the church with a tin tied onto its tail and it frightened the people. Andrew came down the aisle and prayed a most solemn, heart-searching prayer, that if the work were not of God, He Himself would put a stop to it. The people were terrified as the excitement was intense and some even fainted.

Last night again the church was full and Andrew then preached so powerfully and yet so simply on 'the Lamb of God.' He is so very discreet in dealing with souls; about twenty came forward, and others stayed behind. We do feel and realise the power and the presence of God so mightily. His Spirit is indeed poured out upon us.

A teacher in a school in the Bushveld was then visiting Worcester, and was advised by de Vries not to attend the prayer meeting because of her delicate health. But Hessie Bosman insisted, saying that she would go even if it caused her death. It was known that she had prayed oft and long for a revival in South Africa. So she attended the meeting in the school, and was pouring out her heart in the third public prayer of the evening when the phenomenal praying overwhelmed her petitions and she fell on the floor unconscious.

Her friends carried her to the pastorie where she lay unconscious quite some time. Far from causing her death,
the extraordinary experience proved to be a rejuvenation of
her health, for she married a pioneer missionary, Alexander
McKidd, serving God in life and death on the missionfield.[41]

The movement of 1860 stirred every part of the community
of Worcester, old and young, rich and poor, white and Cape
Coloured. Especially were the younger generation blessed,
numbers being brought to genuine conversion, and thereafter
engaging in soul-winning far and near.[42]

A farmer one morning heard loud mourning, and found a
Fingo girl, his wife's servant, in an agony of prayer for the
forgiveness of sin. His wife informed him that the girl had
asked her the day before whether Christ had died for her as
well as for white people. Many Africans on remote farms
experienced conversion in similar circumstances.[43]

It was not long before the movement became general, as
revival spread from Montagu and Worcester to Wellington,
Tulbagh, Swellendam and Paarl. The movement did not get
under way at Wellington until October 1860. There a devout
servant of God had prayed for many weeks and had organized
hours of prayer. Then came the Awakening; the consistory
of Wellington declared in its report to presbytery that there
had been more true moral and spiritual advance in the parish
in a few weeks than in all its previous history.[44]

Tulbagh's minister, like those of Worcester and Wellington
insisted that no special 'means' were employed to promote
the awakening——an important point in the thinking of the
Dutch Calvinists who distrusted Finney's theories of revival
and practices of promotion.[45]

The churches of the Swellendam Circuit felt the impact
of the sudden awakening.[46] For example, the congregation in
Robertson reported an outpouring of the Holy Spirit throughout the parish, prayer meetings springing up everywhere;
and in Villiersdorp the work was equally effective.

The fact that startling awakenings had already occurred
in Montagu, Worcester, Wellington and Robertson but not yet
in Paarl greatly distressed the evangelical scholar, G. W. A.
van der Lingen.[47] To the Cape Town Ring, he reported no
signs of revival, but an awakening soon followed, bringing
(in van der Lingen's phrase) something of 'the glory of the
Church in the first century.'

Van der Lingen gave a revealing report of the impact of
the Awakening on his parish at Paarl:[48]

. . . In no previous year were there as many people who
came to Communion as in this year. . . Family prayers
in the past were held as a duty, or formally. Now they
are alive with attentive reflection. Most of these people
get together in groups of three or four to pray weekly
and many more than half attend the prayer meetings . . .
Many are willing to contribute to the needs of the congregation with their material possessions.

In 1864, Van der Lingen surveyed its progress again:[49]

The prayer meetings are still being held, even though
the numbers have decreased. And a number of those
who have 'tasted of the powers of the ages' during the
Revival are walking worthily. . . One can even sense
an obvious measure of renewed power. All the groups
of three have agreed to assemble also once a month.
Numbers at these monthly gatherings are fairly large.
Our church cannot hold all who come to worship.

Most of the congregations visited by the 1860 Revival were
those of the Cape hinterland which had sent representatives
to Worcester. But the church at Calvinia, two hundred miles
north, had sent no deputation to the Conference.[50] However,
their former minister, Ds. N. J. Hofmeyr, had encouraged
the people to hold prayer meetings on their remote farms
because isolation allowed members to attend church only
quarterly. But everything seemed futile, reported Hofmeyr
(a professor now). Yet the awakening broke out in Calvinia,
transforming the whole population. In a few days time, three
or four prayer meetings were begun in the dorp, and four or
five in the lonely countryside. A missionary concern for the
half-castes and Hottentots developed, and a European farmer
gave up his home in order to live and teach on their location.

The Beaufort West gemeente noted similar impact of the
revival in village and farms and far around.[51] The work had
commenced between 6th and 13th January 1861, many being
instantaneously moved.[52] A prayer meeting often lasting all
day was held four times a week in the dorp, and meetings
were held 'everywhere' on the Lord's day. A 'shaking awake'
occurred in Murraysburg district,[53] followed by hundreds of
startling conversions, the minister averring that there were
not fifty unconverted left in the district. Prince Albert also
was moved in the year 1861,[54] and likewise both Richmond and
Graaff-Reinet,[55] where C. F. J. Muller (grandfather of the
distinguished historian of the same name) left a lucrative law
practice for the ministry and became Professor of Theology,
one of many such motivated scholars.[56]

The Dutch Reformed Church Synod of 1862 investigated the Awakening and its fruits.[57] After detailed discussion in which several told of the happenings in their congregations, all in one accord proposed a grateful recognition that the Awakening was surely the work of the Holy Spirit, and that the Synod should offer thanks for the reviving and pray for the continuance of the same; and it was further resolved that the happenings be made known through pastoral reports.

The extraordinary impact of the Awakenings of 1860 onwards created a perennial expectancy of revival in the Dutch Reformed congregations. In Heidelberg, Cape Colony, for example, a great rejoicing greeted the works of God in the 1860 Revival.[58] Livelier interest in the Lord's service sustained not only prayer meetings but a home visitation and sick visitation ministry, until in 1868 there came a second revival, followed by a third in the next decade, a fourth in 1884, and a fifth movement in 1889 under Dr. Andrew Murray. This pattern of repeated revivals appeared in congregation after congregation for half a century, a typical example being the Groote Kerk in Cape Town, the Mother Church itself.[59]

Prof. N. J. Hofmeyr of Stellenbosch Theological Seminary had declared in his report to the South African Evangelical Alliance that changes wrought by the revival were revolutionary.[60] Fifty young men in the Worcester congregation alone offered themselves for the service. Stellenbosch Theological Seminary, begun in 1859 with the godly John Murray and Nicholas Hofmeyr, was set on its course with a body of truly devoted students. Evangelism flourished. The movement made a lasting imprint upon the life of Andrew Murray, who not only wrote a book for new converts but commenced his wholesome worldwide ministry.

An enthusiasm for missions among the non-European folk developed, as auxiliary societies for missionary interests were established in many places. Within a decade the Dutch Reformed Church had a dozen mission stations in and beyond the Cape Colony and the Boer Republics.[61]

Van der Lingen proposed to the Kerkraad that the ten days between Ascension and Pentecost be thereafter devoted to prayer for revival and to evangelistic preaching. This proposal had far-reaching consequences, and set an evangelistic pattern for the Afrikaans-speaking community.[62] It was the Dutch Reformed denomination which benefitted most by the Awakening of 1860 and thereafter, but it was not long before the English-speaking churches enjoyed a like visitation.

9

REVIVAL IN SOUTH AFRICA, II

In Grahamstown, the veteran William Shaw also prayed for a repetition of the times of revival that he had witnessed a score of years earlier in the land of his adoption.[1] Then, the Revival of 1837 had followed the disaster of war. Now, another disaster had blighted the frontier.

A full sixteen months before the outbreak of the 1857-58 American Revival, in May 1856, a mere child entering upon her teens became a Bantu prophetess. Spirits of dead heroes appeared to Nongquase and charged her to challenge the clans of the Amaxhosa to kill all their cattle, destroy all their grain and consume all the food in the country. Then, on the 18th day of February following, the elderly would be rejuvenated, cattle would spring out of the earth, corn-pits would be most miraculously filled, and the dead heroes would arise to lead their warriors in driving the Europeans into the sea.[2] Chiefs abetted the delusion—hoping that starvation would provoke an irruption into Cape Colony, some have said.

Like the millennial prediction of 1844, it came to nothing. The deluded people slaughtered their cattle and burned their corn. The chiefs neglected to gather their warriors close to the border. Soon starvation made mobilization impossible. The horrors that followed were unspeakable. Hungry hordes wandered to and fro, then sat down and died. For years to come, skeletons of a dozen or a score of victims were found huddled around a solitary tree, where they had died in the shade. The old and infirm were the first abandoned. Families fought among themselves for scraps of food and cannibalism, a rare vice among southern Bantu folk, broke out. Clans numbering tens of thousands were decimated. The Colony was invaded, but by pitifully weakened beggars.

In 1857, awakening had begun in North America. A revival started simultaneously among Europeans in Grahamstown, affecting Bantu and European churches. Commemoration Chapel (seating 1400) was filled Sundays and weekdays for services of worship and prayer.[3] The Bantu congregations received many probationers into membership. Circuit after circuit reported an increase, Healdtown's chapel seating 600 being crowded to excess, three hundred taking Communion and threescore being baptized. It was reported that 'this circuit has participated in the general blessing which Almighty God has been pleased to pour down upon His Church and people both in this and other lands.'[4]

Telegraphic communication existed between United States and Great Britain in 1857, but none with the South African frontier, therefore no link in space could account for the coincidence in time with the American 1857 Awakening.

But the 1858 Revival on the frontier brought numerous gatherings of Bantu under the sound of the Gospel, a very significant factor in the unusual awakenings that followed seven years' teaching.[5] Chief Kama, an earlier convert, had stayed true to his faith during the terrible delusion, and he remained surrounded by his tribe. In the Grahamstown and Kingwilliamstown and Queenstown circuits, and in the sadly desolated Transkei, the Bantu flocked to the missions, and Morley (for example) showed an increase of 600 members, 600 on trial, with overcrowded congregations listening to the Word of God.[6]

A more direct link between the United States and South Africa was forged by the returning of the American Board missionaries from furlough in New England to their work among the Zulus in Natal, even before news of the Ulster 1859 Revival had reached the Cape.

The work of evangelizing the Zulus in Natal had been one of discouragement and even despair to both the American Congregational and Church of England missionaries attempting it. The British Methodists likewise found it difficult. One such pioneer recalled his dismay upon arrival at Port Natal in 1849: 'the work of Christianizing semi-nude savages who brandished spears, shields and knobkerries before us seemed a hopeless task.'[7]

Tyler and his companions had found it very painful year after year to witness the gross ignorance and deep-rooted superstitions, spirit-worship and impure practices of the heathen.[8] So also did the American missionaries.

Already[9] Aldin Grout had told his American supporters that in faroff South Africa there was a longing in Christian hearts for a spiritual awakening, so that prayer for revival in South Africa had begun in the States before South African believers in any numbers had been quickened to pray. Thus it was not surprising that revival came first to Natal.

The first manifestations of Divine visitation in South Africa were not at Worcester in the Cape or Montagu nearby in 1860, but in Natal where at the close of 1858 there were encouraging signs of an awakening, with marked religious interest at nearly all the Zulu stations run by the American missionaries.[10] Aldin Grout reported in 1859 'now we are revived; and the reviving commenced a year and a half ago.' After ten years of patient waiting and longing, the British Methodist mission stations likewise [11]

> . . . witnessed a shaking among the dry bones in the Esidumbini Valley. . . It was a joyful day when five young men came to me and said, 'We have decided to abandon heathenism and serve God.' It was a still more joyful day on which we established a church and sat down for the first time with a little band of native Christians.

The population of Natal at that time was about 170,000,[12] of whom one tenth were of European stock, either English-speaking or Afrikaans-speaking, while less than a twentieth were indentured labourers using Tamil, Telugu or other Indian vernaculars—few of the Indians being Christians.

A vivid insight into the Zulu Awakening of 1859 was given in a letter written by the Rev. Joseph Jackson, a Wesleyan Methodist missionary. Observing that, from Sunday May 22 onwards, many who had been especially prayed for had been converted, he said that on that Lord's Day:[13]

> I rose early this morning to preach to the people, but soon found by their sleepy countenances that they had had but little rest during the night. After the service, I was informed that just as they had been about to separate, while singing the concluding hymn, the Spirit fell upon them in such an overpowering manner that they could not depart, but continued in prayer till break of day.

A man who came from Pietermaritzburg to witness these strange things was seized with conviction, but later 'set at liberty.' The news of the awakening spread far and wide— for most people considered the possibility of such a work of grace at Indaleni as too far-fetched to believe.

Throughout 1859, one full year before the extraordinary awakening among Dutch South Africans, the Zulu awakening continued in power.[14] Far to the west,[15] an awakening began in Botswana among people of different background and speech, the missionaries cheerfully publishing lists of the converts. In 1860, when European churches at the Cape had begun to feel the movement of the Spirit, the Americans reported

Christians at some of the stations became so much
revived that they were unwilling that the meetings should
cease . . . the daily prayer meetings were continued
morning and afternoon through succeeding weeks.[16]

Missionaries noted cases of deep seriousness, reporting
outright conversions apparently occurring at most stations.
Throughout 1861, a 'very hopeful degree of religious interest'
continued in Natal among the Zulu Christians.[17] An increase
of benevolence reported in 1862 indicated a real missionary
concern for others.[18]

Seven years after the original outbreak of revival, 'very
considerable prosperity'[19] in things spiritual was enjoyed.
The statistics of growth indicated more than doubling of the
Zulu church membership.[20] And all this growth took place
before the second wave of evangelical revival reached the
Zulus in Natal through Charles Pamla, Xhosa interpreter
of Taylor, the world-ranging American Methodist preacher,
when the ingathering of converts surpassed the first wave.

Nothing in the records indicated that any of the startling
phenomena which marked the awakenings in Ulster and the
Cape had been witnessed in Natal. The Zulu Awakening was
directly related to the 1858 Revival in the United States, a
movement free of physiological accidents, but marked by
extraordinary praying, intense conviction of sin, immediate
conversions and extended evangelism.

The 1859 Awakening among the Zulus was considered a
promising movement by the missionaries,[21] the Americans
declaring that 'a Christian people have sprung up among the
Zulus . . . a missionary people.'

At the Mission annual meeting at Umtwalumi in early 1860,
prayer was offered for a general outpouring of the Spirit on
all Christian congregations and mission stations throughout
Africa.[22] Postal communications were so difficult that these
Natal missionaries did not know that the answer to their
prayers had already come to Christians at the Cape far to
the south-west, in both the Afrikaans and English-speaking
churches of the Europeans and their Cape Coloured satellite
communities, provoking a missionary out-thrust.

The 1858 Awakening was extended to all six continents by
the remarkable ministry of a very unusual Methodist, the
indefatigable and ubiquitous William Taylor, who proved to
be one of the most versatile evangelists of all time, a true
follower of Wesley who made the world his parish in a way
that few in history ever did.[23]

Taylor was born in Virginia in 1821, converted in 1841, and a year later began to work with the Baltimore Conference of the Methodist Episcopal Church, serving as an itinerant preacher until 1848. In 1849, Taylor followed the Gold Rush to California. Lacking either church or hall, he used a big wooden box as a platform on the wharf at San Francisco, and soon gathered his congregation. Taylor became known up and down California as 'the street preacher.' He returned to the Eastern States and Canada to preach in the aftermath of the 1858 Revival and a few years later heard a call to an intercontinental ministry of unprecedented scope.[24]

In 1863, Taylor of California (as he was known) reached Australia, and commenced evangelizing in the Methodist churches with considerable impact also on other denominations. Most of 1863 he gave to ministry in Victoria and the island of Tasmania; 1864 to New South Wales and Queensland with a side trip to New Zealand; and 1865 to South Australia. His evangelism was very fruitful, for more than six thousand converts were received by the circuits.[25] Taylor decided to visit South Africa, and sailed across the Indian Ocean to fulfil his ambition.

At that time, the spiritual life of the Methodist churches was declining. The European circuits had settled down to a life of formality and there were few conversions. The 1860 awakenings in the Dutch Reformed churches, together with the news of revivals in the United States and United Kingdom, encouraged many Methodists to pray for similar blessing in the Eastern Province and Natal. The answer to prayer came through the visit of William Taylor.[26]

Taylor arrived in Cape Town and began preaching in the Wesleyan chapel, and at Wynberg. He was dismayed by the smallness of the chapels and the even tinier congregations filling a third of their seats. He made his way around the coast to Port Elizabeth and preached there and at Uitenhage and Grahamstown. His meetings were blessed with numbers of conversions, but as yet no real break had occurred.[27]

After stirring times in America and Australia, Taylor found it hard to appreciate the pessimism of his South African Methodist hosts. He told a superintendent in Port Elizabeth that his proposed meetings would be orderly and terminate by ten o'clock each night. This simple remark provoked his host to a burst of laughter, for he averred that the local Methodists could not tolerate any service continuing after eight o'clock. Nevertheless, local people tarried and there were from a dozen to a score of seekers each evening. This was the beginning of a movement among the English-speaking churches, which gained strength in the following months.[28]

The first outbreak of enthusiasm came among Xhosa folk, at a place called Annshaw, some twenty-five miles from Kingwilliamstown. Taylor's interpreter was a young African chief, Charles Pamla.[29] Six hundred people had crowded the mission chapel, mission natives in quasi-European dress, heathen tribesmen in red blankets. Taylor preached to believers on 'Ye shall receive power after that the Holy Ghost is come upon you.' That evening he preached to outsiders on 'Turn ye from your evil ways, for why will ye die?'[30]

Pamla had such a genius for interpretation that he sang a hymn in Xhosa alternately, line by line, with Taylor's English words, though he had never heard the hymn before. A profound stillness fell upon the people, and, when Taylor announced an aftermeeting, two hundred penitents came forward to the front seats, kneeling in contrition.

There were no wild scenes of confusion, but there was simultaneous audible prayer— sighs and groans and floods of tears. William Taylor insisted upon dealing with these inquirers on the spot, and continued with his helpers until midnight. Then Taylor dismissed them, but they were back at sunrise for praise and prayer. Next day, the work continued, Taylor systematically dealing with the inquirers and enrolling them. After his departure, another 165 professed faith, an unprecedented 300 in five days of evangelism.[31]

At Healdtown, a thousand natives crowded the Wesleyan chapel and William Sargent, Methodist missionary, noted:[32]

> Tuesday—what a day! I know not how to record it. I have never witnessed anything that so reminded me of the scenes of Pentecost. . . The people were already in the chapel, engaged in a prayer meeting. Mr. Taylor took for his text 'But ye shall receive power after that the Holy Ghost is come upon you.' The truth told upon the congregation.
>
> At the close, after a season of silent prayer, seekers were invited to come forward, when I suppose that not less than 300 fell upon their knees and began to cry aloud for mercy, among them several Europeans. At first, all seemed confusion. Even the local preachers and leaders seemed petrified. Presently much of the noise subsided and little more than sighs and groans were heard. After a short time, one after another got into liberty . . . they generally rose to their feet, clasped their hands and with eyes sparkling and countenances beaming with joy unspeakable, they broke into a burst of praise.

The missionary occupied his time registering the names of the inquirers professing faith. The meeting extended from 11 a.m. till 4 p.m., as it did again when Taylor preached in the crowded chapel on Thursday. Three hundred inquirers were added to that church within two years.[33]

At Kamastone, in the Queenstown District,[34] hundreds of Xhosa-speaking folk and a number of Hottentots were moved. Simultaneous audible prayer followed the preaching, but no one voice was raised above the others. Taylor guided five prayer meetings and preached six times during that day. The Reverend William Shepstone, the father of a famous son, reported 250 added to the Wesleyan society. It was also reported that some of the converts had been beaten and tied up by their heathen parents, and that only one had drawn back; however, records showed that in 1867 about 200 of them were still persevering.[35]

Gratifying gains were made at Lesseyton as 'indescribable scenes' were witnessed. These revivals also spread to the London Missionary Society stations at Hankey and Kat River, with hundreds of converts registered therein.[36]

Taylor and his interpreter crossed the Kei river and proceeded to Butterworth, where they preached to the Amagaleka tribe. There was an 'awakening of religious life and an outpouring of the Holy Spirit' that increased membership, from 112 to 251, with probationers increasing tenfold; after a year, the membership rose to 413, which represented a 400% gain, plus 286 still on trial.[37]

Clarkebury Circuit recorded its 'unspeakable happiness' in directing weeping penitents to the Saviour, four hundred becoming members with 147 still on trial.[38] This 350% gain was made in a matter of five months.

Taylor continued through the Transkei, preaching with Charles Pamla.[39] The Xhosa-speaking people gave Taylor the name of Isikuni Sivutayo, the Blazing Firebrand, very impressed with a man with broad shoulders and long flowing, patriarchal beard. He stood six feet tall.

At the Shawbury Mission, there was a setback due to some Christian men having been forced to send their daughters to the huts of the chief and his lieutenants (upundhlo). Taylor resolved much of the difficulty but there were no conversions under his preaching,[40] nor were any additions noted in the 1867 returns, though there was a reviving. Osborn Circuit added a hundred members or so.[41] A missionary in the Grahamstown District of the Wesleyan field summed up the movement:[42]

The remarkable characteristic of the Revival is that
the whole land is being blessed. In every place the Word
of God is the power of God unto salvation to many that
believe . . . At some of our native stations, as many as
300, 500 and, in one place, 800 conversions have taken
place. More than two thousand of the native population
have been saved, and certainly more than six hundred
conversions have taken place among the English.

As a matter of record, in two Districts (Grahamstown and
Queenstown) 2763 were added to active membership, with
2360 on trial. The promise of the revival was fully realised
among Bantu folk and Europeans alike.[43]

While continuing his ministry to the Europeans in nearby
Fort Beaufort, Taylor reaped a greater harvest among the
Xhosa-speaking people. 'The awful presence and melting
power of the Holy Spirit on this occasion surpassed anything I had ever witnessed before,' said Taylor. On another
occasion, Taylor preached strongly on the Commandments,
and a couple of hundred in the Healdtown chapel fell on their
knees, crying, sobbing and groaning. The number of converts
in two days exceeded three hundred.

Taylor was concerned that perhaps the cultured lady of
the Rev. Thomas Guard might be offended by what she had
seen. But she assured him that, although she had seen the
pageants of royalty in Europe, and the opening of the great
Exhibition of 1851, she had never seen anything to stir her
soul as much as the revival among these simple Africans.

Taylor found the doors open for a very wide ministry in
South Africa. He travelled around the circuits, seldom staying more than a week in a place. His great success with the
various tribesmen greatly impressed the Europeans.

In Port Elizabeth, a number of Europeans had professed
faith some weeks before the revival had broken out in the
Eastern Province.[44] Then in Uitenhage, the Dutch Reformed
minister put his bigger church at the disposal of the local
Wesleyans, who made good use of the available space.[45] In
the Grahamstown Wesleyan Chapel, built as a result of the
Revival of 1831 and seated for 800, two hundred inquirers
were counselled and added to the church.[46] Meetings among
Europeans in Kingwilliamstown produced ingatherings.[47]

By the time the unusual awakening had begun among Bantu
folk, Taylor had begun his ministry among the Europeans at
Fort Beaufort, in a time of 'Divine favour and mercy,' when
a hundred were added to the church.[48] Among the Europeans
converted in Cradock was the interpreter into Dutch.[49]

A hundred Europeans were converted in Queenstown, an English-speaking town. According to the Rev. H. H. Dugmore, Taylor's converts were of every age from ten to sixty, both married and unmarried, fathers and mothers of families, folks phlegmatic or excitable in temperament, enthusiasts and scoffers, and persons of varied social rank.[50] Membership of the European Circuit at Queenstown increased from eighty to more than two hundred.[51]

For obvious reasons, most of the additions reported during the Awakening were Methodists, but other denominations also shared in the general rise of religious enthusiasm which stirred South Africa, including Presbyterians and others.

The German-speaking Baptists who settled on the frontier among their compatriots founded Kingwilliamstown Baptist Church in 1861, Hugo Gütsche reporting 'times of refreshing from the presence of the Lord' in numerous Awakenings from 1867 onward.[52] There is no record of Taylor having visited the East London district in his itinerary.

On 1st September 1866, Taylor and his party set out for Kokstad and the Griqua territory, occupied by a colony of Afrikaans-speaking half-castes from far to the west, for whom he preached also.[53]

In Natal, Taylor preached in the towns to the Europeans and Pamla preached at the stations to the Zulus.[54] In five weeks, more than three hundred Europeans besides seven hundred Zulus became inquirers, eight hundred standing in the permanent records.

Because Natal Europeans appreciated so little any Zulu Christian workers, Taylor had considered it wise to turn over native work to Charles Pamla as a fully qualified and responsible evangelist. Taylor spent five weeks preaching in Pietermaritzburg, Durban, Edendale and Verulam and thereabouts. Pamla went farther inland.

During William Taylor's journey through the Cape Colony, Kaffraria and Natal, the ministers recorded the names of more than four thousand inquirers professing faith, placed in the care of the Methodist and other churches. Five years' statistics showed the contribution of the Awakening, a total membership of 8247 in 1866, indicating a loss since 1865 of 84; followed by a 10,108 total in 1867, representing a gain of 1861; then 11,367 in 1868, another gain of 1259; followed by 11,524 in 1869, a tapered-off increase of 157.[55] Thus in only two years, almost a 40% increase was recorded by the Methodists alone.

Natal leaders reported 'the great revival of religion' in connection with the ministry of the Rev. William Taylor in 1866; it was said in the Eastern Province that 'the Lord had done great things'; while leaders at the Cape expressed a 'sense of the benefit realised' by the ministry of the tireless Californian.[56] London Methodists happily acknowledged the 'most gracious results in the conversions of sinners and the quickening of societies' in South Africa, commenting:

> After the lapse of more than half a century since the Wesleyan missions were commenced in South Africa, a great and favourable change has taken place in the native work . . . there has been a glorious revival of religion in South Africa in the European and Native population.

In the Awakenings of the 1860s, revival had occurred more or less among people of European or mixed blood or Africans in European hinterlands. Soon the power began to affect the native communities outside the colonies. Within a decade, shortly after the death of Moshweshwe, the Basuto king, a spiritual awakening began at the Paris Evangelical Mission's main station, spreading to all of Lesotho.[57]

Throughout South Africa, in colonies, republics and tribal lands, the work among the Bantu was lasting. Missionaries and native pastors experienced a baptism of the Holy Spirit, and went everywhere preaching repentance and faith, pardon and purity, to illiterate and semi-literate tribesmen.[58]

Mission stations were transformed from Christianizing 'cities of refuge' under missionary direction into Christian communities. Education received a great impetus as native Christians sought learning for their children. An 'era of education,' so designated by Whiteside (Methodist historian), followed the great awakening in South Africa.[59] Converts of the 1860s became the forerunners of a native ministry. Of all Xhosa hymns, a third came from the Revival of the 1860s.

The spiritual sons of William Taylor continued in ministry into the twentieth century and the indigenous bands of local preachers arising from the Awakening became the Wesleyan Native Home Mission. Methodism became the greatest force in evangelizing the Bantu in South Africa: more than a third of all Bantu Christians were recognized as Wesleyan fruit.[60]

Thus the decade following 1860 proved to be a time of real revival among Bantu, Boers and Britons throughout the vast and colourful country, among peoples both civilized and semi-civilized. And the seven years of plenty between 1859 and 1866 were happily not followed by seven lean years.

10

CHRISTIAN ACTION

The population of the United States was approximately thirty million in 1860,[1] of the United Kingdom slightly less. It has been shown that about a million new converts were added to the Churches of each country during the scope of the 1858-59 Awakening, a vast addition to the reservoir of Christian strength, and one that provided resources for a great forward movement in the next half-century.[2]

Not only did the membership of the churches, as well as church attendance, increase by twenty per cent, but there were entirely new developments in the life of the churches, activities taking an entirely new direction in some cases. There were not only new societies, but new kinds of societies in operation. There were reinforcements of older objectives and there were objectives clearly seen for the first time. Most significant in the 1858-59 Awakenings was the rise of the laity to play a fuller part in the affairs of the churches of Protestant Christianity. Bishop Warren Candler said:[3]

> The working forces of the churches were immeasurably increased. The Revival of 1858 inaugurated in some sense the era of lay work in American Christianity. Wesley's system of class leaders, exhorters and local preachers had done much at an early date in the same direction but now the layman's day fully dawned on all churches. No new doctrine was brought forward but a new agency was brought to bear in spreading the old truth through the efforts of men who, if they could not interpret the scriptures with precision or train souls to perfection, could at least help inquiring sinners to find the Lord by relating how they themselves had found Him.

In both America and Britain, the organizers of the union prayer meetings were businessmen warmly supported by clergy who were delighted to find the laymen willing, and gospel meetings were arranged by Christian laymen for their associates in industry, the services, the colleges and the professions.[4] In South Africa, lay people often initiated both prayer and gospel meetings.[5]

G. E. Morgan commented on developments in Britain:[6]

In surveying the vast growth of Home Missions, the conviction gains force that the period following the Revival of 1859 was one of the most fruitful in the annals of Christianity in this country; and also that in these later days, when so many criticize and scepticize about Revival, it cannot be too strongly emphasized that the entire Home Mission Movement was not only inaugurated and manned, but financed by the revival converts and sympathizers.

As a natural corollary of the movement of the laity, the trend toward a practical interdenominational unity developed rapidly. Generally, lay movements are interdenominational, and usually revivals of religion also are interdenominational. Furthermore, in the Awakening of 1858-59, the various denominations were so busy trying to cater for an influx of new members that there was scarcely room for sectarian jealousy. With hardly an exception, the Churches were all working together as one man. Arminians and Calvinists so ignored their differences; Baptists and Paedobaptists were blessed together, and everything was almost too good to be true. By common consent, the doctrinal controversies were left alone, and the idea worked well.[7]

These factors held true in both America and Britain—countries of undivided loyalty— and had considerable force in bilingual South Africa, in which Evangelicals of Dutch or English stock or of Calvinist or Arminian theology were equally benefitted in the Awakening.

With the Revival of 1858 came the successful introduction of the Y.M.C.A. to American cities, and the flowering of the movement in the United States.[8] The influx of converted young men into Christian churches found an excellent outlet in the evangelistic activites of the early Christian associations of young men. The Y.M.C.A. took the initiative in the evangelizing of the masses.

From the beginning of the Revival in Britain, the Y.M.C.A. not only shared in the ingathering, but often sponsored the meetings which brought Christians together for united prayer and united evangelism. A conference of provincial and city Y.M.C.A. delegates met in London at the start of the Revival, and reiterated an early principle of the Y.M.C.A., binding it on all branches—a decided and authenticated conversion to God as the requirement for membership. From that time forward, the Y.M.C.A. increased with the Awakening.[9]

The lasting effect of the 1858-59 Revivals on the Y.M.C.A. is scarcely mentioned in standard histories on the subject.

The year 1864, indeed, is officially recognized as 'the turning point of the Y.M.C.A.,[10] the beginning of certain success.' The 1864 Edinburgh Conference of the Y.M.C.A. laid the foundations of the movement with its liberal provision for all-round requirements of young men, spiritual and social, physical and individual, initiated in evangelism.

In 1865, Andrew Murray became president of the newly-founded Young Men's Christian Association in Cape Town, the first of many such associations in southern Africa; and the movement spread to other parts of the continent.

The most significant and fascinating home missionary development of the 1858-59 Awakening was the birth of the Salvation Army, which extended the evangelistic and social ministry of the more general movement.

The achievements of the husband-and-wife evangelistic team, William and Catherine Booth, during the years of the Revival were notable. Booth's experience in Cornwall taught him a connection between holiness of Christian living and power in successful evangelism, for he preached one to achieve the other.[11] His experience in the Black Country Awakening taught him that the masses could be most successfully reached by their own kind bearing witness. His frustration at the hands of unsympathetic denominational directors must have determined him to shape an organization of his own. He was an interdenominationalist, yet his Wesleyan convictions were strong; so his creation, the Salvation Army, became interdenominational in the support commanded from all manner of Christians, yet denominational enough to be reckoned a convinced Arminian fellowship, more Wesleyan than contemporary Methodists in doctrine and practice.

Prophetically, in the New Year of 1861, a conference was called in Sussex Hall, Leadenhall Street, in the City of London to consider the appalling need of the slums of the East End.[12] The Reverend Baptist Noël there predicted that some far-reaching work was about to begin, and so the East London Special Services Committee began operations.

Six months later, William Booth visited London friends to seek employment in a home mission capacity, and was put into contact with leaders of the East London committee. They invited him to become their evangelist, but four years of success in revival ministry elsewhere elapsed before Booth accepted their invitation. Into this opportunity for service, William Booth poured his passion for soul winning and his experience of ministry in the Awakening. The com-

mittee became the Christian Revival Association; then the
East London Christian Mission; then, as its efforts were
extended, the Christian Mission, which Booth finally named
the Salvation Army.[13]

The Salvation Army thus arose as a lasting extension of
the 1858-59 Revival in its double ministry of evangelism and
social uplift. Many activities developed by Booth had already
been initiated by other workers in the Awakening—its indoor
and outdoor evangelism, its mission to fallen women, to
criminals, its welfare work, and its missionary enterprise.

While the Army bore the indelible stamp of the personalities of William and Catherine Booth, it was cast by them
in the mold of the 1858-59 Revival; and its pioneers entered
country after country, becoming a world-wide movement
still committed to evangelism and social welfare. In 1883
the Salvation Army entered South Africa, and soon adapted
itself to local conditions of urban life.

The mid-nineteenth century Revival brought expression
to a concern for the evangelization of children, as distinct
from their general welfare. This had its effects in church
related teaching as well as in specialized evangelism.

Edward Payson Hammond was born in the Connecticut
Valley in 1831.[14] He was converted seventeen years later,
and participated in the American Revival of 1858. Visiting
Scotland for purposes of self-improvement, Hammond was
asked to preach in Musselburgh in 1860, during the Scottish
Awakening. Having left his greatcoat in the vestry, he went
there but found the door bolted. A tiny little girl opened it
and explained that 'a wheen o'us lassies' were praying there.
Hammond overheard a tiny tot offer so touching a prayer that
tears sprang to his eyes. His ideas were revolutionized.
He became the children's evangelist, and foster-father of
the Children's Special Service Mission. Hammond accomplished his greatest work in revival services in the Vale of
Dumfries and in the city of Glasgow. His success prepared
the way for a fruitful campaign in Boston, followed by great
awakenings in the state of Maine, which made him a sought-
after missioner from Philadelphia to San Francisco. E. P.
Hammond revisited Britain, and maintained a transatlantic
usefulness at a time when the exchange of talent was lively
both ways. He campaigned also in Canada.

But Hammond's lasting work was as a winner of children
to Christ. In the late 1860s, Spurgeon filled the Metropolitan
Tabernacle with 8000 children to hear Hammond preach.

Seventeen years later, Payson Hammond returned to find that many of the child converts had become Spurgeon's most valued congregational officers and workers.

Likewise, the Awakening of 1858-59 infused new vitality into the Sunday School movement.[15] A Chicago businessman, Benjamin Franklin Jacobs, began his Sunday School career during the 1858 Revival, at a time when the Sunday Schools of the country were crowded with children. Jacobs engineered the International Sunday School Convention within seventeen years. Henry Clay Trumbull, likewise active in the Revival, became the leading Sunday School editor in 1875. In Ulster, the Awakening crowded the Sunday Schools, and the upsurge was felt in all three Kingdoms.[16] The statistics of British Churches showed some denominational gains in numbers of pupils in Sunday School as high as 33% to 50% in seven years. Other agencies for child evangelism were springing up.

Sunday Schools multiplied in South Africa after the 1860-1865 Awakenings. Child evangelism was likewise introduced. A children's evangelist, E. C. Millard, acted as assistant to the Rev. George Grubb when the latter visited Cape Town in 1890, invited by the Anglican Church in South Africa. By using the simple methods practised by Children's Special Service Missioners, he won many youngsters to vital faith.

The Mission, in which George Grubb was associated with two other churchmen of different tradition, began in Saint George's Cathedral in Capetown, with Bishop West Jones officiating. After suburban parochial efforts, all three of the missioners combined their ministry in the Cathedral.

Unusual blessings attended George Grubb's ministry, the churches overcrowded and many men converted. He enjoyed great liberty in Evangelical Anglican parishes; in Anglo-Catholic churches a happy graciousness won him approval.

It was said that, in his concluding address, George Grubb called upon the Bishop of Capetown to give the benediction, but His Lordship declined because he was not wearing the proper vestments. Whereupon the Anglican evangelist, in a deep voice heard throughout the Cathedral, called upon 'his dear friend, the Rev. Andrew Murray, to give the parting blessing,' which non-Anglican intrusion provoked an uproar among some High Churchmen but failed to distress any of Grubb's enthusiastic followers, High Church or Low.[17]

The C. S. S. M. thus launched into South African churches continued work into the new century, Frank Millard being the mainspring of its ministry for many decades.

The British and Foreign Bible Society had celebrated its jubilee in 1854. Five years later, the Awakening brought a host of helpers to the band of workers in the noble enterprise. Little credit is given by historians to the cause of the sudden expansion of the 1860s, although it is noted. The circulation of Scriptures among revived and converted multitudes in Ireland soared, and the Hibernian Bible Society became a supporter instead of a subsidiary[18] of the parent society. In 1861, the National Bible Society of Scotland was founded. The 1860s were years of expansion for the Bible Society's Welsh auxiliaries. Advances were made in every direction in England, and by 1863 'there was scarcely a city or town in England which had not its Biblewoman supported by local contributions.'[19] At the same time, the circulation of the Scriptures at home and abroad exceeded two million, a 50% gain over the Jubilee figures. During the War between the States, the presses of the American Bible Society were working at full pressure to keep up with the demand for Bibles, and these were supplied to both armies, while the financial response of civilians increased in proportion. The sale of Dutch Bibles increased in South Africa after 1860, a similar increase in English after 1865.

Similarities and differences existed between the expansion of the Afrikaner nation north and that of the Americans west —for, unlike American pioneers, the Voortrekkers had left their homes already members of a well-established religious fellowship, and they usually carried their religion with them, families maintaining Bible reading and prayer, and on Sunday whole laagers attending worship of a sort, though handicapped by the lack of ministers, a defect of the Calvinist system.

Many Dutch Reformed leaders in the settled Cape were concerned about the spiritual welfare of their compatriots on the northern frontiers of civilization where trekboers, as distinct from the Voortrekkers, had become neglected nomads. The Afrikaners were dependent on the ordained ministers of their Reformed system, and among them there existed no alternatives to the slow-moving ecclesiastical machinery set up by John Calvin for Geneva and the settled society of Europe.

Cape Colony itself was short of ministers. At the time of the 1860 Revival, Robertson of Swellendam was sent to both European motherlands to enlist likely men for service in South Africa. As at the time of the earlier recruitment, he found that Holland lagged far behind Scotland in evangelical fervour, so he enlisted two Hollanders and eight Scots, the latter agreeing to go to the Netherlands to learn the language of the Church.[20] Among them was the redoubtable Alexander McKidd, who later became a renowned missionary. In the Orange Free State and the Transvaal, the settlers and their successors were served by Dutch Reformed ministers who followed them. Andrew Murray the younger, for example, exercised a fruitful ministry in Bloemfontein from 1849 onwards.[21] But the growing churches were understaffed. In Natal, for a further example, the Voortrekkers enlisted the services of both American and German missionaries. The use of a lay ministry, like the Baptist preacher-farmer or the Methodist circuit-rider, was alien to their thinking.[22]

Nevertheless, just as the Awakenings set the pattern for the American frontier, the Revivals set the pattern for the South African frontier. As the Revival of the 1800s provided dynamic for the outreach of the Cape churches to European pioneers and African tribesmen, the 1860 Awakening helped the Stellenbosch Seminary in equipping men for an evangelistic ministry. And the continued influence of Revival was expressed in the revival-and-evangelistic dedication of the days between Ascension and Pentecost in every Nederduits Gereformeerde Kerk.

There was a reaction against such revival and evangelism in the Dutch Reformed Church in the Republics north of the Orange and the Vaal. The Nederduits Hervormde Kerk arose from the work of Netherlands ministers serving the settlers in the Transvaal, ministers who were accused by the Cape Dutch Reformed Evangelicals of being rationalistic.[23] The Nederduits Hervormde Kerk was actually established as a state church by the Transvaal Volksraad which distrusted the links with the Colonial Government which the Cape Church sustained. The Gereformeerde Kerk (or Reformed Church of South Africa) in turn arose from the dissatisfaction of conservatives with Nederduits Hervormde Kerk 'liberalism' and Nederduits Gereformeerde Kerk 'evangelism.'[24]

The last-named body was subject most to revival influence, and the dynamic of revivals enabled it to maintain its lead as the largest body of Afrikaans-speaking Christians. Despite its arrangement with Cape Colonialism, the Nederduits Gereformeerde Kerk expressed an Afrikaner nationalism, while its evangelicalism provided a needed link with the religious life of English-speaking South Africans in its Nonconformist expressions, a warmth of cooperation between Evangelicals of both languages, as contrasted with the incompatibility of Anglo-Catholic English and ultra-Calvinist Dutch, having been a major factor in the fusion of elements of South African nationality. Evangelicalism is more often centripetal.

As in the settlement of Australia, the Anglican settlers were followed by the competitive activity of Anglo-Catholic and Evangelical. The arrival of Robert Gray to become the Bishop of Cape Town[25] further increased the influences of Anglo-Catholic churchmanship, while Evangelical Anglicans remained weak, though not feeble. It is surely significant that the great Awakening of the 1860s which stirred Dutch Reformed and Methodist Churches and others had but little influence upon the Church of the Province of South Africa.

But the Awakening of the 1860s continued to expand through a virile Methodism. Within five years of the Taylor mission, the Methodists had thriving congregations in the Orange Free State and (within fifteen) in the Transvaal. In 1871, the Methodists began ministering to the diamond diggers of Kimberley and from 1881 onward to the gold miners on the Witwatersrand. In 1873, representative government of the Methodists began, and, ten years later, the South African Methodist Conference was formed.[26]

It was not until 1893 that the Presbyterians of South Africa constituted a presbytery. Baptist churches also remained numerically weak though theologically evangelical. Also the Lutherans stayed small in numbers. These churches shared in the movements of revival in all four provinces.

The Afrikaans-speaking Cape Coloured folk divided their religious loyalties between Islam, transplanted from the East, and Christianity absorbed from European neighbours. The Indian immigrants imported into Natal, at first Tamil and Telugu-speaking but increasingly adopting the English, divided their devotional loyalties between Hinduism, inherited from the Orient, and Christianity absorbed from European neighbours and from South India in later years.[27]

11

THE EVANGELIZATION OF AFRICA

The Evangelical Awakening of 1858-59 had an immediate effect upon missionary work in all parts of the world, more particularly in pagan Africa.

In Britain,[1] the Anglo-Catholic section of the Church of England remained antipathetic to the Revival of the 1860s, and there was little sympathy in the predominantly Anglo-Catholic Church of the Province of South Africa.

Anglican missions to Bantu folk arose from a plan made by Bishop Gray to appoint bishops and employ Anglo-Catholic orders to staff missions.[2] The controversial Bishop Colenso also left a successful Zulu Mission[3] which continued to work along evangelical lines.

The Lutherans also supplied a quota of men. As a result of the Revival of 1880 in Norway, the Norwegian Missionary Union was formed, later sending its missionaries to South Africa,[4] as did other Scandinavian missions born in revival.

The Presbyterians sent out choice recruits. Christina Forsyth, a convert of the Revival in Scotland, pioneered in Fingoland.[5] To Africa in 1861 came James Stewart, first a companion of Livingstone on the Zambesi, then an explorer of the highlands of Nyasaland where Presbyterians in later years built a great mission, then to the Lovedale Institution in South Africa to become principal.

In 1872, prayer meetings at noonday were commenced at Lovedale,[6] preparing European teachers and Bantu tribal students for a revival that Dr. Stewart called 'the most remarkable in the whole history of Lovedale.' This movement began in 1874 and continued for years, prompting African students to offer themselves for missionary service.

The impact of the Awakening of the 1860s upon Bantu tribespeople is illustrated by the life of the Xhosa-speaking evangelist, Charles Pamla.[7] His parents were converted in the stirring of the 1830s, and he was born in 1834 in the little town of Butterworth.[8] He attended an Afrikaner school in Bedford and there learned to pray. He was baptized by the same godly Methodist who had baptized his father and mother. In 1861, Pamla enjoyed an experience of the filling of the Spirit, and in 1866 he sold his farm and cattle and engaged in evangelistic work.[9]

Serving as interpreter with William Taylor set Pamla on a course of evangelistic efficiency, for he was not content to be merely an interpreter but immediately preached in his own way the messages of justification and sanctification by faith.[10] In a couple of days of such preaching, he won to the Christian faith a hundred and fifty converts.[11] His ministry greatly angered the heathen tribal leaders, who would have beaten him but for his relationship to the Fingo chiefs.

Charles Pamla was a linguist, fluent in Afrikaans and English speech, and eloquent in Xhosa and Zulu and other Bantu tongues. In Natal, he had opportunity to preach to the Zulus while Taylor ministered to the Europeans. Needless to say, he continued to evangelize after Taylor had left for other countries. The Methodists then appointed him to the Peddie Circuit, where his preaching resulted in the conversion of a chief. Six hundred tribesfolk professed conversion during his first six months at Newtondale.[12]

Pamla was transferred to Lesotho, there ministering until the outbreak of the Basuto War of 1880, which almost cost him his life as an advocate of peace. He returned to Butterworth in the Transkei and ministered the Word with much success. At East London, Pamla's fiery preaching resulted in the conversion of Amaxhosas, Cape Coloured and Europeans. So many Bantu servants of Europeans were detained at the penitent form that angry Europeans complained to the magistrate, who forbade a native drummer to beat the drum to call people to the meetings. When the African police went to arrest whoever was beating the drum, they found a European just converted through Pamla's preaching.[13]

Wherever he ministered, in Queenstown or East London, in Pondoland or Tembuland, it was said that the mantle of William Taylor had fallen on Charles Pamla. Among the Baca on the banks of the Umzimkulu River, Pamla lived in danger of his life because of his challenge to the forces of darkness. Whole kraals of heathen professed conversion. In 1890, Pamla was appointed as superintendent at Tembeni, membership in the area rising from 300 to 5000 in less than twenty years.

European-African contacts were greatest in the South African farms. Dutch Reformed Church missions to non-Europeans had begun in 1826, but this outreach remained feeble until the 1860 Revival swept the Afrikaner churches, which at once increased their missionary concern.

As early as September of 1860,[14] a secular newspaper in Dutch carried a leading article that noted the newly-begotten interest in the missions of the Dutch Reformed churches. In Worcester, sixty pounds was presented to the British and Foreign Bible Society, and there also the missionary interest was so great that Alexander McKidd was sponsored as a pioneer missionary to Bantu folk on the far frontiers.

Ds. Andrew Murray accompanied McKidd and others in missionary pioneering in the northern Transvaal, a thousand miles northeast of Worcester.[15] Paul Kruger's help was given cheerfully. Before the end of the decade, the Dutch Reformed Church possessed a dozen mission stations, two of them beyond the frontiers of the Cape Colony.[16] Mission work was started also in Botswanaland.

At first the congregations of Bantu converts were attached for oversight to European parishes, but in due course and in keeping with Afrikaner tradition, separate congregations of Bantu-speaking believers were formed into autonomous synods,[17] a development which helped promote African talent which otherwise would have lacked opportunity in competition with more sophisticated and educated leadership.

A young Afrikaner, Stefanus Hofmeyr, who had been moved in the 1861 Prince Albert Revival, volunteered to help McKidd in the Zoutpansberg.[18] In 1865, he began working among the Buys Volk, descendants of a notorious freebooter, Coenraad Buys, who had settled in the Transvaal half-a-century before with a number of Hottentot and Bantu wives and their many offspring. For about a decade, Hofmeyr worked among the mixed-bloods and their Bantu neighbours.

Late in 1875,[19] an unusual awakening began in a children's meeting, provoking a week of profound penitence. The movement spread to the adults and affected both half-castes and Bantu, resulting in the conversion of hardened sinners, such as murderers and adulterers. A survivor of the Zoutpansberg Revival (then just a teenager) said:[20]

> The Spirit descended while we were busy praying. All were conscious of the Spirit in our midst. Some cried aloud, others were very afraid and shook out of fear . . . some fainted. Many at that time were converted, even those that wore no clothes. The cattle did not go out to graze for days, for there was no one to take them out.

The awakening continued into its second year and provided native workers for pioneering beyond the Limpopo, north into Rhodesia, out of which rose a great Dutch Reformed mission, Morgenster, an outstanding enterprise.[21]

Within a quarter century, Dutch Reformed missionaries were caring for 20,000 members, 12,000 catechumens and 30,000 children in primary schools, in Cape Colony, the Republics, and beyond.[22] Their work continued to expand.

In 1882, Andrew Murray visited England. At the Keswick Convention he met a younger man, W. Spencer Walton, who had been converted in London, studied his Bible with the Brethren and become associated with the Anglican missioner, Canon Hay Aitken, as a lay evangelist.[23]

Walton had visited South Africa prior to his conversion, so in 1888 he accepted an invitation to campaign in Cape Town. There the Y. M. C. A. Hall became too small, the meetings being adjourned to the Metropolitan Church, thence to the big Exhibition Buildings. Hundreds of people were converted to God and the city was stirred.

The awakening continued in meetings in the country,[24] in Wynberg, Simonstown, Stellenbosch, Wellington, Robertson, Worcester, Towysriver, Grahamstown and Kimberley. Then Spencer Walton returned to England; but in 1889 he helped with Andrew Murray's backing to form the Cape General Mission. The object of the Mission was to evangelize the European population of South Africa, but the sponsors were so committed to Keswick doctrine and dynamic that they soon set up the South African Keswick Convention in Wellington, and other local conferences, to promote holy living.[25]

Walton and his associates were led to pioneer one of the neediest of Bantu areas in South Africa, Swaziland. It was not long before the Mission had become the interdenominational South Africa General Mission, evangelizing Southern Africa, finally designated the Africa Evangelical Fellowship.

Farther north, before and after the 1860 Revival, David Livingstone had been turning the light of exploration and evangelization upon Central Africa. His was the example, and his also was the challenge often given by tongue and pen to which attention was given.

Prior to the 1859 Revival in Britain, the Universities' Mission to Central Africa was founded as a result of a visit by Livingstone to Cambridge, and it performed excellent service before and after uniting with the S. P. G.,[26] which represented dedicated high-churchmanship.

Using South Africa as a base, missionaries in turn moved north into central and eastern Africa. The Paris Missionary Society directed François Coillard to Barotseland, north of the Zambesi. Coillard, an apostle to Southern Africa, himself was converted in a revival in the Jura in 1851,[27] and in 1887, he developed a mission among the Lozi in Barotseland.[28]

Almost a decade passed before the Paris missionaries reported conversions among these pagans. At Kazungula in 1894, Coillard noted in his diary 'the presence of the Lord made itself felt in our prayer meetings.' When the awakening began, the missionaries could scarcely believe it.[29]

On 4th October, Coillard was overwhelmed by the size of the audience gathered at Lealui. 'The benches, the aisles, even the steps of the platform which serves as our pulpit, all were filled, not an inch to spare.' Paris missionaries almost despaired of being able to shepherd such a flock of inquirers presenting themselves in a body for instruction.

The challenge of Livingstone and the dynamic of the 1859 Revival were responsible for the pioneering of the Mission to Malawi by the Free Church of Scotland,[30] which sent to Cape Town in 1861 its main advocate, James Stewart. After a discouraging survey in 1862, little was done until the death of Livingstone, when Stewart and his friends revived their project, a party pushing up the Zambesi to reach Lake Nyasa. The Church of Scotland also entered Malawi,[31] the Dutch Reformed Church of South Africa following into both Malawi and eastern Zambia (Nyasaland and Northern Rhodesia).[32]

Frederick Stanley Arnot was a lad who heard Livingstone speak in times of revival[33] and decided to follow in his steps. He accomplished a great work as a pioneer missionary of the Brethren, making nine long journeys into the bush during thirty years of service before his death in 1914. He led to Africa yet another pioneering missionary, Dan Crawford of 'the long grass.'[34]

In the Central African lake regions,[35] the Zulu-related Ngoni bands had been the terror of their neighbours. Using the tactics of Shaka and his generals, they raided the weaker tribes annually and reduced them to a condition of terror. They wiped out whole clans, devastating vast tracts of country.

Donald Fraser described the Ngoni clans as 'the fighting people' of Central Africa, who had fought and plundered their way through seven hundred miles of inland territory. Either conquering or scattering other tribes, they lived an open life of warfare, without industry. Their social life fell short of civilized standards. Infanticide was practised, twins buried alive, and ordinary domestic tenderness ignored. Husbands were known to have sold their wives to Arab slavers, and uncles to have kidnapped nieces likewise.[36]

William Koyi, a South African Xhosa educated at Lovedale, volunteered in 1876 to serve at the Livingstonia Mission as evangelist. Fearlessly he met an Ngoni war party and persuaded them not only to abandon their raid but to welcome a missionary teacher.[37] The missionaries worked hard to win the Ngoni to the Christian faith, but the progress was slow. The missionaries worked for years without the backing of a civil power. Within a generation they were able to report that civil turmoil had given way to settled peace.[38] How?

Before the end of the century, awakenings to God had been reported from Livingstonia. Donald Fraser told of such an awakening in Nyasaland in 1897, a mass evangelistic rally during which men wept aloud over sin and backsliding. It was a lasting movement, with continuing results and a comprehensive effect, a holy enthusiasm being shown for God's Word by vast crowds attending. Day schools in the mission field increased from twenty to fifty in three years alone, and pupils from two thousand to seven thousand. This movement was still going on in the next century.[39]

During the last decade of the nineteenth century, as South Africans of European stock were preparing for war, there was a movement among them to prepare for the advance of Christianity in the lands of the Bantu folk.

Reports of the remarkable student conference at Mount Hermon in Massachusetts reached South Africa through Dr. Andrew Murray and Miss Ferguson in 1886.[40] In 1890, bands of missionary volunteers were organized at the Stellenbosch Theological Seminary and the Huguenot Seminary, the former contributing more than thirty missionaries, the latter ten.

In 1896, Luther Wishard and Donald Fraser visited South Africa, stirring up missionary interest. In 1898, there arose a band of forty native missionary volunteers at Lovedale, showing that the Bantu response was not inferior.

Robert Moffat before and after 1830 had made contact with the Ndebele people who settled in what became Rhodesia. These Ndebele were a Zulu regiment which feared the wrath of Shaka and went rampaging southwest on the high veld of South Africa until a clash with the Boers sent them over the river Limpopo. In the 1850s, Moffat again failed with the Ndebele, who were defeated by British troops in the 1890s.[41]

In 1890, the British flag had been raised over the land of the Shona, who suffered from raids by the Ndebele. The British South Africa Company welcomed missionaries into Rhodesia.[42] Anglicans[43] and Methodists[44] were quick to enter. The Dutch Reformed also took advantage of the opportunity and built their great missionary enterprise at Morgenster, near Zimbabwe.[45] The American Methodists likewise entered Rhodesia,[46] as did Brethren in Christ from Pennsylvania[47]— missionary enterprises made possible by British imperial policy and power, though scarcely altruistic.

The redoubtable William Taylor, American revivalist and evangelist, was appointed Bishop for Africa by the American Methodist Episcopal Church, and landed at Loanda in 1885. From Angola, Methodist work spread across the continent through the Congo to Mozambique.[48] Angola had been entered by British Baptists and the American Board (Congregational), Christian Brethren and other societies. The American and British societies entered Mozambique more slowly.

In 1877, the British Baptists were challenged to invade the Congo. Unlike their American colleagues, who concentrated upon the lower Congo, the British Baptists pressed inland. Their cause in the Congo was greatly aided by the arrival of George Grenfell, whose earliest impressions of a serious kind dated back to the early 1860s 'when the great wave of awakening which followed the Revival of 1859 was passing over the country.' Grenfell became the greatest of the Congo Baptist pioneers and an able mission director.[49]

H. Grattan Guinness, the revivalist, launched a work in the Congo in the 1870s,[50] the Livingstone Inland Mission, a title which suggested two of Guinness's heroes, Hudson Taylor and David Livingstone, at a time when there was talk of naming the Congo the Livingstone River.

In 1878, the Livingstone Inland Mission proposed a chain of stations from Matadi to Stanley Pool. The Guinness party established stations in the neighbourhood of Matadi.[51] A very enthusiastic worker there was Adam McCall, an experienced hunter who had roamed South Africa, another Henry Richards who commenced a quiet ministry on the banks of the Congo. For six years, Richards saw no results. Illness afflicted him, driving him to seek God in a new way, after which he began to preach the Good News with power, resulting in astonishing response and transformation of the Congolese.[52]

The son of a local chief professed conversion, after which a great movement got under way. As Lukongo carriers on the riverside, passing up and down, saw the people throwing away their idols and turning to God, they were amazed that no ill befell the converts, that the heavens did not fall or the earth swallow them up.

By 1887, more than a thousand converts had been added to the churches. Richards himself organized two services daily. In 1889, no less than 950 were baptized, the Banza Manteke church boasting fifteen hundred members.[53] Converts went out as evangelists to the villages round about pleading with the people to turn from wooden and rag idols to God.[54] The ingathering soon became a folk movement.

Henry Richards thus witnessed an awakening[55]— the first 'Pentecost on the Congo.' Two thousand were baptized during the stirring. In other stations, similar awakenings occurred. By the end of the century, Banza Manteke missionaries had nearly three thousand pupils in sixty schools. Hundreds were still being baptized each year and added to the fellowship. Grattan Guinness transferred the promising field to zealous American Baptists, under whom the awakenings continued, it being said 'We are in the midst of a great spiritual revival upon the field which equals the Banza Manteke Pentecost in intensity and surpasses it in extent . . .'[56]

In 1885, A. B. Simpson, convert of the 1858 Awakening in Canada and founder of the Christian and Missionary Alliance, sent his missionaries to the Congo[57] and began a great work. Henry Grattan Guinness sent out in the 1880s another mission, the Congo Balolo enterprise . . . later part of the Regions Beyond Missionary Union, a worldwide organization.

The Swedish Mission Covenant, a product of the Awakening in Sweden,[58] commenced its Congo operations in the 1880s. The American Presbyterian Mission shared the Equatorial African or northern Congo fields with the Paris Evangelical Mission,[59] and also entered Cameroons.

In the Cameroons, a Baptist mission begun in 1848 and extended by George Grenfell, was transferred to the Basel Mission when the Germans raised their flag in 1887. A mass movement of Bantu towards the Christian faith soon followed, building up in twenty-five years a membership of 15,000.[60]

Throughout the 1880s and 1890s, missions of various kinds, denominational and otherwise, spread throughout the Congo and lands nearby. The Africa Inland Mission was begun in 1895 by Peter C. Scott, who revived Krapf's dream of planting a chain of mission stations across Africa, beginning in the Congo, Kenya and Tanganyika.[61]

In 1886, the Evangelical Missionary Society for East Africa was formed in Berlin. Its main sponsor was Pastor Friedrich von Bodelschwingh of the Inner Mission at Bielefeld, a leader in the German Evangelical Awakening. It soon moved across the newly acquired German territories, sharing opportunities with older German groups in East Africa.[62]

In 1862, the explorer Speke declared that the kingdoms of Uganda were by far the most attractive in all of Africa to missionary enterprise.[63] Stanley was of the same opinion and his challenge stirred the Church Missionary Society to enter Uganda, a task by no means easy.[64]

Alexander Mackay, a convert of the Revival of the 1860s in Britain, and a party of pioneers arrived in Zanzibar in 1876, but only two of them established themselves in Uganda, two dying of fever and two being murdered.[65] The entrance of a militant Roman Catholic mission added to their troubles, which increased when the friendly king Mtesa died and was succeeded by a vicious son Mwanga. Mwanga was responsible for the murder of James Hannington, Anglican bishop, in 1885. Converts of the Christian missions refused to submit to Mwanga's practice of sodomy. So the Kabaka roasted three martyrs slowly to death, and burned alive thirty-two young men in one funeral pyre. Perhaps two hundred martyrs died in the fire, and another bishop perished through fever.[66]

Yet the mission gained a foothold. In 1888, the Baganda themselves overthrew Mwanga, but the Muslims counter-revolted and drove out all the missionaries and dispersed the Christians. Civil war ensued, until the very men who had been so persecuted by Mwanga replaced him on his throne; then in 1890 the area passed under British control, a Uganda protectorate being established in 1894.[67]

Alfred Tucker was appointed bishop in 1890,[68] the year that Alexander Mackay succumbed, but the mission was still precarious until 1893 when a strange chain of circumstances changed the whole situation.

A Baganda reader, Musa, announced his firm intention of apostasizing to heathenism, and this so discouraged the local missionaries that one, George Pilkington, sought mental and spiritual recovery on an island in Lake Victoria.[69]

Far away in South India, a Tamil Christian had found the secret of the victorious Christian life, becoming a successful revivalist who won many thousands to Christ in Tamilnad and Kerala.[70] He penned a tract upon the work of the Holy Spirit,[71] a tract which found its way to Pilkington on a tiny

island in a lake in East Africa. The message transformed
Pilkington's life and ministry. He returned to his labours a
changed man, and like Tamil David, saw the message provoke
a great awakening, with hundreds of conversions and revival
in churches. Roscoe, a colleague of Pilkington, described the
outbreak of the revival at Mengo after the return of Pilkington
from the island of Kome' thus: 'We are in the midst of a great
spiritual revival . . . after the morning service, fully two
hundred stayed behind to be spoken with.'[72]

The revival spread throughout Uganda.[73] In fifteen years,
the number of native lay teachers increased from 75 to 2032,
communicants from 230 to 18,041, baptized Christians from
1140 to 62,716, and catechumens from 230 to 2563.[74]

George Pilkington lost his life in a Sudanese uprising in
1897. Baganda Christians became ardent native evangelists,
reaching tribes around them and adding to evangelical growth
in East Africa.

About the same time as the Uganda Revival, a spiritual
awakening was reported from Jilore, north of Mombasa.[75] An
Anglican missionary reported an hour of preaching followed
by a three hours 'endless song of praise.' In 1894, the
Church Missionary Society reported from Jilore: 'A season
of revival a year and a half ago produced permanent effects
in the spiritual earnestness of the converts.'[76]

By the 1880s, the Church Missionary Society had extended
work into Kenya, and in 1891 the Church of Scotland Mission
among the Kikuyu developed into a considerable enterprise.
Kenyan achievements fell short of the successes in Uganda,
where there was no tribal displacement by settlers.

Thus, fulfilling the dream of missionary pioneers, from
Cameroons across the width of continental Africa to Kenya,
the chain of mission stations had become a reality. South of
that line were the great majority of Bantu folk, among whom
Christianity was becoming the major religious force, making
sure that the teachings of Christ, not the creed of Islam,
should prevail among the Bantu-speaking peoples.

In Canterbury Cathedral in 1864,   during the Revival in
England, Samuel Adjai Crowther was consecrated Bishop
of the Niger Territories.[77] In post-revival times, the Faith
spread rapidly in his jurisdiction in Nigeria. However, he
was compelled to rely upon less committed and qualified
African helpers, corruption and confusion being found in his
diocese in the later years of his quarter century of service,
after which there was a slow recovery.

Rapid growth of the Wesleyan Mission in Lagos occurred in the post-revival decade. Mary Slessor, converted in the afterglow of the 1859 Revival in Scotland,[78] came out in 1876 to Calabar and served for nearly forty years in the United Presbyterian mission. In 1887, a Presbyterian from the North of Ireland pioneered in eastern Nigeria, the Qua Iboe Mission—working among Ibibios, not Ibos— resulting from Samuel Bill's interdenominational enterprise.[79]

Support for the Baptist cause in Liberia languished with the Civil War in the United States, but Negro Baptists took up the burden of support in post-war years.[80] The Methodist cause also declined until William Taylor, designated Bishop for Africa, revived it, the mission operating with white and Negro workers.[81]

In Sierra Leone, the first three bishops succumbed to fevers within two years. The Sierra Leone Pastorate was established with native-born ministers.[82] The Methodists also suffered attrition through disease, and built up a self-supporting ministry in the second half of the century.[83]

The sprawling territory known as French West Africa was pioneered in 1862 by the Paris Evangelical Missionary Society, which entered through Senegal.[84] About the same time, West Indian Anglicans opened a work in the French Guinea.[85] British Wesleyans established a foothold in French Dahomey and in the Ivory Coast. The interior provinces, in the shadow of Islam, were largely untouched.

The greatest successes were won within Bantu-speaking Africa. How were the battles fought, and with what dynamic? Not only were many of the societies that pioneered Central, East, and South Africa the direct products of the Evangelical Revival in the homelands, not only were many of the pioneers either converted or called in these revivals, but in so many cases the greatest expansion of the faith among the Bantu peoples came through the outbreak of just such evangelical awakenings on the African mission fields.

12

MOODY AND THE STUDENTS

The impact of the 1858-59 Awakening was felt in the field of evangelism for more than forty years—the span of D. L. Moody's ministry—and continued on until the outbreak of World War I, before which disaster another worldwide awakening had become interdenominationally effective.

As the figure of Charles Grandison Finney dominated American evangelism in the middle third of the nineteenth century, so the figure of Dwight Lyman Moody dominated the final third, not only in the United States but Britain. Finney was a well-educated scholar; Moody an uneducated countryman who never learned to spell or punctuate his pungent speech. This they had in common, that they were full of zeal to win men and women to Jesus Christ.

In Northfield, a pretty village in rural Massachusetts, family circumstances scarcely suggested a career as a world evangelist for Moody.[1] His father had died when Dwight was four years old, leaving his mother and eight other children (including twins born posthumously) without provision. Nor did family religion suggest it. All the Moody children were christened in the local Unitarian Church. As an eighteen-year old lad in Boston, Moody was professedly converted. It proved to be a simple rather than a profound experience, for when he was examined for admission to church membership, he had so little to say that his candidacy was deferred until he had learned a little more.[2] A little over a year later, Moody moved to the frontier town of Chicago. It was here that his great career began.

The Awakening of 1857-58 in Chicago made a profound impression on the life of the zealous young man from New England.[3] The churches of every denomination were packed to overflowing, yet the rapid growth of the town provided all the raw material for evangelism needed.

In Chicago, Moody became interested in winning young folk to Christ through the Sunday School and through the Young Men's Christian Association. So successful was he that he became an expert in 'drumming up' scholars for

Sunday School.[4] In 1858, he started a Sunday School of his own in a vacant saloon, and before long it was the largest Sunday School in Chicago. All the while, he continued active in his business as a salesman.

Moody's Sunday School developed into a church. In 1860, Moody decided to give up his business income (then bringing him $5000 a year) and to 'live by faith' (which brought him $150 the first year).[5] In 1864, the congregation occupied its own building on Illinois Street, and next year Moody was elected president of the Y.M.C.A. in Chicago. He remained a layman.

His first trip to Britain Moody made in the year 1867, seeking out leaders of the evangelical movement there, such as C. H. Spurgeon, George Müller, George Williams, Lord Shaftesbury, R. C. Morgan, Henry Varley, Harry Moorhouse, and those who seemed to Moody to have something to share with him in the work of the Lord.[6]

Events in Chicago encouraged Moody to revisit Britain. In 1868, the great Farwell Hall of the Y.M.C.A. was burned. Harry Moorhouse, a product of the Revival in Manchester, several years earlier, came to visit Moody, and was asked by him to preach—a mistake, everyone thought at first. Moorhouse preached for a week on the love of God, using the text, John chapter iii, verse 16.[7] He profoundly moved D. L. Moody, whose preaching was never the same again, and who became a preacher of a new message in a new spirit.

Moody had been married in 1862 to a young English-born girl, Emma Revell. In 1870, he met a helpmeet of a different kind, Ira D. Sankey, who became his soloist in his world ministry. In 1871, a great fire destroyed the city of Chicago, reducing to ashes fifty churches and missions. In 1871, while visiting New York, Moody experienced a mighty enduement of the Holy Spirit, an answer to two old ladies' prayers.[8]

In 1872, Moody paid a second visit to Britain. After a night of prayer in Dublin, Henry Varley said to him: 'Moody, the world has yet to see what God will do with a man fully consecrated to Him.' That comment startled Moody.[9] His visit brought a local awakening in a North London church and a number of invitations to return to Britain for a wider ministry followed. An Anglican clergyman, William Pennefather, sent him an invitation by letter to America.[10] Moody tried to settle again in Chicago, but he felt restless until he decided to return to Britain and win 10,000 souls to Christ there.

Moody persuaded Sankey to go along. Their plans made, in June 1873, the Moody and Sankey families arrived in Liverpool to learn that Pennefather had died.[11] Moody crossed to York and commenced meetings on short notice. The response was slow but definite. There was still no movement in the next campaign, in Sunderland. But in Newcastle-on-Tyne, Moody and Sankey's evangelism enjoyed success.

From there, the evangelists proceeded north to Scotland. A turning point in Moody's ministry came in their Edinburgh Campaign. Despite the local Calvinistic conservatism, the evangelist won the enthusiastic approval of the people, both inside and outside the churches. The ministers studied the movement carefully, then began to back it without reserve. Moody introduced the noonday prayer meeting of the 1858-59 Revival again. His evening meetings were crowded, taxing the largest auditoriums.[12]

After three weeks in Dundee, Moody began a mission in Glasgow that made a lasting impact on the city. Not only were thousands converted, but the United Evangelistic Committee transformed itself into the Glasgow Evangelistic Association and maintained a dozen subsidiary organizations of evangelism and relief work.[13]

Thus encouraged, the evangelists crossed over to Ireland. The Belfast Mission of the Moody and Sankey team commenced in the autumn of 1874. A daily noonday prayer meeting was begun in a Donegall Square church. The evening meetings attracted an enormous attendance of young men. The Anglican, Presbyterian and other ministers reinforced them. Dublin's Roman Catholic majority noted Moody's own avoidance of affront to their faith, and proved friendly, if not enthusiastic.[14] Again, there were several thousands of professed conversions. The Irish had seen the greatest expression of evangelism since the '59 Revival.

The Manchester, Sheffield, Birmingham and Liverpool Missions followed, each with success. They were moving towards a climax in London. Twenty thousand people nightly heard them in the Agricultural Hall in Islington. While William Taylor of California continued there, D. L. Moody preached in a tabernacle in Bow to the poor and in the Opera House in the Haymarket to the rich each evening. The London meetings lasted twenty weeks and attracted 2,500,000.[15]

As in Scotland, Moody's work in England gave birth to many Christian enterprises besides giving a breath of revival to existent organizations. It made such an impact that

Friedrich Engels, the collaborator with Karl Marx in his Communist propaganda, explained the whole business as a plot of the British bourgeoisie to import Yankee revivalism to keep the proletariat contented.[16]

In August 1875, Moody returned to the United States and commenced a campaign in Brooklyn in October, followed by a greater in Philadelphia in late November. Vast crowds attended, for news of success in Britain had enthused the American church people. In February 1876, Moody held a campaign in New York, where the New Yorkers attended in tens of thousands, many responding.[17]

Moody returned to Chicago to campaign in the winter of 1876, and received a hero's welcome from a city which claimed him as a son. Early in 1877, he commenced ministry in Boston, another city of his youth, but there he encountered opposition from both Roman and Unitarian sides. A year later, he was still campaigning in New England. Sankey parted from him to conduct a singing ministry in England, but failing there returned to work with Moody as before. In 1880-81, together they ministered in cities across the country as far as the Pacific Coast.[18]

In Newcastle-on-Tyne, Moody began his second British campaign in October 1881, again moving north to Edinburgh for six weeks, then to Glasgow, in which metropolis he held forth for five months. He then conducted short series of meetings in Welsh cities and towns and in provincial cities in England.[19] In 1883, Moody conducted an eight months' mission in London. Two large temporary structures were built, one in North London and the other in South London. As soon as a three weeks' mission had been completed in one, it was soon transferred to another location on the same side while the other building was being used across the river.[20]

After 1884, Moody conducted his evangelistic campaigns in smaller American cities,[21] besides giving much of his time to educational promotion at Chicago and Northfield, and to Bible conferences. It was rare for him to visit non-English-speaking countries, though in 1894 Moody preached in Mexico City, contributing to a most significant year.[22]

Moody conducted a great campaign in 1893 at the World's Columbian Exposition in Chicago. Approximately two million visitors attended this evangelistic series at the World's Fair, sponsored by Moody with the help of his Bible Institute. Points of preaching were chosen on the north-side, west-side and south-side of Chicago, and, on Sunday mornings, Moody rented a huge circus tent near the lake front. To reach those speaking French, German, Polish and other languages of Europe, Moody invited Monod of Paris, Stoecker of Berlin, Pinder of Poland, and other European notables to conduct special meetings, and he also shared ministry with Thomas Spurgeon of New Zealand, Henry Varley of Australia, John McNeill of Scotland—famous English-speaking evangelists, and warm admirers of Moody.[23]

In Kansas City, Missouri was held Moody's last series, commencing November 1899. His committee was composed of Anglican, Baptist, Congregational, Disciples, Methodist and Presbyterian ministers.[24] There were the usual great crowds, but Moody showed signs of exhaustion. He told his friends: 'This is the first time in forty years of preaching that I have had to give up my meetings.' He rushed home and lingered little, leaving his loved ones 22nd December 1899, mourned by multitudes who rejoiced in his works.

Moody's ministry was a puzzle to unbelieving scholars. The distinguished historian, William Warren Sweet, insisted that 'the attempts of sociologists and psychologists to explain him seem trite and foolish.'[25]

It seems appropriate to point out that Dwight Lyman Moody was an evangelist, and that his organized campaigns of evangelism were not necessarily 'revivals' in the historic sense of the word, and that his calling cannot therefore be described as a revivalist, if such a word is also used to describe the ministry of men such as Evan Roberts.

Among classes that despised his homely ways, Moody stirred up supercilious enemies, yet he also inspired both loyalty and esteem in the best products of the universities. A man is known by his associates and his friends. Moody's co-workers were extremely able men. He made use of the musical talents of Philip P. Bliss and George C. Stebbins, besides those of Ira D. Sankey. Associated with him in preaching were men like D. W. Whittle, Reuben A. Torrey, A. C. Dixon, and J. Wilbur Chapman, Americans; and from Britain, Henry Varley, John McNeill, Henry Drummond, G. Campbell Morgan, and F. B. Meyer.

The story of what God had accomplished through Moody in Great Britain and the United States created quite a great interest in evangelism and revival in Australia, New Zealand and South Africa,[26] even though the American evangelist was never to visit these southern commonwealths. His influence was as great among Afrikaners as English-speaking.

The organ of the Dutch Reformed Church published in Cape Town devoted much material in its columns to the ministry of Moody and Sankey.[27] Not only was Andrew Murray vitally interested, but other ministers both English-speaking and Dutch-speaking, returning from Britain with enthusiasm for the wholesomeness of Moody's work, imparted a hunger and a zeal for like results in South Africa.

In the 1870s, therefore, there were reports of evangelical awakenings in Cape Town, Stellenbosch, Wellington, Montagu and Swellendam. Out of this movement came the evangelistic tours of Dr. Andrew Murray in the dorps of sections of the Cape, the first in 1879, the second five years later, the third in 1886, the fourth in 1887, the fifth in 1888, the sixth in 1890, the seventh in 1891 and the eighth in 1897.[28]

Andrew Murray was not the only Reformed minister who reaped a harvest of converts in the country. The Dutch Reformed Church had been so thoroughly stirred by the 1860 Revival that evangelism was taken as a matter of course, hence the Synod of 1876 devoted time and attention to special services for evangelistic preaching.[29]

From 1884 onward, a significant awakening developed in Umvoti County in Natal, around Greytown, in which James Turnbull was the Dutch Reformed minister. The widespread movement started among the Boers, and whole families of farmers professed conversion. As a result of this, a deep concern for the spiritual welfare of their English-speaking neighbours developed among the Boers. David Russell (of Pietermaritzburg) was invited over to Greytown to direct an evangelistic outreach in which hundreds became inquirers and three hundred joined the churches.[30]

In Greytown, an English-speaking merchant commented that 'Nothing short of a miracle could have brought about a change like this so soon after the battle of Majuba.' The farmers of Umvoti County became much concerned also regarding the masses of Zulus in that part of Natal. Ardent efforts were made to evangelize the Bantu farm population through meetings organized by laymen, with much success attending the gatherings.

David Russell, who had commenced a lively ministry as a layman in 1878 in Durban, went on to become an ordained Presbyterian minister as well as one of the best-known of all South African evangelists, preaching throughout various English-speaking countries, his ministry lasting for three-score years.

Also of deep significance to South African Christianity was the Keswick Convention for the Deepening of the Spiritual Life, an evangelical movement with a truly worldwide influence, budded at gatherings in London, Oxford and Brighton in 1873, '74 and '75, and blossomed into early maturity at a Lake District resort in 1875; but the seed was sown in the great Revival of 1858-59 in the English-speaking world. Its origins may be traced to the American Middle West.

William Edwin Boardman had published at the height of the Awakening of 1858 a treatise upon the 'Higher Christian Life.' He was a zealous young Presbyterian businessman when he started his search in the 1840s for a holier life. His book was a huge success on both sides of the Atlantic (circulation, 200,000), being published in Britain in 1860.[31] It produced its greatest effect in the Old Country.

The year 1860 dated the conversion of a young English clergyman, Evan Hopkins, and it was not long before a copy of Boardman's treatise found its way into the eager hands of Hopkins, then engaged in an engrossing revival ministry. It was on 1st May 1873 that Hopkins with fifteen other people met in Mayfair to discuss the subject of the deepening of the Christian life. He entered a fuller experience so real that his wife was the first to follow him into it.[32]

In July 1874, a conference was conducted at Broadlands estate in Hampshire, the seat of Lord Mount Temple, the leaders being Mr. and Mrs. R. Pearsall Smith. Before he could participate in a conference announced for 1875, Smith suffered a nervous breakdown, brought about by charges more serious than the indiscretion which provoked them.[33] It is of interest that Pearsall Smith's daughter married Lord Bertrand Russell, which added to his anti-Christian bias.

Meetings for promoting Scriptural holiness were begun at Oxford in August 1874, with the help of Canon Cristopher. The Convention at Oxford was followed by a larger one at Brighton, begun on 29th May 1875.[34] Henry Varley, of 1859 Revival fame, spoke several times. D. L. Moody in London sent the good will and prayers of eight thousand people then attending his mass meetings.

The Vicar of St. John's, Keswick, Harford Battersby, had been active in the 1860 Awakening in Carlisle.[35] He attended the Oxford Convention, committing himself. He invited his friends to the Lakeside town, and thus began the conventions for deepening of the Christian life that gained for 'Keswick' a unique place of leadership in the evangelical world. A majority of its leaders were either evangelists or converts of the 1859 Revival, as were a number of new speakers.

Canon Harford Battersby continued to preside until his death; Evan Hopkins emerged as the leader; William Haslam ministered; Theodore Monod participated. After an address by Evan Hopkins, Handley C. G. Moule was moved to stand publicly as a seeker after blessing, and as Principal of Ridley Hall, Cambridge or as Bishop of Durham, he warmly addressed the Keswick Convention thirteen times.[36]

Andrew Murray entered a deeper experience at Keswick in 1882, and became a mouthpiece of its message all over the world.[37] In 1887, a new speaker was F. B. Meyer, converted during the Revival in the 1860s in London.[38] Another was Charles Inwood, the Irish Methodist evangelist, whose ministry extended its message far and wide.[39]

The Keswick Convention became a missionary force after Reginald Radcliffe in 1886 borrowed its tent for a missionary meeting. Hudson Taylor and Eugene Stock used the Keswick platform to enlist young people for the mission fields. The Keswick line of teaching was supported within the United States by such evangelical leaders as D. L. Moody, Reuben Torrey, Adoniram J. Gordon, A. B. Simpson and J. Wilbur Chapman, but it never became the unifying force in United States that it had become in Great Britain.

Keswick borrowed its evangelical ecumenism, with its slogan 'All One in Christ Jesus,' from the Revival of 1858-59 and the movements which followed it. Unlike certain other products of the Revival, the Keswick Convention maintained its evangelical and evangelistic character.

Andrew Murray thus became a spokesman for Keswick in South Africa, and not only won the unchurched through his evangelism but nominal Christians to a greater commitment. Through his influence, an annual convention for the deepening of the spiritual life was organized at Wellington.

Keswick theology, mediated through a tract written by a Tamil evangelist, stirred up George Pilkington in Uganda and through him provoked an extraordinary awakening that added tens of thousands to the Anglican mission churches of East Africa.[40]

A Keswick speaker, Charles Inwood, brought the same message to Malawi, and witnessed another extraordinary revival of the Presbyterian churches and ingathering of the heathen, less than twenty years later, a comparable work of grace in Central Africa.[41]

The influence of D. L. Moody was profoundly felt among Christian students. Moody was not a theologian. His own theological convictions were strongly conservative, but he maintained cordial friendships with men of other points of view, including Professor Henry Drummond. But until the 1880s, Moody had avoided ministry to students, chiefly because he felt himself academically unequipped.

'There never was a place,' said Moody, 'that I approached with greater anxiety than Cambridge. Never having had the privilege of a university education, I was nervous about meeting university men.' He was not concerned without good reason, as events quickly proved.[42]

Well might Moody be anxious, for there were many high-spirited students lying in wait for him. There were hoots and cheers, fire-crackers and guffaws, but Moody kept his temper. His student sponsors had heavy hearts that 5th of November in 1882, but next day a ring-leader, Gerald Lander of Trinity College, called to apologize.[43]

Although seventeen hundred students had been counted in the first meeting in the Corn Exchange, only a hundred attended the second in a seated gymnasium, but they included Gerald Lander. On Wednesday, before a larger crowd, Moody gave an evangelistic appeal and after repeating it saw more than fifty men make their way to the inquiry room. One was Gerald Lander—afterwards Bishop of Hong Kong.

Next night, a hundred or more waited behind for counsel. All through the week, clear-cut conversions were professed by intellectuals and athletes, many of them proving to be both deep and lasting. The final meeting in the Corn Exchange brought eighteen hundred hearers, and concluded a mission which proved to be the beginning of a worldwide, interdenominational student movement.

The next day, without the benefit of a Sunday start, Moody opened his mission in the Corn Exchange in Oxford, which was filled to overflowing. Bolder, he quenched attempts at rowdyism several nights running and gained a hearing for his messages. Audiences moved from Clarendon Assembly Rooms to the Town Hall, where Moody gathered inquirers in an aftermeeting, and a number made personal decisions for Christ.[44]

Helping in Moody's evangelism, the two Studd brothers of cricketing fame, J. E. Kynaston Studd and Charles T. Studd, addressed one of Moody's Stepney mission meetings, and a young man named Wilfred Grenfell was converted.[45]

Sir Montague Beauchamp, William Cassels, D. E. Hoste, Arthur and Cecil Polhill-Turner, Stanley Smith and C. T. Studd, all Moody's helpers and some his converts, offered themselves to work in China under the China Inland Mission, They first became a remarkable witness team, named the Cambridge Seven, touring the British universities with their message, stirring up the students; then they sailed east.[46]

Meanwhile, in the United States and Canada, the Young Men's Christian Associations had become the main vehicles of religious life on the campuses of North American colleges and universities. The first Y.M.C.A.s for students were organized in the University of Michigan and the University of Virginia in 1858, during the Revival. Within ten years, there were forty such associations; and an Inter-Collegiate Young Men's Christian Association was founded in 1877.[47]

Two years earlier, a young man named Luther Wishard moved to Princeton University and found fellowship in the Philadelphian Society, a Christian union.[48] One of his friends therein was T. W. Wilson, known in class as Tommy, but better known later as Woodrow Wilson who carried his deep Christian idealism to the Presidency of the United States of America during critical times.

Luther Wishard became the mainspring of student Young Men's Christian Associations, and within another ten years there were two hundred and fifty associations on campuses with twelve thousand members.

A friend of Luther Wishard, Robert Mateer of Princeton, became leader of an Inter-Seminary Missionary Alliance which held its first convention in 1880 with two hundred and fifty students from thirty or more seminaries present;[49] these missionary-minded students, like their Y.M.C.A. friends, were strongly evangelical and evangelistic.

Luther Wishard, as organizer and evangelist of the Inter-Collegiate Y.M.C.A., had tried hard to interest Moody in collegiate ministry, but had been rebuffed by the modest Moody, conscious of his academic deficiencies.[50] In 1884, after Moody's powerful impact on Cambridge became known, Wishard pleaded again with Moody, who consented to preach at a few colleges in 1885, including Dartmouth, Princeton and Yale. His college-slanted sermons, he knew, were few. He looked for help from his many faculty friends.

Meanwhile Stanley Smith, the Cambridge oarsman, and C. T. Studd, the Cambridge cricketer, had visited Edinburgh University in 1884 to make an impact on the four thousand

students. Moody invited Kynaston Studd to spend an academic
term in the autumn of 1885 in North American colleges, of
which he visited twenty in thirteen weeks.[51] One of those he
then challenged to a dedication of heart and life at Cornell
University was John R. Mott, a law student who had been
converted in a revival in Pottsville, Iowa at age 14.[52]

An outcome of Moody's growing interest in the student
world was the convening of a college conference at Mount
Hermon in Massachusetts in the summer of 1886, when some
two hundred and fifty students from one hundred colleges
attended, and Moody was as popular as any eminent lecturer.
This first conference was entirely unprogrammed, and the
students followed a course of lectures and activities which
came about 'as the Spirit directed.'[53]

One of the college delegates was Robert P. Wilder, son
of a retired missionary to India, who had already formed a
student foreign missionary association at Princeton. The
Wilder family, whose head had been one of the Williams
College group of missionaries in the early 1800s, had been
praying that a thousand students from American universities
might be enlisted for foreign missionary enterprise.   To
every student who would listen, Robert Wilder presented
the call of missions.[54]

Wilder succeeded in persuading Moody to set aside time
for missionary talks, and this combination of prayer and
presentation had its effect.[55] One hundred delegates signed a
declaration signifying their willingness to serve overseas.

Robert Wilder and John Forman toured the universities
and succeeded in enlisting about two thousand volunteers
for missions. Moody was first cautious about the exuberant
enthusiasm of the youngsters, but he continued to help them.
The volunteers increased their own numbers to about three
thousand in the academic year, 1887-88.[56]

Professor Henry Drummond of Edinburgh crossed over
the Atlantic and addressed the students. He received a welter
of invitations to address scientific societies, but refused
almost all of them. He returned to minister in American
universities, Williams College being stirred, Dartmouth
suspending all classes, Princeton pre-empting his time from
morning till night, Yale giving him one of the busiest weeks
of his life. Even Harvard heard him graciously. Drummond
was attacked by conservatives for his attempt to bring both
religion and science into harmony, and, although Moody had
lined up with the conservatives, he stood by Drummond as

a zealous evangelist and a great scholar. Drummond so extended his student ministry around the world.[57]

Luther Wishard returned the British visitors' calls by touring the universities of Cambridge, Oxford, Edinburgh and Glasgow in the spring of 1888. The summer he spent in Germany, France, Switzerland and Sweden. Wishard extended his journey around the world, reporting conversions and calls to service everywhere.[58]

James B. Reynolds, another student volunteer, crossed the Atlantic to Oslo University. He also visited Stockholm, Lund and Copenhagen in 1889. In 1891, Robert Wilder visited universities in Britain, enlisting three hundred volunteers for missionary service.[59]

In 1893, a conference was called at Keswick, attended by a hundred delegates from twenty universities, and from it was created the Inter-University Christian Union.[60] Donald Fraser, later a successful missionary in Central Africa, became its first secretary.

The Student Volunteers sought to enlist every Christian in the objective of evangelizing the world. Their watchword was 'the evangelization of the world in this generation.' In their main objective, they were hugely successful, for in half a century, more than twenty thousand students reached the foreign mission fields of the Church, an astounding and heartening achievement. The greatest of church historians, Kenneth Scott Latourette declared his measured opinion that it was through the Student Volunteers in the various countries that a large proportion of the outstanding leaders in the spread of Protestant Christianity were recruited.[61]

In due course, the Student Volunteer Movement began to make its impact upon the students of South Africa, Afrikaners and English-speaking alike. Another movement which made a contribution to church life, interdenominationally and bilingually, was the Christian Endeavour Societies.

In the winter of 1880-81, there was a time of revival in Williston Congregational Church, in Portland, Maine. Its pastor, Francis E. Clark, wishing to conserve the blessing, organized a 'Young People's Society of Christian Endeavor' to call youth to greater dedication and service, training the young folk to participate in church activities.[62]

By 1895, there were thirty-eight thousand C. E. Societies in the world, with 2,225,000 members. The movement was evangelical, evangelistic and church-related, suited to the climate of the day, which was evangelical and ecumenical.

13

CONTINUED SOCIAL IMPACT

Following the mid-century Awakening, Britain maintained the lead assumed fifty years earlier in undertaking social reform and relief. There were many reasons for this.

It is an American historical opinion that the 1858 Revival had little effect on the social welfare of the American people.[1] Rather its effects were suspended while the nation's energies were being consumed by the War between the States, a war with far-reaching social after-effects.

During that war, Christians engaged in social action; the United States Christian Commission brought spiritual good, intellectual improvement, and social and spiritual welfare to Federal troops; there were Christian organizations also that cared for the welfare of Confederate soldiers.[2]

Negroes were given as much protection as war permitted. Suddenly, in the course of hostilities, slavery was swept away.[3] What Christians were striving for by peaceful agitation became mandatory almost overnight by military decree. Emancipation, however, did not occur in a moral vacuum.

In post-war years, the American Evangelicals found British social enterprises ready to adopt. The 1858-59 Evangelical Awakening, while it was primarily evangelistic, had developed a humane spirit as liberal as its theology was conservative. Commenting on a single outcome of the great Revival, G. M. Trevelyan affirmed that it had 'brought the enthusiasm of "conversion" after Wesley's original fashion to the army of the homeless and unfed, to the drunkard, the criminal and the harlot,' treating 'social work and care for the material conditions of the poor and outcast as being an essential part of the Christian mission to the souls of men and women.'[4] This tribute belongs to the 1858-59 Awakening as a whole, not only to a very worthy part.

One of the first effects of the Awakening of 1858-59 was the creation of new and intense sympathy with the poor and suffering. 'God has not ordained,' protested Lord Shaftesbury, 'that in a Christian country there should be an overwhelming mass of foul, helpless poverty.'[5]

A revival school of Christian philanthropists soon arose, seeking to go straight to the heart of the slums with its practical Samaritanism, yet always ready to cooperate in all wise legislative improvements. So, as this Awakening intensified the fervency of faith, denominational schemes, organizations and committees were multiplied; numberless philanthropic institutions, asylums, homes, refuges, and schools were founded.[6]

As before, Shaftesbury was spokesman for evangelical social reform.[7] He originated more Royal Commissions of social investigation than any parliamentarian in all British history, extending benefits to all classes of working people.

During 1864 and 1867, Industrial Extension Acts were passed, practically universalizing provisions of workmen's protection. In 1865, Lord Shaftesbury tackled the problem of agricultural gangs and so relieved the children of the countryside from a bondage as brutal as that endured by their townsfellows in earlier decades. In 1872, Shaftesbury worked for the abolition of use of children in brickyards. His most striking victory was passing legislation forbidding the use of little boys to clean house and factory chimneys.

The Seventh Earl of Shaftesbury was not without faults, of course. As an aristocrat of class-conscious times, he upheld the superiority of his order, detested trade unions, and was occasionally a narrow-minded diehard. He bitterly opposed the Salvation Army and refused to reconsider an opinion hard to excuse.[8]

There is an immediate connection between an evangelical awakening and educational hunger.[9] In Great Britain in 1815, elementary schools were entirely private. Two decades later, Lord Ashley (later Shaftesbury) petitioned the Queen to provide education for the working classes. As insisted by Evangelicals, the State contributed a measure of support to elementary schools. In 1870, their recommendations were fulfilled in an Education Act, setting up public day schools. A million or more were in attendance in England in 1870; two million or more in 1885.[10] This had a profound effect upon the countries of the overseas Empire.

During the 1859 Awakening in Dublin, some members of a brilliant family named Barnardo professed to accept Christ as Saviour in the Metropolitan Hall series.[11] Two of these Barnardo brothers tried to persuade their younger brother, Tom, but he scoffed. Nevertheless he attended the meetings and witnessed the striking demonstrations of spiritual conviction. These he explained away as emotional hysteria and psychological phenomena, yet in spite of his subtle arguments he was set to thinking. An address by John Hambledon in the same place some weeks later caused him such conviction that long after midnight he sought, in great distress and with many tears, his brothers' help. Young Barnardo heard a call to missionary service and soon volunteered— but tragic discoveries in the dismal East End of London led him into his life-work, the founding of Dr. Barnardo's Homes, the world's largest private orphanage system. Other great orphanages were founded throughout the country.[12]

Young and Ashton, in their study of British social work in the nineteenth century, specified Evangelicalism as the 'greatest single urge' of humanitarianism, saying that the sentiment of human benevolence and its practical expression derived directly from religious influence. 'It came from the quickened knowledge, born of religious revivalism, that all men were the children of God and loved by Him.'[13]

The same forces were at work in American experience. A Christian man, John Augustus, a cobbler in Boston, offered in 1841 to bail out a drunkard. The Massachusetts Court agreed to it and, in the next two decades, this Christian man bailed out two thousand people who might have otherwise become criminals.[14] By the time of the Awakening, the vital experiment had succeeded. The example was followed.

The Probation of First Offenders became law first in the State of Massachusetts in 1878, and a similar law passed in Britain in 1887, though preceded there by the Youthful Offenders Act of 1854, and the Discharged Prisoners Act of 1862, likewise through Christian prompting.[15] Sarah Martin and Mary Carpenter, who achieved so much for the care of prisoners in Britain, were both dedicated Christian women who had before them Fliedner's example from Germany.

The Awakening of 1858-59 had an immediate effect upon the ancient practice of prostitution. It was a far cry from medieval days when the Bishops had licensed a row of houses of ill-fame near London Bridge; and a long time since the Puritans of Cromwell's day had made fornication a felony, punishable by death on the second occasion.

The industrial revolution aggravated the problem. Slum squalor and drunkenness made many women reckless. By the mid-nineteenth century, venereal disease was rampant in London, and in the 1860s became the target of regulative legislation, approved and disapproved on moral grounds.[16]

One of the first startling stories from the Ulster Revival of 1859 was that of a prayer meeting being held by the newly converted inmates of a brothel. A policeman reported seeing a group of fourteen prostitutes making their way to a home of rehabilitation, the result of a visit to a prayer meeting in Belfast. Dr. Hugh Hanna in the same city noted that prostitutes were prompted to seek salvation after seeing the falling off in business.[17]

In the earlier months of the 1860 Revival in the city of London, attempts were made to reclaim the prostitutes who frequented the West End. A series of evangelistic meetings was held for prostitutes only, arranged at midnight or later. At the outset, many fallen girls burst into tears when addressed by the saintly Baptist Noël who talked very tenderly to them. The sponsors took a score of penitents to houses of rehabilitation. A thousand women were rescued in a year of the operation of the mission.[18]

The work was carried on by a rare champion. In bereavement, Josephine Butler sought to share the greater pain of other unfortunates, and thus found her life work in social welfare in London. In visits to prisons, where she shared in the menial tasks of the women, Josephine Butler was confronted with the evil of state patronage and regulation of vice. She dedicated herself in righteous indignation to the abolition of the evil. Concentrating upon the inequality of suspected women before the law, Josephine Butler worked for repeal of the obnoxious legislation that made government the official supervisor of iniquity.[19]

By the year 1877, more than eight hundred committees (provincial and metropolitan) had gathered eight thousand petitions with more than two million signatures submitted to Parliament. A Select Committee of Parliament (1879 onward) reported adversely, so Mrs. Butler rallied Christian forces in prayer 'so that the prayers of the people of God would be as the incense of Aaron, when he ran between the living and the dead.' The Acts were suspended in 1883, and repealed in 1886.[20]

'No other woman in history,' said the social reformer, Dame Millicent Fawcett, 'had such a far-reaching influence or effected so widespread a change in public opinion.' Other victories, by Ellice Hopkins and by Bramwell Booth with his journalist-associate, W. T. Stead, were won.[21] In a major crusade against the white-slave traffic, Stead demonstrated (in a morally innocent but technically guilty way) that young girls could be inveigled into involuntary servitude of the most vicious kind. His crusade was followed by national and international action carried on by the League of Nations.

For ninety years, the charge was reiterated by enemies of the 1859 Revival that the excitement brought about a sad increase of sexual promiscuity. Even Charles Dickens was guilty of declaring that 'the most immoral scenes take place on Sunday nights.'[22] There was much evidence to the contrary, but the prejudice persisted.

Most of the instances quoted by observers of the Revival concerned the reform of professional prostitutes rather than promiscuity and its outcome, illegitimacy. There were no compulsory registrations of births in Ireland in those days, but the Scottish figures indicated a decrease in rural cases, and a considerable reduction of the annual increase in urban areas; the all-Scotland figures showed a tiny fractional rise in illegitimacy year by year, except in 1860, when the 1859 Awakening had its full effect.[23]

A charge of increased promiscuity is easy to make in the absence of statistics to contradict selected examples of sin. Since the first publication of the present author's studies on the subject, this charge has not been repeated. Without a doubt, the excitement of the times provided more temptation for young people, in sympathetic reaction, not more sin.

In the year 1859, the young Swiss businessman Henri Dunant followed the French Emperor Napoleon III to North Italy, hoping to arrange business contracts. Unwittingly he found himself a spectator at the bloody battle of Solferino, fought between the armies of the French and Austrians.

Henri Dunant was of a prominent evangelical family and already active in the Young Men's Christian Association of Geneva.[24] Among those who had made a profound impression upon his thinking were Elizabeth Fry, famed as a prison reformer, and Florence Nightingale, famed as a military nurse.[25] Dunant was expert in both business and evangelism and maintained his family interests.

Dunant was horrified by the suffering of the wounded and dying on the battlefield. He helped as best he could in the days that followed, noting the sincere if unskilled efforts of local people to alleviate their suffering. He wrote 'A Memory of Solferino' and published it in 1862, sending it to statemen and leaders throughout Europe. As a result, a Geneva Convention was held in 1864 and from its findings and decisions came the Red Cross Movement.[26]

Not everyone expected to help proved willing. Some of the military leaders resented the intrusion of civilians on the battlefield. To Henri Dunant's sorrow, even Florence Nightingale withheld her support,[27] saying that the succor of the wounded in war was the business of government. But there was enough help forthcoming to speed the Red Cross on its mission of mercy and it spread throughout the world, by no means an evangelical agency but an evangelical idea whose time had come.

Timothy L. Smith, in his able study of 'revivalism' and social reform, made a pertinent observation concerning conditions in the United States at that time:[28]

> The rapid growth of concern with purely social issues such as poverty, working men's rights, the liquor traffic, slum housing, and racial bitterness is the chief feature distinguishing American religion after 1865 from that of the first half of the nineteenth century.

The United States was being rapidly industrialized, and the Christian Gospel was beginning to influence the situation. Evangelical sentiment was expressed by Mrs. Barnardo thus: 'The State should deal with it, but does not: the Church of Christ must!'[29] Responsibility of the State was recognized.

The social influence of the 1858-59 Awakening carried over to the mission fields of the world. The influence of the missionaries was circumscribed by their relationship to the holders of power: in other words, in India and in southern Africa, the missionaries could appeal to the British as the colonizing or protecting power, either directly or by stirring up the evangelical conscience at home; whereas, in China or Japan, the missionaries had no lobbying lever.

Generally speaking, the colonial powers were indisposed to interfere with their subjects' way of life, providing the government and commerce were not disrupted thereby. They welcomed the aid of the missionaries, but supported them only up to a point, and, in certain countries, they opposed them and ardently defended the native religion and culture.

The missionaries were scarcely ever able to achieve results in such fields as the rights of working men, for the simple reason that the working force was nowhere as near full development as in the industrialized countries. There were other factors also, the gap between employers and employed in standards of living, which was considerable in countries of homogeneous race as well as in those where the race factor further complicated matters.

There was little that the missionaries could do regarding sexual morality. They discouraged polygamy among their own converts, but were unable to alter public opinion about the matter. They discountenanced primitive puberty rites as breeders of immorality, but their rules were not binding outside their followings. They disapproved of promiscuity, but what did that matter to the tribes people who tolerated it? Their influence was not fully effective until cultural disintegration occurred, and the detribalized people sought a more suitable way of life in modern times.

It was necessary, therefore, for the missionaries to concentrate upon education and medical services, for in every country there was manifested a minimum of objection to such benefits to all classes, including the lowest. And in these two fields, they were second to none.

The 1860 Revival's effect on South Africa has been noted. Not only did the Awakening move the Afrikaners to engage in missionary activities on their northern frontiers, schools being founded along with churches, but the Taylor Awakening profoundly moved the Xhosa and Zulu communities, leading to 'an era of education' among them, to quote an historian.[30]

It was many years before the rest of Africa was opened up for education. But it is significant that the earlier the missionary penetration, the higher the proportion of the population in school today. Even so, education was a mission by-product, and not the major emphasis of missions. Most missionaries engage in it automatically. And the same was true of medical work. The missionaries built hospitals all over Africa and provided the only worthy medical service.

It was after the 1858-59 Revivals in America and Britain that medical missionaries were activated in all India.[31] The Scots initiated medical evangelism in clinics and hospitals from 1860 onwards.[32] Seven medical evangelists in 1858 became 140 in less than forty years, with 168 Indian doctors assisting them. Women's medical work began following the Revivals,[33] and ardent evangelical Christians started medical colleges in north, central and south India. A survey in World War II showed that 90% of all nurses in India were nominal Christians, four-fifths of whom trained at mission hospitals.

It is possible to document the missionary contribution in education and medicine likewise in China, Japan and Korea. Timothy Richard, founding father of Chinese universities, was a convert of the Revival of 1859 in Wales. The medical missionaries laid the foundation of a Chinese medical service.

Even in Latin America, Evangelical missionaries provided so much of the initiative in establishing schools, teachers' training, and model higher educational campuses, despite the opposition of the religious establishments therein. They also provided medical services in areas of greatest need.

In the homelands of Evangelical Christianity, the step-by-step improvement of social conditions, the leavening of the lump by the Christian conscience, was accompanied by a development of a social impetus by Society itself, so that it was no longer necessary for Christians to initiate ideas for new social improvements—they simply joined efforts with other enlightened citizens. Their ministry of pioneering was channeled more and more into needier fields abroad. There, where the social conscience was often feeble, they were free to combine their urgent evangelism with urgent social betterment, their hosts accepting the former so long as it was accompanied by the latter.

This Christian service was so very different from the practice of the Communists, who were often committed to the worsening of conditions so that bloody revolution would follow the frustration of social progress.

Arnold Toynbee has described Communism as a Christian heresy, and certainly it sprang out of the Christian social conscience rather than out of Islam or Buddhism, even though it reacted bitterly against many basic Christian beliefs and practices.

Marx was in London during the great Revival of 1860 onward.[34] Marx founded his International in 1864 and stayed in its company or at the desks of the British Museum. He was a contemporary of Lord Shaftesbury and of his reforming friends, and he was still a resident of London when D. L. Moody came to preach.[35] He derided the Moody campaigns, if his friend Engels be accepted as a reliable authority. Marx became so obsessed with his dogma that he learned to hate Christians for doing good and so delaying the day of violence. He was impatient with the evolutionary methods of all Christian social reformers.

Christian socialists found the Marxist spirit very different to their own temper and motives. They disagreed with Marx about God, about the nature of man, about the Christian morality and the purpose of life—about so many things that it was obvious that they agreed in only a few points, the need of reform of society and its regulation. They believed that man could not live by bread alone.

14

THE FIFTH GENERAL AWAKENING

The worldwide Awakening of the early twentieth century came at the end of fifty years of evangelical advance, following the outpouring of the Spirit far and wide in 1858-59 and the 'sixties. Thus it did not represent a recovery from a long night of despair caused by rampant infidelity, as was the case in the days of Wesley. It seemed, rather, a blaze of evening glory at the end of 'the Great Century.'[1]

It was the most extensive Evangelical Awakening of all time, reviving Anglican, Baptist, Congregational, Disciple, Lutheran, Methodist, Presbyterian and Reformed churches and other evangelical bodies throughout Europe and North America, Australasia and South Africa, and their daughter churches and missionary causes throughout Asia, Africa, and Latin America, winning more than five million folk to an evangelical faith in the two years of greatest impact in each country. Indirectly it produced Pentecostalism.

Why did it occur at the time it did? The ways of God are past finding out. One can only surmise. A subtler form of infidelity had arisen, a compromise between Christianity and humanism. A more sophisticated interpretation of human conduct, inspired by Freud, spoke of God as an Illusion.

The prescient widsom of its Author may also account for the sudden spread of the Revival of 1900-1910. Within ten years, the awful slaughter of World War I had begun, and a gentler way of life passed into the twilight of history.

Arnold Toynbee, reminiscing, recalled the trauma of the time, when half his classmates perished in battle. Oneself was a child when the news of the Battle of the Somme threw every family in his native city into mourning for the finest of their fathers and sons and brothers killed in action.[2]

The Awakening was a kind of harvest before the devastation of Christendom. It was Sir Edward Grey who lamented in 1914 that the lights of civilization were going out one by one, not to be lit again in his lifetime. The upheavals of war unloosed the times of revolution on mankind. A biographer of Wilbur Chapman observed:[3]

As we look back over these extraordinary religious awakenings which . . . so quickened the churches and so effectively pressed the claims of God upon the consciences of multitudes, we cannot escape the conviction that God in gracious providence was reaping a spiritual harvest before He permitted the outburst of revolutionary forces that have overwhelmed the world, impoverished almost every nation, produced economic and social chaos, and stained with dishonor the pride of Christian civilization.

In the history of revivals, it has often been noted that such restoral periods are a warning of, and synchronize with, impending judgment. The harvest is gathered before the field is doomed to death.

The early twentieth century Evangelical Awakening was a worldwide movement. It did not begin with the phenomenal Welsh Revival of 1904-05. Rather its sources were in the springs of little prayer meetings which seemed to arise spontaneously all over the world, combining into the streams of expectation which became a river of blessing in which the Welsh Revival became the greatest cataract.

Meetings for prayer for revival in evangelical gatherings such as Moody Bible Institute and the Keswick Convention greeted the new century—not surprisingly.[4] What was remarkable was that missionaries and national believers in obscure places in India, the Far East, Africa and Latin America seemed moved at the same time to pray for phenomenal revival in their fields and world wide. Most of them had never seen or heard of phenomenal revival occurring on missionfields, and few of them had witnessed it at home. Their experience was limited to reading of past revivals.

The first manifestation of phenomenal revival occurred simultaneously among Boer prisoners of war in places ten thousand miles apart, as far away as Bermuda and Ceylon. The work was marked by extraordinary praying, by faithful preaching, conviction of sin, confession and repentance with lasting conversions and hundreds of enlistments for missionary service. The spirit of Revival spread to South Africa in the throes of economic depression.[5]

Not without significance, an Awakening began in 1900 in the churches of Japan, which had long suffered from a period of retarded growth.[6] It started in an unusually effective movement to prayer, followed by an unusually intensive effort of evangelism, matched by an awakening of Japanese urban masses to the claims of Christ, and such an ingathering that the total membership of the churches almost doubled within the decade. Why did the Japanese Awakening occur in 1900? It would have been impossible four years later when Japan became involved in momentous war with Russia. Significantly also for the evangelistic follow-up of the general Awakening, the Torrey and Alexander team found that unusual praying had prepared a way for the most fruitful evangelistic ministry ever known in New Zealand and Australia,[7] and the unprecedented success of the campaigns launched Torrey and Alexander (and later Chapman and Alexander) on their worldwide evangelistic crusades, conventionally run but accompanied by revival of the churches.

Gipsy Smith experienced much the same kind of response in his Mission of Peace in war-weary South Africa, successful evangelism provoking an awakening of the population to Christian faith. Gipsy Smith extended his ministry.[8]

Meanwhile worldwide prayer meetings were intensifying. Undoubtedly, the farthest-felt happening of the decade was the Welsh Revival, which began as a local revival in early 1904, moved the whole of Wales by the end of the year, produced the mystic figure of Evan Roberts as leader yet filled simultaneously almost every church in the principality.[9]

The Welsh Revival was the farthest-reaching of the movements of the general Awakening, for it affected the whole of the Evangelical cause in India, Korea and China, renewed revival in Japan and South Africa, and sent a wave of awakening over Africa, Latin America, and the South Seas.

The story of the Welsh Revival is astounding. Begun with prayer meetings of less than a score of intercessors, when it burst its bounds the churches of Wales were crowded for more than two years. A hundred thousand outsiders were converted and added to the churches, the vast majority remaining true to the end. Drunkenness was immediately cut in half, and many taverns went bankrupt. Crime was so diminished that judges were presented with white gloves signifying that there were no cases of murder, assault, rape or robbery or the like to consider. The police became 'unemployed' in many districts. Stoppages occurred in coalmines, not due to unpleasantness between management and workers, but because so many foul-mouthed miners became converted and stopped using foul language that the horses which hauled the coal trucks in the mines could no longer understand what was being said to them, and transportation ground to a halt.

Time and again, the writer has been asked why the Welsh Revival did not last. It did last. The most exciting phase lasted two years. There was an inevitable drifting away of some whose interest was superficial, perhaps one person in forty of the total membership of the Churches. Even critics of the movement conceded that eighty percent of the converts remained in the Churches after five years.[10]

But there was a falling away in Wales. Why? It did not occur among the converts of the 1904 Revival, other than the minority noted. Converts of the Revival continued to be the choicest segment of church life, even in the 1930s, when the writer studied the spiritual life of Wales closely. Two disasters overtook Wales.[11] The first World War slaughtered a high proportion of the generation revived, or converted, or only influenced by the Revival, leaving a dearth of men in the churches; the coal mines of Wales were hit in the 1920s by tragic unemployment, which continued into the thirties in the Depression; and the class under military age during the war, infants during the Revival, espoused the gospel of Marxism. The Aneurin Bevans replaced the Keir Hardies in the party.

There was yet another reason. The Welsh Revival took scripture knowledge for granted, and preaching thus deemed superfluous was at a minimum. The Welsh revival constituency was ill-prepared for a new onslaught of anti-evangelicalism which captured a generation of otherwise disillusioned Welshmen. The province of Ulster moved into the place held by the principality of Wales as a land of evangelistic activities.

The story of the Welsh Revival has often been told. Most Christian people, including scholars, have been unaware of the extent of the Awakening which followed in the English-speaking world—in the United Kingdom, the United States, Canada, South Africa, Australia and faraway New Zealand.

The Archbishop of Canterbury called for a nationwide day of prayer.[12] Thirty English bishops declared for the Revival after one of their number, deeply moved, told of confirming 950 new converts in a country parish church. The Revival swept Scotland and Ireland.[13] Under Albert Lunde, also a friend of the researcher in later years, a movement began in Norway described by Bishop Berggrav as the greatest revival of his experience. It affected Sweden, Finland, and Denmark, Lutherans there saying that it was the greatest movement of the Spirit since the Vikings were evangelized.[14] It broke out in Germany, France and other countries of Europe, marked by prayer and confession.[15]

It is difficult to count converts in the Church of England, but, in the years 1903-1906, the other Protestant denominations gained ten percent, or 300,000.[16]

When news of the Awakening reached the United States, huge conferences of ministers gathered in New York and Chicago and other cities to discuss what to do when the Awakening began. Soon the Methodists in Philadelphia had 6101 new converts in trial membership; the ministers of Atlantic City claimed that only fifty adults remained professedly unconverted in a population of 60,000. Churches in New York City took in hundreds on a single Sunday— in one instance, 364 were received into membership, 286 new converts, 217 adults, 134 men, 60 heads of families.[17]

The 1905 Awakening rolled through the South like a tidal wave, packing churches for prayer and confession, adding hundreds to membership rolls—First Baptist in Paducah added a thousand in a couple of months and the old pastor died of overwork. Believers' baptisms among the Southern Baptists rose twenty-five per cent in one year. Other denominations shared equally in the Awakening.[18]

In the Middle West, churches were suddenly inundated by great crowds of seekers. The 'greatest revivals in their history' were reported by Methodists in town after town; the Baptists and others gained likewise. Everyone was so busy in Chicago that the pastors decided to hold their own meetings and help one another deal with the influx. Every store and factory closed in Burlington, Iowa, to permit employees to attend services of intercession and dedication. The mayor of Denver declared a day of prayer: by 10 a.m., churches were filled; at 11.30, almost every store closed; 12,000 attended prayer meetings in downtown theatres and halls; every school closed; the Colorado Legislature closed. The impact was felt for a year.[19]

In the West, great demonstrations marched through the streets of Los Angeles. United meetings attracted attendance of 180,000. The Grand Opera House was filled at midnight as drunks and prostitutes were seeking salvation. For three hours a day, business was practically suspended in Portland, Oregon, bank presidents and bootblacks attending prayer meetings while two hundred department stores in agreement closed from 11 till 2.[20]

Churches of the various denominations, town or country, were moved from Newfoundland to British Columbia across Canada, in spontaneous prayer or ardent evangelism.[21]

Church membership in the United States in seven major Protestant denominations increased by more than two million in five years (870,389 new communicants in 1906) and continued rising.[22] This did not include the gains of the younger denominations of Pentecostal or Holiness dynamic whose rate of increase was considerably greater.

It is naturally difficult to estimate the gains in the Dutch Reformed Church in South Africa, for most converts therein already possessed family affiliation. The Methodist Church increased by thirty percent in the three years of revival.[23] No doubt, the same patterns applied in New Zealand, Australia and South Africa, all stirred by the Welsh Revival.

The writer has visited all the States of India, has addressed more than a million people there, and has lectured in twenty of their theological colleges, and to hundreds of missionaries and national pastors. And yet he encountered only one who knew of the extent of the Indian Revival of 1905-1906, a retired professor of theology. Yet the Awakening in India moved every province and the Christian population increased by seventy percent, sixteen times as fast as the Hindu, the Protestant rate of increase being almost double that of the Roman Catholic. In many places, meetings went on for five to ten hours.[24]

In Burma, 1905 'brought ingathering quite surpassing anything known in the history of the mission.' The A.B.M.U. baptized 2000 Karens that year, 200 being the average. In a single church, 1340 Shans were baptized in December, 3113 in all being added in the 'marvelous ingathering.'[25]

The story of the Korean Revival of 1907 has been told and retold. It is less well-known that the Revival came in three waves, 1903, 1905 and 1907—the membership of the Churches quadrupling within a decade, the national Church being created from almost nothing by the movement. Since then, the Korean Churches have maintained the impetus.[26]

The revival campaigns of Jonathan Goforth in Manchuria have been recorded and published, but the extent of the Awakening in China between the Boxer Uprising and the 1911 Revolution has not been apprehended. China's greatest living evangelist, survivor of the China-wide Awakening of 1927-1939, told the writer that he had not even heard of the Awakening (in every province in the 1900s) apart from the post-Boxer revulsion. Yet the number of Protestant communicants doubled in a decade to quarter of a million, twice that figure for the total Evangelical community.[27]

In Indonesia,[28] the numbers of Evangelicals, 100,000 in 1903, trebled in the decade of general Awakening to 300,000, and in subsequent movements of phenomenal power, the number of believers on one little island (Nias) surpassed the latter figure, winning two-thirds the population. Protestant membership in Malagasia increased sixty-six percent in the years of Revival, 1905-1915. And pioneering success was achieved in the newly-opened Philippines.

The Awakening had limited effect in the Latin American countries: unusual revival in Brazil, phenomenal awakening in Chile, with Evangelical membership in both countries starting to climb—until in our times it passed the number of practising Roman Catholics; pioneering continued in other republics with sparse results but promise of future harvest, since realised.[29]

The Edinburgh World Missionary Conference recognized that more progress had been made in all Africa in the first decade of the twentieth century than experienced hitherto. Protestant communicants in the African mission fields increased in 1903-1910 from 300,000 to 500,000, there having been many awakenings in various parts in those years.[30] But the full impact of the Welsh Revival was not felt until the war years, when phenomenal revival occurred among the Africans. In the next half century, the increase was double that of the general population.

It was most significant that the Awakening of the 1900s was ecumenical, in the best senses of the word. It was thoroughly interdenominational. The foregoing narratives have provided instances of Anglican, Baptist, Brethren, Congregational, Disciple, Lutheran, Methodist, Presbyterian and Reformed congregations sharing in the Revival. There is a total lack of evidence of any response on the part of Roman Catholic or Greek Orthodox communities, but this is not surprising, for it was so in the days of the Puritans, of Wesley, of Finney, and of Moody. Only in the mid-twentieth century, when their changing attitude to Scripture has accompanied a changing attitude to dissent, have heretofore non-evangelical church bodies been affected by evangelical movements.

During the Welsh Revival, there occurred charismatic phenomena—uncanny discernment, visions, trances—but no glossolalia. There was an outbreak of speaking in tongues in India in the aftermath of the Awakening. In 1907, there was speaking in tongues among converts of the Revival in Los Angeles, from which Pentecostalism spread widely.[31]

There is no telling what might have happened in society had not the First World War absorbed the energies of the nations in the aftermath of this Edwardian Awakening. The time, talent, and treasure of the people were pre empted in any struggle for national existence, and what little is over is devoted to the welfare of the fighting men and the victims of war. This was the case in World War I.

Even so, no one could possibly say that the Awakenings of the 1900s in Great Britain or the United States were without social impact. In Britain, there was utter unanimity on the part of observers regarding 'the high ethical character' of the movement. The renewed obedience to the four great social commandments reduced crime, promoted honesty, inculcated truthfulness and produced chastity. Drunkenness and gambling were sharply curtailed. It was the same in the United States, for a wave of morality went over the country, producing a revival of righteousness. Corruption in state and civic government encountered a setback which was attributed by observers in church and state to the Great Awakening. For a dozen years, the country was committed in degree to civic and national integrity, until new forces of corruption triumphed again in the 1920s.[32]

In such awakenings, it seems that the individual response is much more immediate than the social response. British church leaders acclaimed 'the high ethical character of the movement.' The then largest denomination in the United States declared in review that the public conscience had been revived, overthrowing corrupt officials, crossing the party lines, electing Governors, Senators, Assemblymen, Mayors and District Attorneys of recognized honesty. The people of Philadelphia 'threw the rascals out' and put in a dedicated mayor. Washington Gladden, the 'father of the social gospel,' was assured that the general awakening was creating a moral revolution in the lives of the people. In other countries, profound impressions were made.[33]

What was the social effect outside Western Protestantism? On mission fields, the missionaries multiplied their schools and hospitals. In twenty years, pupils in Christian schools in India doubled to 595,725; 90% of all nurses were Christian, mostly trained at mission hospitals. In China, missionaries pioneered secondary and higher education and laid the foundations of the medical service; the beginnings of the African educational systems and medical service were due likewise to the missionary impulse.

15

THE MISSION OF PEACE

Prayer meetings were held in the Moody Bible Institute in Chicago and elsewhere at the turn of the twentieth century for another awakening all over the world in the new era. Traceable to this intercession were the world-girdling series of evangelistic campaigns of Torrey and Alexander and of Chapman and Alexander, who succeeded D. L. Moody in mass evangelism, as well as a series of phenomenal Awakenings that included the Welsh Revival of 1904-05.

War was raging in one corner alone of the world at that time, in South Africa, and world attention was focussed there. The measures taken by the British Army to break resistance and bring the war to a merciful close brought more bitterness to the out-fought Boers than did the actual fighting in 'the last war of gentlemen,' for many thousands of women and children had died in epidemics in relocation camps.

Yet out of tragedy came lasting good from these concentration camps.[1] Both Afrikaans and English-speaking ministers served heroically the tens of thousands of noncombatants held in these widely scattered refugee camps by force.[2] Thousands of their civilian population attended daily services and made lasting professions of faith in deep revivals of religion.[3]

There was much sympathy in Europe and America for the defeated Boer people and prayers were offered for their spiritual recovery. While the countryside of the High Veld was being pacified, the captured commandos were still being shipped from South Africa to the islands of St. Helena and Bermuda in the Atlantic and to military posts in Ceylon and India, where they were confined in prisoner-of-war camps.[4]

British and Foreign Bible Society workers made a point of contacting the contingents of prisoners-of-war at their ports of embarkation, Durban for the Indian Ocean sailings and Cape Town for the South Atlantic. They distributed New Testaments in Dutch to the saddened soldiers of the Boer republics, forced to leave their beloved country for the first time, a new experience for land-loving men.[5]

At Cape Town, a Bible Society agent (Nuttall) stood and addressed the prisoners-of-war by means of an interpreter, offering them the gift of the Scriptures in their accustomed language, 'that God's Word may comfort and counsel you in this hour of need,' and he reported that 'both they and I wept together.' An old farmer arose, with tears in his eyes, to thank the Bible Society.

With these prisoners-of-war went ministers of Reformed Churches of the Transvaal and Orange Free State and Cape Colony, sharing their imprisonment and ministering with the goodwill of the British military authorities.[6]

On the island of Bermuda, where Ds. J. A. van Blerk and Ds. J. R. Albertyn ministered, there came a stirring revival of religion.[7] And on the island of St. Helena, Ds. A. F. Louw preached powerfully to discouraged men, and witnessed a response that brought many conversions.[8]

Among the prisoners-of-war on St. Helena were two young Student Volunteers, already prisoners for two years.[9] They deplored the past neglect of pagan Africa within easy reach of enlightened South Africans, and affirmed their conviction that Afrikaner missionaries were needed to work in the Bantu territories to the north. Thereafter a rising interest in such missions was reported among the non-student majority of the prisoners-of-war.

Ds. Louw led 6.30 a.m. prayer meetings daily attended by a hundred prisoners, as many as thirty of whom took part in prayer.[10] Once the main body of prisoners had been stirred, the range of their intercession included faraway parts of the African continent, as well as India and Ceylon, where their captive comrades were confined.

The awakenings on Bermuda and St. Helena continued without let-up until the cessation of hostilities in 1902. Burghers in the prison camps had to face a problem of conscience as the price of repatriation, that of taking the oath of allegiance to the British King, Edward VII. A majority of them, whose parents or forbears had been British subjects at one time or another, signed.[11] Ships brought the hopeful men home, a home which was ready in congregation after congregation to share their spiritual experience.

Ds. D. J. Viljoen was shipped with prisoners-of-war to India in 1901,[12] holding shipboard services for an interested group daily.[13] The prisoners were sent to Fort Ahmednagar in the Maratha country, where a thousand men were detained behind thick walls and barbed wire.[14]

Viljoen commenced worship services, at first enlisting prisoners with experience of lay ministry and using them for visitation, prayer meetings, catechism and church services, but not for the sacraments. Classes also and young folk's meetings were organized.[15]

A small group of deeply spiritual men came together daily in prayer. Their minister sent them among the indifferent prisoners in the camp, where sometimes their witnessing was resented. Ds. Viljoen and his helpers concentrated on evangelism. In spite of poor attendances at first, the results were encouraging, and within a few weeks, he was busy in daily services. There was a genuine revival among Christian soldiers, and there were many conversions of those who had been strangers to God's grace. A great awakening ensued in the camp.[16]

Fort Ahmednagar became a place of praise and prayer, singing sweeping the camp in daytime and the voice of prayer muting the murmurs of the night.[17] The Christians were impressed by the need of the Hindus around them, and eighteen of them became missionaries to African tribesmen on their release. The awakening continued in camp till war's end.

It is of interest that within four years many of the Indian communities round about for whom they prayed experienced a startling revival. A godly Indian educator, Pandita Ramabai, became interested at this time in revival, and in June 1905 a strange but powerful movement began at the Mukti schools in Kedgaon, with the same startling phenomena witnessed by Ds. Andrew Murray at Worcester in 1860.[18] Extraordinary awakenings occurred in churches and schools in Ahmednagar, Poona, Aurangabad, and Bombay, until all the missions in the Maratha country felt an impact.[19]

It was the same in Boer camps in the other parts of India. Ds. A. P. Burger, minister of Middelburg in the Transvaal, was taken prisoner in February 1902 and was sent with two thousand others to a prison camp at Shahjahanpur, Uttar Pradesh.[20] He began regular worship services, and taught school classes every day. The pattern of revival was repeated. At night, the Moslems and Hindus nearby listened to the hearty singing of five hundred or more newly-revived prisoners-of-war. There were similar reports from Boer chaplains in Sialkot, in the Punjab—now Pakistan. [21]

There were many candidates for missionary service in the Indian camps. A prisoner-of-war, when lying wounded and bleeding in the field of battle, reproached himself that he was willing to do so much for his country and so little for missions.[22] He volunteered at the Ahmednagar camp, as did so many others in similar establishments.

In Ceylon, there were five thousand Afrikaner prisoners-of-war at Diatalawa under close guard.[23] Prisoners suffered from boredom and from sickness, a typhoid epidemic killing many. Afrikaner prisoner-chaplains held services and helped the distressed. A little prayer group of men grew into hundreds and then into thousands. The result was the conversion of hundreds and the creation of a missionary burden.[24]

One prisoner-of-war was converted to God after some five months under the ministry of Ds. George Murray. He prayed daily for guidance regarding his life after the war, and as an answer received the words: 'As the Father hath sent me, so send I you!' To which he replied, 'Here am I, send me.'[25]

In Portugal, internees from the Transvaal border were held in camp,[26] and again awakenings were experienced. It was the same in civilian camps within South Africa, where women, children and old men were held. By May 1901, these civilian camps were catering for totals of 19,680 Europeans and 18,079 Africans.[27] A letter from the veteran Ds. William Robertson reported 4419 in Aliwal North, 4722 in Bloemfontein, 1441 in Brandfort, 3456 in Bethulie, 2077 in Heilbron, 3788 in Kroonstad, 2070 in Kimberley, 2678 in Norvals Poort, 2711 in Springfontein and 4320 in smaller camps.[28] In all of these was maintained a vigorous spiritual ministry.

After two and a half years of fighting, peace came again to South Africa. It was greeted with mixed emotions. Most English-speaking South Africans respected their Afrikaner opponents too much as soldiers and citizens to engage in any cheap gloating over a victory by overwhelming forces. And peace was welcomed by the Afrikaans-speaking folk, long convinced of the impossibility of victory over the British Empire but saddened by defeat and bitter over the deaths of the women and children in the relocation camps.

Shortly after the cessation of hostilities, the principal of the Lovedale Institution (James Stewart) asked significantly in an editorial:[29]

> What can the Church militant do to heal the sore between two brave peoples, and bring this land within the Kingdom of the King of Kings? A revival of true spiritual religion, reaching Boer and Briton alike, would do more towards raising the standard of national righteousness than can be readily imagined.

The hunger for spiritual awakening in all of South Africa was manifest among Afrikaans-speaking people also. As early as 1903, Dutch Reformed leaders, writing in a missions journal,[30] were reporting signs of revival communicated to the churches from the camps. From every side came word of renewed spiritual life during the annual Pentecost week of meetings in 1903, a year of economic depression.

Already, the 'revival of religion' among the prisoners-of-war and internees and refugees was beginning to be felt in the home churches. A rising tide of spiritual interest was reported throughout 1903,[31] a typical account referring to the excellent attendances at meetings for prayer and worship, and an increased earnestness concerning spiritual matters. Ds. C. V. Nel, for example, held a ten days' campaign at Riebeek West under the auspices of the Student Christian Association and reported 'showers of blessing' during which more than one hundred past and present students had 'given themselves to the Lord.'

The little book on the power of prayer, which had been circulated in South Africa in High Dutch before the outbreak of Revival in 1860,[32] was reissued in 1904 and this was followed by a call to prayer signed by the leaders, J. R. Albertyn, G. F. Marais, A. F. Louw and H. P. van der Merwe.[33] Letters and articles on Revival appeared in both the Afrikaner and English language religious journals.[34]

In 1902, an earlier attempted rapprochement between the Church of Scotland and the Dutch Reformed Churches had been politely rebuffed.[35] Spencer Walton, beloved by Briton, Boer and Bantu in South Africa, commented upon postwar conditions in South Africa, admitting that racial hatred between the two European communities was very bitter and that the country as a whole was in a deplorable condition.[36]

In 1904, a deputation of Scottish Presbyterian leaders set foot in South Africa and were well-received by the Dutch Reformed ministers and people.[37] It was a wise and choice expression of brotherhood, for the Dutch Reformed Church still cherished gratitude to Scotland for evangelical blood-transfusions of evangelical Calvinism common to both.

Keswick also provided a link between British Evangelicals and Afrikaans-speaking brethren.[38] Mr. Albert Head exercised a ministry of sincere reconciliation at the Wellington Convention, and later Dr. F. B. Meyer came out to South Africa 'to Boers and Britons . . . to bind the two peoples closer together through the Gospel.' [39]

Within five years, there was such a great improvement in British-Boer relations that a Union of South Africa was proposed to unite the warring republics and colonies in a single self-governing national entity. While there were many political and economic factors in this development, not least was the vast improvement in the spiritual relations between Dutch Reformed and English-speaking Churches.

There were two main factors in the spiritual uplift, first the success of a Mission of Peace to South Africa by a British evangelist in 1904,[40] and second, the stirring of extraordinary revival in Afrikaans and English-speaking churches by the news of the Revival in Wales and elsewhere.[41]

> The hearts of the people have been turned to God in earnest prayer for a revival of religion . . . from Cape Town to the Limpopo . . . a line of earnest prayer with deepening intensity for a quickening of spiritual life and the conversion of sinners.

A converted gipsy, Rodney Smith, had made quite a name for himself in popular evangelism in the English-speaking world. His graciousness reflected his Master. Born in 1860, converted in 1876 in his native England, he served for some time in the Salvation Army before entering upon a worldwide evangelistic ministry.[42]

Gipsy Smith had been invited to South Africa before the outbreak of the 1899 Anglo-Boer War.[43] He arrived in Cape Town in April 1904, but was coldly received by the Dutch Reformed people. His sponsors in the English-speaking Churches found difficulty in locating some suitable building for the only likely auditorium in the city was the Groote Kerk of the Dutch Reformed Church, and that was definitely refused a local committee,[44] such was the state of feeling before the Mission.

But after Professor Nicholas Hofmeyr of the Stellenbosch Seminary called upon Gipsy Smith and invited him to address the students, there came a change of attitude. At first, a cold and critical indifference was shown, but the warmth of his personality soon disarmed the critics.[45]

A deserted corrugated-iron building, Fillis's Circus, was seated for three thousand and packed out from the beginning. Gipsy Smith was noted for the tenderness of his preaching and the balm of Gilead was poured into hurt hearts along with the preaching of the Good News.[46]

Following the huge attendance at the first meeting, Gipsy Smith was given a reception by Members of Parliament and other civic leaders.[47] The old corrugated-iron building was rechristened the 'consecrated-iron building.' Men were in the majority from the beginning of the mission, even in the inquiry room.[48]

Gipsy Smith asked his Cape Town sponsors to collect all drinkers and drunkards off the streets, and bring them to a midnight meeting in the old circus building.[49] Between ten p.m. and midnight, charabancs were sent around the city, loading men in various stages of intoxication. Two thousand noisily greeted the evangelist, some waving bottles of liquor. From his opening word Rodney Smith held their attention and there were many who professed conversion, including one who gave himself up to the Pretoria police as a murderer in whose place another had been hanged.[50]

There were more than three thousand people counselled in Cape Town's Mission of Peace.[51] A conference for students and a public rally were held in Stellenbosch, adding to the results of the Cape meetings.

In a concluding Cape Town rally, pastors told of congregations revived, prayer meetings alive and crowded, and whole families won.[52] The Cape Town Mission had attracted vast crowds not hitherto seen in any religious gatherings, Methodist editors affirmed, and yet conversions were being reported in continuing church services all around the Cape and its hinterland.[53]

On his way to Kimberley, Gipsy Smith held a meeting for Dr. Andrew Murray in Wellington, a tenth of the audience of 1500 making decision.[54] On May 14, the Kimberley Town Hall was filled, a wave of religious enthusiasm following in which the Town Hall was crowded to the doors upon every occasion, the sign 'Full Up' greeting the hundreds who had not come early enough.[55]

> In Kimberley, the like had never been seen before... At times, the feeling was intense; strong men wept like children... Results far exceeded all expectation ... British and Dutch mingled together, as they had never done since the war. There were cases of those who had been actually fighting against each other on the battle-field, one pointing the other to the Lamb of God.[56]

Thirteen hundred inquirers were instructed, a third of them Dutch Reformed, half of them young people. Fullest cooperation was given by the churches of the Diamond Fields, and family life was greatly strengthened by the movements continuing in the denominations.

Night after night in Bloemfontein, the Town Hall was over-crowded in a way unprecedented in the Orange Free State capital. Men, again predominating in the audience, 'trembled under conviction of sin.'[57] Local editors gave the campaign a column and a half of comment and news daily.[58] The Dutch Reformed ministers played a major part in the Mission, in which 266 of 570 counselled were of Reformed preference. As elsewhere, Afrikaner and English-speaking were found working together, sometimes a 'man in khaki' kneeling beside a former 'burgher on commando.' Gipsy Smith, Free Church evangelist, Anglican Bishop Taylor Smith, the Dean of the Anglican cathedral and the local Roman Catholic priest had 'tea together.'[59] And when a bitter attack on Gipsy Smith's preaching for instantaneous conversion was made later in the local press, it was answered by the Roman Catholic priest strongly defending the evangelist.[60]

Johannesburg, which had accumulated in only eighteen years a population of 160,000, was the venue of the next Mission of Peace, which was sponsored by the Witwatersrand Church Council.[61] A big tent had been erected in Krugersdorp and a special train took the people there. Crowds increased from 2500.[62] Afrikaner correspondents announced that 2337 inquirers had professed faith, 980 of Dutch Reformed prefer-ence, 450 Methodist, 290 Anglican, 240 Presbyterian, 145 Baptist and 101 Congregational, 131 being of other loyalties.[63]

As in Cape Town, an effort was made to reach the city's alcoholics.[64] A Salvation Army band led a march of 4000 witnesses, and a hundred workers visited bars and canteens, the tent being filled again for a midnight meeting.

During the Pretoria Campaign, 10th to 17th July, it was learned that President Paul Kruger had died in exile over-seas. Gipsy Smith announced a memorial service which was largely attended. Among the inquirers after the Lord Whom the dour old President had served in his own faithful way was a grandson of Oom Paul, and a Boer general was numbered among the nine hundred others professing conversion.[65]

In Ladysmith, ten days of prayer meetings preceded two nights of preaching, but there were few inquirers registering their decisions.[66] If there was an explanation, none was ever published. Ladysmith had been besieged, as was Kimberley.

The Town Hall in Durban was crowded out for the Mission of Peace, 24th July onwards.[67] More than eighteen hundred nightly attended meetings sponsored by some forty Durban churches. The local press supplied a friendly editorial and

many columns of news about 'the wonderful ingathering.'
There were eight hundred inquirers counselled, a quarter
being referred to Methodist churches.[68] Durban ministers
reported quickening of church life in worship services and
in prayer meetings. However, from the week following the
start,[69] angry letters appeared in the press regarding the
evangelist's strictures on intoxicating beverages and on the
theatrical profession.[70] A storm brewed in the foothills, and
burst upon the evangelist in the provincial capital.

In Pietermaritzburg, Gipsy Smith met with 'a most bitter
opposition' from the people in the liquor and theatrical and
gambling professions.[71] Hit elsewhere by the response of the
crowds attending the meetings, they denounced him as 'King
of Bunkum,' 'a Fraud,' 'the Biggest Humbug in South Africa.'
One newspaper proved hostile at first,[72] the other friendly.
Again there were record crowds and commitments reported
by the hundreds among inquirers. The sponsors noted 'What
a gracious work of God it has been!'[73]

The Natal missionaries of the American Board reported
as an overflow from the Durban Mission an unusual local
awakening among the Zulus at Amanzimtoti, in which there
were confessions of sin and conversions to God.[74]

Gipsy Smith, accompanied by his wife and daughter, sailed
from Durban to East London,[75] where a wave of quickening
and revival was expected in church circles. Rain fell all
Sunday and continued to handicap the mission, but the Town
Hall soon became crammed from wall to wall.[76] One minister
announced that 275 inquirers had applied for membership in
his church.[77]

The final campaign was held in the Feather Market Hall
in Port Elizabeth, the biggest of all available buildings in
South Africa.[78] Despite bad weather, 2000 gathered and the
Mission grew till a thousand were counselled.[79] The Mayor
presided over the final meeting on September 13.[80]

The Gipsy Smith Mission of Peace did not escape the usual
criticisms which plague itinerant evangelists. A resident
minister commented:[81]

> A few critics . . . those who know the price of every-
> thing and the value of nothing . . . have, as usual, been
> shouting evil and slanderous reports from the lofty plat-
> form of an invincible ignorance . . . chiefly regarding
> the financial results of his mission tour. Everybody
> knows that the Gipsy receives while in South Africa
> exactly the same stipend that he receives at home.

> The Evangelical Free Church Council (in England) pays
> his expenses, and the whole of the balance is remitted
> to them, to be used for extension and aggressive work
> where poverty prevents people from paying necessary
> expenses in a series of evangelistic meetings.

The aggregate attendances at the Gipsy Smith Mission of
Peace in South Africa exceeded three hundred thousand, and
converts and inquirers 15,000 or more.[82] One denomination
as a sponsor 'endeavoured faithfully to garner the results of
Gipsy Smith's Mission,' and enjoyed its greatest numerical
growth of the decade.[83]

The Mission was most effective in English-speaking and
bilingual communities, yet there were instances of indirect
influence in drawing together Afrikaans and English-speaking
(chiefly Dutch Reformed and Methodist) ministers in the
dorps—to reconcile the less evangelical proved much more
difficult.[84]

Gipsy Smith returned to Great Britain, soon to become involved in the Welsh Revival. The news of the Welsh Revival
of 1904 had an electrifying effect upon Christians of both
European stocks.[85] Already in South Africa in that year, the
Commission for Special Evangelistic Preaching of the Dutch
Reformed Church had issued a call to Prayer for Revival
in South Africa.

Dutch Reformed and Methodist and Presbyterian organs
gave news reports not only of the Welsh Revival but also of
the awakenings in Scandinavia, the United States, and India,
and other countries.[86]

Dr. Andrew Murray, Professor Hofmeyr and Ds. Botha
initiated a Conference on Revival for ministers, held at the
Stellenbosch Seminary in mid-May 1905, its main topic the
ministry of the Holy Spirit in the world and in the Church.
An observer wrote:[87]

> . . . the Lord has spoken with a powerful voice these
> days to His Church on earth by what He did in Wales . . .
> Without much prayer, faithful prayer, we cannot expect
> the great works of God here as in Wales unless we ask
> with great sincerity great things from God.

Revival thus became the major topic in the South African
Christian journals by the middle of 1905, and continued so
to be featured throughout 1906, with reports from home and
abroad and even a letter from Evan Roberts in Wales. Soon
phenomenal local awakenings appeared in the Cape Province,
in both Afrikaans and English-speaking churches.

At Whitsuntide, the Methodists at Wittebergen sponsored a week of prayer which provoked an unusual response, with intercessors attending at four in the mornings.[88] A month later, a great revival in the Dutch Reformed Church gemeente at Villiersdorp was reported by both Afrikaans and English religious journals.

Some 'indescribably wonderful' happenings occurred on the evening of Sunday 23rd July 1905 according to reports from Villiersdorp itself by Ds. E. G. Malherbe.[89] About a hundred and thirty young people were engaged in a Christian Endeavour service when an 'outpouring of the Holy Spirit' upon the whole company took place, resulting in an intense conviction of sin, anxious concern, repentance with tears, earnest prayers, and calling out for salvation.[90]

Each evening following, the people gathered in meetings of up to three hours' duration, and attendance increased from 350 to 500. Sometimes a score of people prayed at the same time audibly, so great was the individual preoccupation with God.[91] Already more than a hundred outright conversions had occurred, including the roughest and the most reckless of sinners. Some testified openly with power, urging their friends to respond and praying for them by name. Among the residents professing conversion were six young people who had been charged with murder—one of whom, Karl Zimmerman, later became a pioneer missionary to the Tiv in Nigeria.

The whole congregation at Villiersdorp was changed. The revival transformed the Young People's Society, which soon increased from 22 to 62 active workers. Yet quite a number of the converts were fifty years of age or more. The minister reported that the revival was spreading and appealed for help to fellow ministers. Three months later, he observed:[92]

> It is surprising to see how God's Spirit takes control of the gathering without human pressure being used. It is a usual occurrence for several people to pray simultaneously, yet always in good order and earnestness, ... arising from a concern for the unconverted.

This revival movement began to influence thirty other Dutch Reformed congregations, chiefly in the Cape Province in both eastern and western sections.

News of the Villiersdorp Revival caused the Christians at Prince Albert to begin meetings for prayer in the various homes until these proved too small, when they adjourned en masse to the schoolhouse.[93] On the Sunday evening, an extraordinary work of the Holy Spirit began among the young people. Children of the parish filled another building also and phenomenal happenings occurred among them, astounding the leaders seeing such amazing workings of the Holy Spirit. Whole households of people professed conversion.

On 7th August, the Young People's Society of Villiersdorp visited the church at Fransch Hoek and told the people of the great spiritual work in their dorp.[94] Hence much prayer was offered for a similar visitation in the Huguenot colony. Within a month, 'the drops began to fall.' Some young people decided to hold a prayer meeting the following day in a private home. To their astonishment, forty-two intercessors arrived, although no announcement had been given. Next day, the meeting for prayer filled the consistory room and, becoming too small, was moved to the old school building and thence to the big church, with as many as six hundred present.

Although the movement had originated among the Young People's Society, older folk were deeply moved, including scores over eighty remembering the revival of 1860.[95] The church was crowded for a thanksgiving meeting on Sunday. Meetings that followed became difficult to close, crowds dismissed from a service re-entering another door. The attraction was not the preaching but an irresistible urge to 'marvel at God's Spirit' at work among the people.

The leaders at Fransch Hoek reported that the awakening changed the lives of older Christians also. 'The cold in soul became warm in heart, wayward children returned to the Father, misunderstanding were set right.' An old Boer arose to say: 'I never could forgive the English. Now I must!'

The records of the period of many Reformed congregations confirmed the scope of the revivals. A visit of enthusiastic Christian young people from Villiersdorp created a stir in Heidelberg, Cape Province, according to a centennial report given by the Dutch Reformed congregation there. Conviction brought about by the sudden death of two younger people accelerated the movement.[96] Undoubtedly, Dutch Reformed folk, pastors and people, shared in the Welsh Revival.

Similar extraordinary awakenings were in evidence in the English-speaking congregations. William M. Douglas, appointed as the Methodist connexional evangelist following Gipsy Smith's Mission of Peace, witnessed 'a great uplifting' during August at Somerset East, 'an echo of the Revival in Wales.' Husbands and wives, mothers and daughters, young and old, sought salvation.[97] Times of refreshing were experienced also at the historic town of Graaff-Reinet.[98]

At the Wellington Convention, presided over in late September by Dr. Andrew Murray, the Rev. W. M. Douglas shared ministry with Albert Head of England and participated in extraordinary happenings.[99] A couple of hundred people engaged in prayer from 10 p.m. until 1 a.m. when half those present retired, but the remainder continued with a fresh intensity. Like the 1905 Keswick Convention in England, the Wellington Convention was the largest for several years and was long remembered for its memorable happenings in the lives of its supporters.[100]

The Methodist weekly published a stirring account of a spontaneous revival in Simonstown on Cape Peninsula, where the main instrument was the fiery preaching of the Rev. J. McAllister of the Methodist Church of South Africa.[101] It was marked by an intense conviction of sin. Another 'gracious awakening' during the spring of 1905 (November)[102] occurred at Woodstock following the October movement at Simonstown at the opposite end of the peninsula.

Meantime, the Rev. William M. Douglas was witnessing a 'work of God in Aberdeen' in October in which a profound impression was made on the whole town, bringing Dutch and English closer.[103] And in November, Douglas wrought a remarkable work in Port Elizabeth, where the greatest results were seen among the Christians.[104] At Seymour,[105] there were 'striking and convincing proofs of the genuine and deep work of the Holy Spirit.' This was the beginning of a lifetime of effectiveness for William Douglas.[106]

The Baptist, Congregational and Presbyterian churches shared in the upsurge of revival. The reporting of unusual happenings by the religious press must not be interpreted to mean that only these places were benefitted. It seemed that the outpouring of the Spirit, so notable in Wales, brought about a rising tide of spiritual interest, not only in South Africa, but throughout the world.

Minutes of the Grahamstown District Methodist Synod assembling in 1906 at Graaff-Reinet took note of much cause for thankfulness for the good work going on in the various churches of the district. 'The spirit of prayer is abroad,' it was reported, and it was noted that in missions held there had been great blessing, with sinners converted and saints strengthened in the faith.[107]

It is very difficult for the historian of major evangelical awakenings to assess the numbers of accessions to state churches or folk churches made in any given movement.

For example,[108] the 1859 Revival resulted in hundreds of thousands of conversions in Scotland, but the statistics of the Church of Scotland failed to show the benefit in the way that the statistics of the Methodist bodies in England did, so many Scots converts having been already members of the state church by family connection.

In the same way, the statistics of the Dutch Reformed in South Africa failed to show the difference between a member of the folk church by infant baptism and juvenile confirmation and one converted in evangelism or revival in the church.

It was different with the Methodists of South Africa, who kept careful statistics of all their accredited members in local societies as well as of probationers on trial. Methodist Conferences from 1901 until 1910 showed an interesting graph —from an increase in membership of nearly 7% in 1902, possibly due to the presence of many British Methodists in the Army and Navy, additions dropped to 2% in 1903. In the years of the revival, the increase in membership grew to nearly 8% in 1904, 14% in 1905 and 8% in 1906, a thirty per cent increase in three years. The three years following the period of harvest showed practically no gains until 1910. There is every reason to believe that the increase clearly demonstrated in the Methodist statistics was true of other evangelical Churches.[109]

Though not directly involved in the Boer War, Rhodesia suffered its sorry impact. European congregations in both Salisbury and Bulawayo were hindered by a lack of interest in spiritual matters, the numbers of communicants in 1900 being deplorably small, while the work among Africans faced 'anxieties, difficulties and disappointments.' In 1901, depression was reported in Salisbury and anxiety in Bulawayo. In 1902, a big incursion of new residents into Salisbury augmented European congregations, but, in Bulawayo, matters were at a standstill, ministers alternating between hope and despair, while work among the Africans showed no worthwhile progress or some little decline.[110]

This state of affairs persisted into 1903 and 1904, with a continued depression among English-speaking Christians and a rising interest among the Africans.[111] In 1905, David Russell conducted evangelistic campaigns in both Salisbury and Bulawayo, the church members being quickened and some outsiders being converted to God. So the movement of 1905 was only a recovery, although a definite awakening followed among Africans, both Shona and Ndebele.[112]

16

THE AFRICAN AWAKENINGS

Just as the colonial settlers in the American Colonies so seldom displayed an interest in the conversion of their own American Indian neighbours, save under the impact of spiritual awakenings, so the colonial settlers in South Africa seemed indifferent to the evangelization of nearby Bantu tribespeople, except in times of evangelical revival. During the last quarter of the nineteenth century, Dr. James Stewart of Lovedale commented:[1]

> Missions in South Africa are supported mostly by the home country. The colonial churches do little for the heathen, and the colonists for the most part are indifferent and ignorant of the subject.

To explain the seeming indifference, the Scots missionary pointed out that distance often lends enchantment to a view, hence the faraway American and European Christians showed more interest in Africa; that the colonial church folk often suffered the vexation of unsatisfactory native servants and tended to care less about the natives' well-being; that the missionaries from overseas themselves were often to blame for neglecting to create an interest in missions among their colonial neighbours—a thing to be deplored because such colonial folk were known as liberal givers to good causes of all kinds.

The effect of the 1860 Awakening on the Dutch Reformed Church and that of 1866 on the Methodists has already been noted. Dr. Stewart went on to point out that the various South Africa-based missionary enterprises had already reaped a harvest, citing the Dutch Reformed missions in Zoutpansberg and the Anglican and Methodist missions elsewhere.

It was difficult to draw a proper comparison, he said, between the work of overseas missionaries and that of South African churches among their heathen peoples, for so many Dutch Reformed congregations maintained a native mission, their ministers sustaining double charges, while Methodists often combined European and African country circuits into a single pastoral unit.

Soldiers on both sides of the Anglo-Boer War came into contact with the degradation of heathenism and saw the uplift of Christian missions. In 1903, about a hundred evangelical British soldiers were reported returning to South Africa to serve the common Lord of Boer and Briton in reaching the Bantu folk with the Good News.[2]

Soldiers serving in the Republican cause had even better better opportunity of observation. When the Boer commandos engaged in mobile warfare against overwhelming British armies, General J. C. Beyers was directing commandos in action in the low veld of the northern Transvaal during the month of September 1900.

Active on commando were several deeply spiritual leaders, including Ds. A. P. Kriel as well as General Beyers himself. Nightly, on commando, they led in Bible study and prayer.

Between Lydenburg and Waterberg,[3] burghers on patrol near Thabini located missionaries of the Swiss Mission in a lonely station, and gladly they attended a Sunday service. One of the three, J. F. Naude, addressed a crowd of three hundred natives. He and J. A. Retief were impressed by a missionary couple serving twelve thousand Africans. They were dismayed at the thought of thousands dying without even hearing the Word of God, and felt convicted that they themselves as a privileged people had not done all that they could have done. Distressed to find foreigners from overseas with a greater concern, they decided to convene the burghers in Pietersburg to discuss the matter further.[4]

On September 28, the meeting took action and decided to send (as soon as peace was restored) a missionary to the Zoutpansberg or Waterberg districts. Men stood up to make their vows of missionary service or support after the war.

The General arranged another meeting, and at Warmbad on October 3 a larger conference met, deciding how to implement their vows. After cessation of hostilities, a hundred demobilized men contacted the Cape Missionary Committee and were assigned the care of Bethel, a mission station near Pietersburg, ten serving there with Hendrik Hofmeyr.

These awakenings in the relocation camps and prisoner-of-war camps overseas led to a general spiritual awakening in the Afrikaans-speaking Christian community everywhere. This twentieth century awakening soon began to take on a missionary form, for the Dutch Reformed missions journal jumped from two thousand to six thousand circulation in but a few months' time.[5]

A hundred and seventy-five of the prisoners-of-war soon volunteered for missionary service, a total which ultimately passed the two hundred mark—'a remarkable outburst of missionary zeal' and a 'cause for wonder' throughout the world of missionary enterprise.[6]

The leaders of the Dutch Reformed Church, suddenly convened for a welcome emergency, were amazed and delighted with the influx of candidates, for the number of the Dutch Reformed missionaries serving in various parts of Africa had been severely reduced by fever and distress, so that more than a hundred candidates were needed immediately.

At a conference in Stellenbosch on the 16th of October, 1902, it was decided to build a college to prepare the candidates for missionary service, and within four months the Moderator of the Cape Synod, Ds. J. H. Hofmeyr, opened the college in Worcester with Ds. A. F. Louw as principal.[7]

Already in Lesotho, a movement was under way, for the Paris missionaries reported additions of 1178 to bring the total of communicants in 1902 to 12,676, a rapid growth.[8]

In 1903, there was an awakening among African students studying at Lovedale. In eight days of meetings, attendance averaged 600 or so[9] and 242 inquirers registered decision. In 1904, a most significant General Conference of missionaries operating throughout Southern Africa was convened. From it stemmed a great missionary advance as well as real cooperation between the denominations and societies.[10]

The visit of John R. Mott in 1906 resulted in a drawing together of Anglican, Baptist, Dutch Reformed, Methodist, Moravian, Presbyterian and South Africa General Mission ministers at Lovedale. The conference not only healed the wounds of war but resulted in a great movement of the Spirit, marked at first by an intense stillness in the assembly.[11]

Charles Pamla was a veteran in his seventies at the time and retired to supernumerary status only when he became an octogenarian in 1913. He itinerated again as the Methodist connexional evangelist.[12] At times his congregations exceeded one thousand, and as many as two hundred 'came forward.' There were threescore converts from paganism, and double that number of youngsters professing their faith for the first time, and twelve times as many restorations from backsliding in Bensonvale.[13] Then followed campaigns in Zulu and Xhosa and Sotho towns, and in Aliwal North, Burghersdorp, Colesburg, Kimberley, Winburg, Parys, Kroonstad and Capetown. Pamla added in all 25,000 to the Church.

In 1911,[14] the South Africa General missionaries reported an extraordinary awakening in Tembuland, in the Transkei, marked by intense conviction of sin, many confessions—including some of murder—and heart-warming restitution. A severe challenge to Christianity was reported in 1914 by the same Mission to the north in Gazaland through a revival of African paganism.[15] A year or so later, in April 1915, there began a quickening among the Christians,[16] a turn of the tide. Three months later, Rees Howells sailed for South Africa. Coming from the 1905 Revival in Wales,[17] he stressed the confession of all known sin and total commitment to God, as Evan Roberts had done in 1904.

On 10th October 1915, an evangelical awakening began in earnest at Rusitu.[18] In the New Year, the missionaries were experiencing a measure of reviving throughout Gazaland. At Rusitu, it was said, 'not a soul comes into a meeting without coming under conviction of sin.' Throughout May and June, the awakening spread across the field, affecting tribesmen in Rhodesia and Mozambique all of 1916—the forerunner of awakenings in other fields.

In 1917, the missionaries happily gathered at Mount Tabor in Natal for a revival conference which produced its own 'showers of blessing'[19] among missionaries and Africans. Rees Howells next visited Lutubeni in Tembuland, in the heart of the Transkei. By 1918, an evangelical awakening was in fullest force among the Tembus, Walter Searle writing of 'another gracious visitation of the Holy Spirit.'[20]

The revival in the Transkei spread to Swaziland in mid-1918. The movement made a deep impression on the people, including royalty—letters written at the time confirming reports given the writer by high-born Swazi Christians who vividly recalled the king humbling himself in church:

> At Ezulwini, the power of God came down on the very first meeting ... the next two days I shall never forget. We were in the church eleven and twelve hours a day dealing with the people ... from 6 or 7 a.m. until midnight. For two days and nights, many could not eat or sleep, either because of conviction of sin or the great joy that flooded their hearts when sins were forgiven.[21]

Jeremia, a former Lovedale student and a henchman of the Swazi King, had been ill for several years, scarcely able to walk. Praying under conviction, he suddenly leaped to his feet and danced for joy, running hither and yon—healed of his infirmity.[22] There were many startling events.

The blessing overflowed to the heathen, eighty repenting in a week as real fear fell upon the people. The same effects were seen at Bethany where, in a few days, 120 made their profession of faith. Meetings at Mbabane had similar effect. Rees Howells and his colleague Medill assured all fellow missionaries that 'in every way, it was like the Welsh Revival.'[23] The missionaries simply said 'the power in the meeting was indescribable.'

The awakening spread in 1919 to Zululand and again Rees Howells became the outstanding evangelist.[24] Awakenings were notable at Mseleni and Makowe, where there were many 'confessing sin, with weeping.'

Before long, by the middle of 1919, 'renewal of life' was reported from Christian communities in Natal, Swaziland, Tongaland, Zululand, Pondoland, and Tembuland.[25]

In the first decade of the twentieth century, the Hottentots and the Hereros revolted against German rule in Southwest Africa, slaughtering the German (but not Boer or British) settlers.[26] The retaliation was severe, the Hereros reduced to a fifth of their numbers. It was not until 1910 that a turning to Christianity occurred among them.[27]

Meantime, the discipling and indoctrination of the tribes of Malawi had been going on apace. The brave but bloodthirsty Ngoni warriors were learning to live in peace.

The conventions at Loudon increased in power year by year, until 1910, when Rev. Charles Inwood, of the Keswick Convention, visited the country.[28] For months before, the missionaries had roused the expectations of the native Christians until about a hundred prayer meetings were being held. In them, Christians confessed their shortcomings and prayed for the power of God upon the convention. And up to three thousand admission tickets were distributed by the elders, to encourage and control attendance.[29]

The addresses were given in English, translated into Tembuka, with little outward response at first; but a spirit of prayer and confession fell upon the elders. On the Saturday morning, a young man began to sob hysterically and was removed. A period of silent prayer followed the set address.[30]

> Then an elder began to pray, confessing before all the sin of having cherished a spirit of revenge for an evil done him. Then another began to pray, and another and another and another, till two or three were praying together in a quiet voice, weeping and confessing, each one unconscious of the other.

> And then suddenly there came the sound of 'a rushing wind.' It was the thrilling sound of two thousand five hundred people praying audibly, no man apparently conscious of the other. I could think of no better image to describe the noise than the rushing of wind through the trees. We were listening to the same sound as filled that upper room at Pentecost. Not noisy or discordant, it filled us with a great awe.[31]

Some began to cry out in uncontrollable agony, so the missionaries judged that an unwholesome physical excitement would break out unless the meeting were controlled. Fraser started a hymn but each person for a while 'sang what was uppermost in his mind and heart in a volume of tumbling waters' until all at last united in the words of a psalm of confession. The benediction was pronounced and the vast congregation dispersed in utter silence to pray.

Better to control the meetings, the womenfolk were asked to meet in the school quadrangle and the men in the big church. In both gatherings, 'torrents of prayer' flowed as the whole audience engaged in simultaneous prayer. On Sunday about 7000 gathered, thousands of heathen having heard of the astounding events. An evangelistic message was given and again the overwhelming response. In the afternoon, 1250 communicants partook of break and wine, a eucharist indeed with overflowing joy.

In the weeks following, at Chinde's, Ekwendeni, Bandawe and Livingstonia, Charles Inwood preached at conventions 'with the same mighty and awe-inspiring results,' while the local missionaries held a series of local conventions.

There were permanent and ethical fruits, for feuds were healed, debts paid, bitter quarreling gave way to brotherly kindness, prayer became joyous, candidates volunteered for Christian service, and the heathen were brought into the Christian faith. Although the intense fervency of revival died away, the Malawi Church inherited a memory of

> the rapture and power that comes when God reveals Himself to men, a longing for renewed displays of His glowing presence, an intense conviction that there is no power in the world so irresistible as the Holy Spirit.

It was the same in Zambia. Dan Crawford, a Scottish Brethren missionary, met a man carrying a string with more than thirty knots—each of them representing a convert won for Christ. On investigation, his converts were found meeting among the rocks at Lofoi, praising God.[32]

In the eastern provinces, following the Dutch Reformed revivals at the end of the Anglo-Boer War, came a great ingathering into the Reformed Mission, baptized members increasing from 600 to 2029 between 1903 and 1910.[33]

The great breakthrough in missionary work in the Congo, according to Bishop Stephen Neill, came about when African evangelists were sent out in village ministry.[34]

> The system of village evangelists was developed everywhere in Protestant missions; first, and with greatest success, at Luebo among the Baluba . . . The Kasai region is thickly populated. In 1904, Luebo already had forty out-stations, each provided with a literate evangelist. Church membership stood at 3000.

The mission station at Luebo was only ten years old, and it included among its American Presbyterian missionaries several American Negroes. As a 'city of refuge' in strife, the population had reached 10,000. By the year 1901, the American Presbyterians were reporting a 'Pentecost on the Upper Congo,' with crowds of six thousand listening to the preaching on Sundays.[35] In the following year, the Mission claimed a total of 854 members, with 382 new converts.

On 11th May 1902, there came a remarkable revival at the Luebo station, with forty additions to church membership. In packed out services,[36] five hundred soon became church members: another nine hundred were receiving instruction. In 1903,[37] a new church was dedicated at Ibanj in the same field, a thousand seats provided. In the thanksgiving offering, fifty thousand cowrie-shells (about $42 in value) were received. Some said that the area had now become evangelized.

By 1906, 9000 were members, 2000 preparing for membership, 6000 in young people's societies, and 20,000 pupils in various schools. That year, 2180 were added to the church, 'a church of spontaneous growth . . . originated in itself and the Holy Spirit.'[38] In 1914, more than a third of all Protestant communicants in Congo (30,000) were Kasai Presbyterians.

In Kifwa, thirteen churches baptized 648 converts in 1906, giving instruction to eighteen hundred more in preparation for baptism.[39] The Congo Balolo Mission, commenced by Grattan Guinness, experienced an abundant harvest at its stations in the Congo, particularly Bonginda.[40] It was stated that 'this African Revival has been remarkable for the spirit of prayer demonstrated, Saturday evening prayer meetings being crowded in preparation for the fruitful Sunday services.' A peculiar feature was the occurrence of prophetic dreams.

In 1906, Alliance missionaries in the Congo commented: 'We need an outpouring of the Holy Spirit to reveal and convict of sin and to quicken, and for this we are praying.'[41]   In 1907, a marked revival began at the Alliance mission stations at Kinkonzi and Yema, reported in 1908 as 'fruitful revival.'[42]

After a period in which the work languished, Baptists at Banza Manteke[43] reported an outbreak of conviction of sin, followed by conversions—a Congo resumption of progress.

In 1897, the American Disciples of Christ had sent out a scouting party to the Congo but received little encouragement from Belgian officials. Fraternally, the American Baptists turned over one of their stations to their Campbellite friends and from there the enterprise spread. The wave of revival reached the Disciples' field, 1912 being their 'greatest year,' a revival at Lotumbe being their 'most notable event.'[44]

In 1908, after speaking to tens of thousands of men in his crowded meetings in Britain, C. T. Studd (of cricketing and missionary fame, himself in middle age) heard the call of Africa, and came out to the Congo to found the Heart of Africa Mission, later the Worldwide Evangelization Crusade.[45]

The Christian and Missionary Alliance began its Angola work in 1910,[46] and (by way of Northern Rhodesia) the South Africa General Mission entered the country, supplementing American and British missions established decades before. In Angola, in areas pioneered by Christian Brethren of the Garenganze Mission under F. S. Arnot, an awakening commenced among the tribes.[47] In the north of Angola, the revival among related tribes in the Congo affected Baptist work.

In southern Cameroon, from 1906 onward, the American Presbyterians witnessed a wonderful transformation of the M'bey people, regarded as thieves and cannibals by nearby tribesmen.[48] The Bulus also experienced a great awakening. Likewise in Cameroon, American Presbyterians reported 'most encouraging signs' of spiritual awakening, together with increased zeal in all evangelistic work in 1906.[49] The year following was even better, more than eight hundred men, women, and children having confessed Christ in a single church, where the attendance averaged a thousand.[50] It was announced that practically all those churches having native pastors had come to self-support in the previous two years.

In 1908, church attendance was reported on the increase, Sunday services at Elat attracting sixteen hundred people; at Lolodorf a thousand.[51] In 1909 was reported their 'greatest advance' upon that field, and a 'marvelous growth' in their churches, fed by a 'continuous revival.' Attendance at the July communion was 1200 at Batanga, 1600 at Efulon, 1700 at Lolodorf, and 3500 at Elat.   There were 2000 inquirers.

German missionaries reported a revival of interest in Christianity in Tanganyika fields. In Ostafrika, from 1888 to 1906, the fighting was almost continuous between Germans and native tribes,[52] sometimes a hundred tribes in revolt.

Near Mombasa,[53] the Church Missionary Society noted 'evident signs of the working of the Holy Spirit' in Freretown, but later news from the area proved disappointing:

> There had always been a marked difference between the dioceses (Uganda and Mombasa) while they agreed in methods of work and in the type of men which they attracted to their staffs. In Uganda, more attention was paid to the training of African teachers and evangelists and there were fewer, but reasonably well-equipped, mission stations ... while in Kenya less emphasis was placed on the training of indigenous workers, and the European was often found working single-handed in an isolated station.[54]

By late 1905, Christians in Uganda recognized that there was a need of numerical increase as well as spiritual uplift. Attendance had dropped and Christians were falling back into their old ways.[55] A 'cycle of prayer' was arranged for a month throughout the diocese of Uganda. Prayer was offered for the Bishop and clergy and workers, native and European both, various areas receiving attention from intercessors. The New Year of 1906 thus began in marked expectation.

In Uganda, awakening to spiritual life occurred in Toro country, resulting in intense conviction of sin and followed by awakening to missionary responsibility. In the year following, the Toro churches were still crowded out, communicants at Kabarole alone increasing from 1208 to 1376 in five years, the Christian constituency from 2286 to 4118. It was said that the ingathering of new converts caused a lowering of spiritual standards.[56]

Bishop Tucker reported in March, 1906, that[57]

> We are in the midst of the Mengo Mission services, which are being attended by vast crowds—between 3000 and 4000 at a single service. The preparatory work of prayer and visiting has resulted in much blessing and we are earnestly praying that large numbers of backsliders —some of whom we have not seen for years and who are daily attending services—may be restored.

This revival attracted the largest attendance of Baganda till then reported for any purpose, religious or otherwise. Morning meetings exceeded four thousand in attendance all week through, and aggregate attendance was more than 50,000. Many were the conversions. Such was the deepening of spiritual life that the impact was felt over East Africa.[58]

Late that year, it was reported that church attendance by non-Christians was up by 33%. So great a change was experienced by inquirers that many postponed baptism as unimportant, later instruction reversing this trend. Local statistics reflected fewer revival additions than expected, an epidemic of sleeping sickness being the reason.

In West Africa, less than sixty thousand communicants and a hundred and thirty thousand adherents of Evangelical churches and missions became nearly eighty thousand and a quarter of a million respectively between 1904 and 1909.[59]

The 1900s were times of pioneering for two interdenominational missions, the Sudan United Mission and the Sudan Interior Mission,[60] the former founded in 1904 by Karl Kumm, and the latter in 1893 by Rowland Bingham.[61]

In the first decade of the twentieth century, there were many encouraging signs in the Yoruba country in Nigeria. A railway had been built from Lagos to Ibadan in 1902, and communications were vastly improved.[62] Christianity made great strides in Abeokuta, where the C. M. S. enterprise had been founded in the wake of the 1860 Revival in England. The chief of the Ake attended church regularly, as did Egba chiefs.[63] Chief Ogbaloko appealed to his household to give up idolatry, and several basketfuls of fetishes were burned. A Jebu community asked, not for financial help but for one to train their young men, educational and medical help.

Likewise, in Nigeria, there was great awakening seen in the Niger Delta, an extraordinary visitation of the Spirit marked by an agonizing conviction of sin among people whose notions of sin had hitherto been discouragingly feeble.[64]

A people's movement in Nigeria followed the Awakenings of 1905. Within a decade, the number of inquirers under instruction for membership in the Church Missionary Society Niger Mission rose to 20,668, a far cry from less than a thousand at the beginning of the century.[65]

In 1914, in Soba country, the Church Missionary Society enrolled two thousand inquirers who had abandoned their idols and fetishes, one town alone registering six hundred seekers after God.[66]

The American Presbyterians opened up a new work in Fulasi and, a year later in 1914, reported the blessing of 'the right hand of the Most High,' average attendances on Sundays in the first quarter being 636, in the last quarter 1399, native Christians supporting twenty-five evangelists in the surrounding Nigerian countryside.[67]

There was not much to report in French Dahomey,[68] but Togoland was administered as a German territory in the early 1900s, and its colonial government began building good roads to open up the country. The mission work of the North German Missionary Society, based on Bremen, was supplemented by German and British Methodist missions. In 1913, the Bremen missionaries reported 1535 baptisms, an encouraging number.[69]

In Ghana also, there was marked improvement of the spiritual life of the churches, following the worldwide 1905 Awakening. The Wesleyan Methodists multiplied sevenfold in the next quarter of a century. African prophets arose to reach the tribes in the interior.

One among the many, a native prophet unrelated to any mission arose to preach in the hinterland of the Ivory Coast and Gold Coast. William Wadé Harris, a native of Liberia, influenced by some Anglican missionaries, came to Christian faith and felt a call of God to preach. Without foreign support or sanction, he began to itinerate with a message of the One True God, the observance of the Lord's Day, the destruction of all symbols of idolatry, and the renunciation of adultery. He won thousands of followers, as did others who copied him in method and message.[70]

Unlike the nativist Bantu prophets of South Africa, Harris urged his disciples to seek instruction from the missionaries, the Methodists gaining thereby a constituency which increased to more than a hundred thousand.

In 1906, the Church Missionary Society in Sierra Leone began to withdraw its European missionaries and replace them with suitable African clergymen.[71] The jubilee of the Anglican Sierra Leone Pastorate was celebrated in 1913. The Colony proper had become more than half Christian, less than a sixth Muslim, the remaining third being pagan; but its hinterland was almost totally pagan, a few Muslims.

The Methodist Episcopal work in Liberia enjoyed a time of awakening. At Grand Cess, 200 people gathered for 5 a.m. prayer meetings, 700 for class meetings and 1200 for the preaching services on Sunday, continuing thus into 1909.[72]

Awakenings in Liberia continued into the next decade. A young woman dreamed that God had commanded her to put away ju-jus and seek God. The result of her obedience was the turning of many to righteousness, a Kru preacher taking over the care of the new church. Another awakening occurred in Kru territory after the believers had sought deliverance from a fearful drought. About forty young people professed conversion, and the enthusiasm spread to the nearby towns. Men and women would rise from sleep at midnight and hurry several miles along the beach for prayer. No building could accommodate the crowds attending the preaching.[73]

While the Awakening of 1905 was spreading all over the world, Ethiopia was almost a closed country, so far as Evangelical Christianity was concerned. In 1905, a Galla convert educated in Stockholm, Onesimus by name, returned to Addis Ababa and was welcomed by Emperor Menelik, who permitted him to work among his own people. By using the Swedish and Amharic texts, he presented a Galla Bible.[74]

The Evangeliska Fosterlands Stiftelsen's missionaries in Ethiopia, which had five stations in Shoa and Wallega provinces with three hundred converts before the beginning of the twentieth century, reported 'great growth in a hard field' in 1914, the number of stations doubled, two thousand converts, and seventy-five native evangelists, rejoicing the hearts of the pioneering Swedes.[75]

Between 1913 and 1919, a remarkable ingathering of Muslims into the Christian Church was reported in Ethiopia. The distribution of Scriptures by the British and Foreign Bible Society triggered a movement which involved 10,000 baptisms.[76] The leader of the movement was an ex-sheik, Zacarria by name. Dissatisfied with the formality of the Coptic Church, about five hundred teachers formed Bible study groups. The death of Noaye Kristos, leader in 1924, somewhat checked the movement.

In North Africa, shadowed by Islam, 'the glory of the impossible' occurred also—for in 1903,[77] an awakening in the mission-sponsored college at Assiut in Egypt provoked fifty students freely to offer themselves for missionary service. By 1906 in Egypt, there were signs of an evangelical awakening, for a town of about twenty thousand in Upper Egypt (Nachaileh) became the scene of an 'amazing work' which thronged the assemblies of the Christians, emptied the resorts of vice, and converted thieves, robbers and drunkards, with 'at least one convert in every household.'[78]

In Algeria, the French evangelist from Paris, Reuben Saillens, addressed an audience of 1200 in Algiers on the subject of Revival in Wales, that meeting on 27th November 1905 being the precursor of lasting blessing. And in 1906, Saillens reported 'the most encouraging time ever known in Algiers.' A local theatre was crowded nightly by two thousand and many were the converts counselled in French.[79]

Thus the evidence indeed is overwhelming that throughout the African continent Evangelical Christianity rapidly advanced in the first decade of the twentieth century. There were many factors in that growth, but not least among them was the phenomenon of evangelical revival appearing among African congregations.

It was reported, in 1910, at the Edinburgh Missionary Conference that 'by far the greatest progress of Christianity in Africa has been achieved in the past decade.'[80] This was a great leap forward in Africa, and its impetus was fully sustained, for the missionary expert, David Barrett, has assessed it thus: [81]

> The fact is that, since around 1910, Africa has been the only one of the world's six continents in which the entire Christian community has expanded uniformly at a rate over twice that of the population increase.

And Bishop Stephen Neill added: [82]

> On the most sober estimate, the Christian is reasonably entitled to think that by the end of the twentieth century Africa south of the Sahara will be in the main a Christian continent.

Without depreciating the efforts of missionaries of other segments of the Christian faith, one may highly evaluate the contribution of Evangelicals, missionary and national, and give proper credit thus to the outbreak of the Awakenings.

17

EXTENDED SOCIAL IMPACT

Britain's Royal Geographical Society, which had erected a memorial obelisk to David Livingstone at the place where he died on the 4th of May, 1873, declared that the world was indebted to Africa missionaries not only for their work in educating and civilizing the natives, but also for the many important geographical explorations they made.[1]

Livingstone's name stands foremost among the great explorers of Africa. His father-in-law, Robert Moffatt,[2] and London Missionary Society pioneers blazed the trail of exploration before him, and later missionaries shared equally with the foremost professional geographer-explorers the privilege of opening up Africa.

Coillard explored the upper Zambesi,[3] Arnot penetrated the Garenganze[4] and discovered the source of the Zambesi, and Bishops Mackenzie and Maples, Drs. Stewart, Laws, Young, Elmslie and others opened up section after section of the unknown interior.[5]

George Grenfell, gold medallist of the Royal Geographical Society, mapped much of the Congo.[6] And, according to the explorer Speke,[7] other missionaries were the pioneers in mapping the legendary mountains of Kenya and Kilimanjaro, and were the first to explore the great lake systems.

A volume could be written about the explorations of the pioneer missionaries in other parts of the continent of Africa. The secular explorers were often well-equipped and well-financed by interested supporters in the world of business. The missionaries accomplished their explorations as a sideline, operating on a financial shoestring.

The missionaries were the pioneers of health and sanitation, of clinics and hospitals.[8] The first Protestant medical missionary to land in Africa was J. T. van der Kemp.[9] As early as 1823, the Moravians established a leper colony.[10] In the midst of incredible hardships, David Livingstone found time to report upon disease and medicines.[11] And from the compassionate efforts of the pioneers, a complex of mission hospitals and medical service ultimately grew.

From the beginning, missionary societies declared war
on the slave trade. At times, whole communities of rescued
slaves came under the jurisdiction of ordinary missionaries,
who used every possible means to protect their charges. They
further sought to influence civilized governments to assume
responsibility for controlling and abolishing the slave trade.
At home, their boards brought pressure on the legislative
conscience of parliaments and executive acts of governments.

The missionaries represented a constituency which protested the ghastly cruelties inflicted upon helpless Africans
by Europeans in the slave trade. Their successors likewise
protested the cruelties inflicted upon Africans by Europeans
in the rubber trade of the Congo Free State.[12] It was not surprising, therefore, that missionaries endeavoured to deliver
primitive tribespeople from the unchecked terrors of their
own tyrannical chiefs or scheming witchdoctors, opposing
the smelling out of witches, trial by ordeal and brutal torture
or execution at the whim of a chief.[13]

The records of the past are attested, by explorers and
travellers as well as missionaries. The following account of
Xhosa custom has been substantiated by the narratives of
Taylor of California and of Tiyo Soga, the first university
graduate of his race, and by observers other than its writer:

> The whole clan was assembled and seated in a circle;
> the witchfinder, who was fantastically painted and at-
> tired, went through certain incantations; and when all
> were worked into a state of frenzy he pointed to some
> individual as the one who had by bewitchment caused
> death or sickness among the people, murrain among the
> cattle, blight in the crops, or some other disaster. The
> result to the person so pointed out was confiscation of
> property and torture, often causing death. The number
> of persons who perished on charges of dealing in witch-
> craft was very great. The victims were usually old
> women, persons of eccentric habits, men of property, or
> individuals obnoxious to the chief. Any person in advance
> of his fellows was specially liable to suspicion, so that
> progress of any kind toward what we should term higher
> civilization was made exceedingly difficult by this belief.
> No one except the chief was exempt from being charged
> with dealing in witchcraft. The cruelties practised on un-
> fortunate individuals believed guilty were often horrible.[14]

These atrocities were not isolated instances, occurring
in a corner of Africa. A Mukama of Bunyoro, a kingdom of
Uganda, was buried in a grave lined with the living bodies

of his wives and domestic retainers whose arms and legs had previously been broken to prevent their escape.[15] Such incidents can be found in the writings of explorers, traders and travellers as well as missionaries, and happened not only in South Africa but the Congo and East and West Africa.

Next to preaching the Good News, the chief missionary method was elementary education, considered the beginning of modern civilization. Bantu folk had developed a system of education through puberty rites to equip the young for life in the tribe, but there was no 'reading, writing or arithmetic.' At the time of the missionary contact, a majority of Bantu folk south of the equator possessed no alphabet or other form of writing, no set of numerals, no almanac or calendar, no notation of time, no measurement of length or capacity or weight.[16] The missionaries tackled the educational deficiency and found pupils as eager as any in the world.

As a matter of course, missionaries played their part in the reducing of the languages of the Africans to writing; they prepared translations of the Scriptures, taught the people to read and write, opened schools for the youth, established hospitals for the sick, introduced arts and crafts, and built up law-abiding Christian communities. What they had first accomplished for the Bantu folk in Southern Africa, they extended all over the continent.

The missionary attitude to the capabilities of the Bantu folk was one of enthusiasm, for example: [17]

> These South African native peoples . . . are probably the finest black race in Africa. They have proved it as warriors and thinkers. The slave trade never touched them. They are monotheists and were uninfluenced by the idolatry and fetish-worship of most Africans . . . they have proved strong enough to survive contact with civilization. They have it in them to survive as a people, being neither merged nor submerged among Europeans. All this we may well hold as proved. We therefore must take count of them as a growing factor in the development of Africa. They may spread material non-Christian civilization; this may mean future disaster. They may spread Christian civilization; this was Livingstone's ideal.

Southern Africa from the Zambesi to the Cape benefitted first and foremost from the work of missions in education. Local governments, in provinces and territories of Southern Africa, had established excellent educational facilities for children of European settlers. The education of the Bantu was left entirely to Christian missionaries, who at the turn

of the twentieth century maintained 1860 schools of all grades
with 110,895 students attending them. This represented almost half of all the schools maintained throughout the African
continent and fully half its number of students.[18]

From the time of the awakenings in the English-speaking
churches in the Eastern Province, the Methodists extended
their programme of schools for the Bantu. From the time
of the consecration of Bishop Gray, the Anglicans promoted
a school system. The awakenings among Dutch Reformed
churches had the same indirect effect, those who had been
touched and challenged going forth to teach their less fortu-
nate Bantu neighbours to read and write. And the overseas
missionaries, whether from United States, Scotland, England,
Germany, Scandinavia or France, operated such a successful
programme of elementary education of their charges on their
mission fields that the governments of all the provinces and
territories came to recognize the desirability of education
for all the African peoples.

A government inspector declared that[19]

> A visit to Lovedale would convert the greatest sceptic
> regarding the value of native education. The great or-
> ganizing power of Dr. Stewart appears on every side.
> The staff is large and able and the civilizing effects of
> the whole institution is remarkably felt. It may have its
> defects, but the scheme at present is the most complete,
> the largest and most successful of its kind in the country,
> and the institution as a whole is probably the greatest
> educational establishment in South Africa.

By 1903, the Lovedale Institution maintained by the United
Free Church of Scotland reported a total of 753 students,
drawn from every part of Africa south of the Zambesi. It
possessed nine industrial departments as well as a wide
range of classes for intellectual training. The missionaries
there trained altogether 4616 students in nine schools.[20]

Anglicans maintained schools and colleges in the Transkei
territory, Zululand, and up-country. Wesleyans operated
schools among the Xhosa; the American Board maintained
several boarding schools in Natal and Zululand, with 530
students.[21] The Huguenot College at Wellington in the Cape
was maintained for Afrikaans-speaking girls who (550 strong)
were to be found engaged as school teachers and the like in
various mission stations. In Lesotho, the Paris missionaries virtually became a local government educational
agency.[22] In Botswanaland, the missionaries maintained the

only educational system. In Swaziland, the schools were begun by the missions. In Rhodesia, mission schools provided the only programme of education for the Africans.

In South Africa, African enterprise was not lacking, for a Zulu chief, John L. Dube, who had graduated from the Tuskegee Schools in the United States, set up a flourishing industrial school enterprise in Natal for Zulus, with a couple of hundred industrial apprentice-students, a Christian school that was patterned after the Hampton Institute in Virginia which produced Booker T. Washington.[23]

By the turn of the twentieth century, social engineers were beginning to urge Governments to establish a state system of schools for Bantu folk with compulsory attendance and special training in technical and industrial skills. The experts said:[24]

> Excellent work is carried on at some of the larger missionary institutions. The work is almost entirely in the hands of missionaries of various denominations, but it is recognized by the state and is aided and supervised by the Government.

One such expert, John Tudhope, observed in his report:

> If the natives are to be preserved, it must be through an enlightened system of education, fitting them to take their proper place in the political system, sharing its duties and responsibilities and also its privileges. But they cannot be expected to achieve this without careful preparation. No nation has ever passed from heathenism to civilization per saltum. It is only by a slow and sometimes painful process that this can be accomplished, and the natives of South Africa are no exception to the general rule. The efforts of individuals and missionary societies, supplemented by government aid, have shown us what can be done and results are sufficiently encouraging to warrant us going further in this direction.

Missionaries were equally influential in other parts of the continent. As late as 1875, there existed in Malawi, 'no schools, no teachers, no pupils and nobody who could read.' In thirty years, things changed. The Church of Scotland maintained a successful educational system based at Blantyre, with 57 schools and 3643 scholars; the United Free Church of Scotland, centred upon Livingstonia, maintained an even more remarkable system of schools, 15,765 pupils attending 207 institutions. In Ngoniland, southwest of Lake Nyasa, the Zambesi Industrial Mission maintained 37 schools with 1600 pupils. The Paris Evangelical Mission in Barotseland served 1200 pupils in ten schools.[25]

In Central Africa, at the turn of the century, the Zambesi Industrial Mission cultivated thousands of acres, largely in coffee and cotton, and useful trades were taught in forty schools based on ten principal stations.[26] This mission had not only won hundreds of Bantu folk to Christian faith but also provided them a livelihood, after Ngoni raids had all but destroyed them.[27]

In Rhodesia, Zambia and the Congo, American Methodists promoted industrial schools, along with their evangelistic enterprises. Other such industrial schools were established by various societies throughout Bantu Africa and beyond in the West African countries. It is interesting to note that Cecil Rhodes persuaded British South Africa officials to donate land for the missionary societies in Rhodesia and encouraged educational and medical services.[28]

In the Congo, the American Baptists were maintaining 109 schools with 3285 pupils, while their British colleagues there reported slightly higher figures, between them a majority of the total of 10,471 scholars and 318 schools operated by the evangelical missions together.[29] In the French Congo and in German Cameroons were many missionary schools also, each serving the converts and inquirers.

In Angola, American Congregationalists and Methodists maintained a total of 32 schools with several thousand pupils receiving instruction.[30] The first party of Americans included a Negro educated at the Hampton Institute.

The German missionary societies in German East Africa (Tanganyika and Rwanda-Burundi) started their elementary school system in the country, ably seconded by the Church Missionary Society and other foreign missions. The Anglican Universities' Mission maintained a first-class school system on the Island of Zanzibar and the German-controlled mainland with 146 schools and 5079 scholars.

The Church Missionary Society in the British East African territory (Kenya and Uganda) were maintaining a total of 262 primary schools with 26,847 pupils. The educational policy of the Society was largely concerned with the elementary schooling of the entire body of inquirers and converts. Sir Harry Johnston, British explorer and administrator, estimated that 200,000 of these had been taught by the mission teachers to read their Bibles and school-texts. Thus were the foundations laid for the modern school system.

George Pilkington, the able Anglican leader in Uganda, made a notable comment: [31]

It is astonishing what an educational value this reading of God's Word has; the pupils' very physiognomy seems to be changed by it, so that it is almost possible to tell a reader by his outward appearance. And in no other way does the reality of God seem to impress itself so forcibly on the native mind as by the daily poring over the pages of the New Testament at first mechanically and then with more glimmering of meaning, until at last the Divine message of love is intelligently grasped, and perhaps driven home by some sermon or meeting or the faithful words of a friend; and another catachumen is added to the rolls and (we trust) another soul to the company of Christ. It is a noticeable and deeply instructive fact that profession of conversion never, or hardly ever, has been made by a Muganda who cannot read, except—of course—a few special cases of blind or old.

The reported opinion of Theodore Roosevelt provided an insight into the judgments made in the early 1900s:[32]

As soon as native African religions—practically none of which have hitherto evolved any substantial ethical basis—develop beyond the most primitive stage . . . they tend to grow into malign creeds of unspeakable cruelty and malignity and immorality . . .
Even a poorly taught and imperfectly understood Christianity, with its underlying foundations of justice and mercy, represents an immeasurable advance on such a creed. Where, as in Uganda, the people are intelligent and the missionaries unite disinterestedness and zeal with common sense, the result is astounding.

In 1908, another observer, Winston Churchill, added to this vindication of missions, contrasting the grotesque and pitiful welcome his party received from primitive people in other parts with the experience of entering Uganda—'another world' of 'clothed, cultivated, educated natives.' In his African tour, Churchill claimed that he had never seen better order or happier homes than in Uganda, 'where a few years ago the pioneer missionaries were mercilessly put to death.'

So too in West Africa, where the missionary societies were operating nearly a thousand schools between the Benin Gulf and Gambia, with about forty thousand pupils.

This missionary educational enterprise was the forerunner of present-day national school systems, and it was maintained from the start by men of unquestioned dedication, supported by the voluntary giving of Christians in the more privileged nations. This is worth remembering.[33]

In African tribal education, the child was educated for the community, without a thought of individual gain at the expense of the family, tribe or community.[34] In Western education, whether in missionary or government schools, the pupil became an individualist in a competitive system. He developed a scorn for superstitious practices of all sorts.

Missionary effort in Africa produced much of the disintegration of tribal societies. Chiefs who, for reasons of personal and tribal benefit, welcomed the missionary, seldom foresaw the inevitable result of the founding of a church— the transfer of loyalty to what appeared to be a higher way of life, and the depreciation of the old ways. Even though the missionary was an alien, the sharing of spiritual fellowship produced a spiritual kinship with him which the impact of less kindly Europeans could not destroy.

Missionary education, though a by-product of missions, produced a younger generation which soon felt itself superior to its elders, reversing an age-old and natural relationship. The African pupil became an inhabitant of two worlds, one the world of Western thought and technology, the other the world of his ancestors, his parents and elders, and most of his age-group. Of his own volition, he admired the one with respect and fear, and the other he despised with familiarity and contempt, though holding his family in an impatient affection.

Mission schools, though by no means the last word in either technology or education, introduced not only better animal husbandry and agricultural methods, but inculcated much-needed ideas of personal and social hygiene, prophylaxis against disease, and improvement of diet, resulting in a vast enlargement of living standards which in turn soon challenged superstitions against which missionaries spoke.

In some cases, African peoples who had held other tribes in a kind of serfdom rejected the new set of values as inimical to their position, whereas the subject peoples welcomed the innovation. In most cases, the subject peoples forged ahead—as in the case of the Shonas in Rhodesia, the Bahutus in Rwanda and the Ibos in Nigeria. In South Africa, the pro-Christian, pro-education Xhosa far outshone the traditional red-blanket Xhosa, producing Transkei's African elite.[35]

In the areas of European settlement, the rise of an African educated elite disturbed the status quo. The first generation educated African endeavoured with enthusiasm to enter the world of the European. He was not welcomed, except as an inferior. The second generation of African scholars entered vocational training and became nurses, orderlies, printers, carpenters, bricklayers, agriculturists, technicians, and teachers, a skilled working class with plenty of work to do.

The third generation, reaching for higher education, soon channeled their frustrations into political activism and so emerged as the African elite. It was said by critics that the only change involved in national independence was the exchange of the leadership of the European for the leadership of the African elite. There was this difference; the African, whether born into a backward, tribal village or into a partly-educated working class or into the most privileged African circles, could rise to the level of his abilities and education. This became true in the Transkei as well as Tanzania.

Where African nationalism had been captured by Leninist propaganda, anti-missionary sentiment (already latent) was fostered strongly among the peoples who owed so much to missions; yet national leaders (in Kenya and Nigeria) were quick to recognize the debt to missions.[36] Bohannon stated:

> The great debt that Africa owes to missionaries is that in a situation in which the forces of trade, colonial government, and the missions themselves were creating cultural havoc, it was only the missions that began to rebuild. Whatever any individual Westerner may think of the missionary edifice, every African knows that it is to missionaries that they owe the beginning of the African educational system.[37]

What was the motivation of the missionaries? It was a spiritual and altruistic one, primarily. It was obvious that missionaries did not go out to Africa for health or wealth. Between 1878 and 1888, half of the Baptist missionaries in the Congo died of disease, between 1835 and 1905, nearly a third of all the Wesleyan missionaries to West Africa.[38]

The missionary, with exceptions, was not the conscious agent of colonialism. He often indeed supported the extension of European civil power in Africa, but generally his support was due to his view of Christian responsibility.

The motivation of the African in accepting the missionary contribution has also been analysed. Many African chiefs hoped to gain access to the more sophisticated weapons of warfare, to farming equipment, tools and information as a result of their welcome to the alien missionary. Improved seeds and hybrids ensured better crops, for everyone.

In the same way, the motivation of the convert in embracing the Christian faith has been studied. In some cases, it was purely spiritual. In other instances, the adherents of Christianity saw some material gain in adopting the new way. Missions provided education, and education seemed to be the simplest way of entering the 'civilized' world with its promise of an escape from manual labour and its hope of recognition as one belonging to a superior society.

Secular critics have condemned the nineteenth century missionary for his obvious lack of an enlightened motivation conditioned by mid-twentieth century anthropological and sociological conclusions. It might be asked——Who in the colonial period between 1815 and 1914 possessed any such enlightenment? How was a missionary from Europe or America supposed to anticipate the findings of mid-twentieth century science? It is much more reasonable to recognize that the missionary was the product of nineteenth century society but one deeply moved by first century principles, by eternal verities believed by Christians.

The missionary often confused western values with eternal verities. His converts sometimes did the same. But modern missionary polity is no longer concerned with westernizing converts. It is a recognized objective to convey and commit Christian principles to other societies and let the converts work out their own harmony of faith and tradition. After all, Western Christianity also is only a Christianity imperfectly adapted by its adherents.

When missionaries sought to abolish African practices, polygamy, witchcraft, human sacrifice, bride-purchase and trial by ordeal and the like, it was not for political reasons but because they were intolerable to Christian thinking. The attack however, had a political effect, for it soon brought down a tribal way of life based thereon.

One of the handicaps of the missionary enterprise arose from missionary rivalries. Among Evangelicals, with some exceptions, a very general comity of operation was practised, due to the fact that such mission societies shared the same view of the Church as a body of believers which existed in various organizational forms. This was heresy to the Catholic (Roman, Greek or Anglo-Catholic) who considered the Church as a visible unity, and denied——until the change of ecumenical climate——that the Evangelicals were in the Church at all. Most inter-missionary rivalries were attributable to this Catholic-Evangelical divergence in policy, though there were exceptions to this rule, such as a French-Reformed versus English-Wesleyan dispute in Lesotho.

The Congo may be taken as an example of the fullest of missionary comity among Evangelicals, who divided up the country with a minimum of friction. The 1946 missions map of the Congo displayed this remarkable comity. The Roman Catholic missions in the Congo were not only outside these comity arrangements but were in a recognized competition for the loyalty of the African Christians.[39]

The civil war in Uganda in the 1890s between supporters of the English-Protestant and French-Catholic missionaries demonstrated the extreme of inter-missionary tension. Only in the post-war 1950s and 1960s did the traditional rivalry of Protestant and Roman Catholic abate somewhat. On Uganda, Bishop Stephen Neill described the conflict as 'a grievous and highly unedifying chapter in missionary history,' but Professor Latourette noted that 'the arrival in 1879 of the White Fathers . . . brought division and rivalry . . .' It is known that Cardinal Lavigerie, a truly great missionary director, regarded Protestant missionaries as dangerous, heretical rivals in the field. That commenced the conflict.[40]

At the mid-nineteenth century, a missionary presented himself at the kraal of a chief whose people had never before seen a European. The chief, after assuring himself of the visitor's lack of political ambition, generally granted his request for land to build a mission church and school; the witch-doctor was offended; the chief was hopeful of benefit to the tribe. Soon a crisis developed when the missionary's following grew in numbers. Sometimes the chief expelled the missionary; more often, the chief's son, educated in mission school, succeeded to the chiefly stool and supported him.

Complications followed the arrival of the first traders or settlers. Upon occasion, the resident missionary became a defender of the tribesmen against the rapacity of his kinsmen.

Meanwhile, the church school was raising the level of the 'civilization' of the tribe. Inevitably, the educated African began asking questions which the settlers or traders or the colonial government deplored. Often the missionary was blamed. He himself defended his charges but discouraged violent revolt. His position made him a kind of mediator. Ardent nationalists soon left him far behind. When the winds changed, the missionary was often the first non-African to accept the change. After the fever of revolution had passed, African leaders reassessed the work of the missionary and generally asked him to stay on as a guest of African society, a teacher in the emergent African states.

18

BETWEEN WARS AWAKENINGS

In the 1920s and 1930s, when the Western world enjoyed a post-war boom and suffered an unprecedented economic depression, and evangelism therein—with rare exceptions—was cramped by a debilitating malaise of churchly enemia, the younger churches of Asia and Africa experienced surge after surge of spiritual power, issuing in revival of true believers, restoration of backsliders and nominal church members, the awakening of the masses round about, and folk movements as well as healthy indigenous evangelism. The same period witnessed a startling growth of crypto-Christian movements and of independent African Churches. All this occurred in East Africa, Central Africa, South Africa, and West Africa, among black African peoples, and was paralleled among white Africans in the South by healthy revival and sane evangelism.

The most outstanding, far-reaching, and long-lasting revival-awakening began in a newly-opened mission field in one of the remotest countries of the African continent. In the year 1925[1] the first Anglican missionaries entered the twin kingdoms of Rwanda-Burundi and gained a foothold at Gahini, where an effective medical and evangelistic ministry was begun. It was pioneering work of an elementary sort.

The Ruanda General and Medical Mission was an auxiliary arm of the Church Missionary Society, itself an evangelical Anglican foundation,[2] its auxiliary sponsored by the most ardent evangelical sector of the Church of England to operate on Biblical, Protestant, and Keswick lines. Its pioneers included Dr. A. C. Stanley Smith, son of Stanley Smith of the Cambridge Seven who served in China. Its sponsors found their best support among Keswick Anglicans.[3]

There were many key personalities gathering in Rwanda for the outbreak of spiritual power—European and African. One such was Joe Church, a medical missionary supported by the Cambridge Inter-Collegiate Christian Union; another was Blasio Kigozi, a Muganda from Kampala in the Ugandan kingdom;[4] and they all formed a vanguard in experience.

Suffice to say, although individual leaders entered into new experiences in the late 'twenties, it was not until the 1930s that any significant movement was reported in the Rwanda-Burundi field.[5] Awakenings were occurring elsewhere in Africa.

In the Congo, now the Republic of Zaire, a catechist of the (British) Baptist Missionary Society, Simon Kimbangu, began an itinerating ministry, preaching repentance and claiming a gift of healing. The British Baptists disavowed the healings, and offered increasing opposition to Kimbangu, who was finally arrested by the Belgian authorities because of anti-European dissidence in a minority of his followers. Meanwhile, the following of Simon Kimbangu increased until it became the largest African Independent Church on the continent, with half a million adherents in the 1960s.[6]

American Baptist missionaries and national pastors at Sona Batu avoided unnecessary opposition to the Kimbanguist movement, which spared them the massive defections that other missions suffered. Their Congolese churches experienced a quickening and an ingathering, winning a thousand a year in that locality, 1500 in 1922, 3000 in 1923, and 2400 in 1927. In 1925, the churches in the Kingila district with a total of 3000 members defected en masse, but there were 1190 baptisms of believers in other parts of the field. In 1927, the Bambala tribe invited the missionaries to come and preach in a huge tabernacle constructed for their visit. The response in profession of faith enabled them to start a flourishing church in this tribal movement.[7]

In the Banza Manteke field, the Kimbanguist movement had lesser impact, but an awakening was reported in 1923 resulting in the number of baptisms rising from a few hundred a year to a thousand annually in 1923 and 1924. An old chief in the Ntondo field tried to burn down a church building, and beat, fined and imprisoned the women of his village for attending services. He later repented, and a movement of declaration of faith begun in 1926 was accelerated in 1927.[8]

Far up the Kwilu river, six hundred miles by road from Kinshasa, there were significant stirrings at Vanga in 1924. There had been much drunkenness and immorality, but now the people in groups began to bring in baskets full of fetishes to be burned. The number of baptisms of believers trebled in the years following. This tribal movement proved to be the preparation for an extraordinary movement of the Holy Spirit, a classic revival, in the 1930s.

The year 1927 was significant for awakenings in West
Africa also. An example may be taken from Nigeria, in the
field of the Qua Iboe Mission, founded by Samuel Bill—a
convert of Moody's first campaign in Belfast. The details
of the 1927 movement were first given the writer by one of
the Qua Iboe missionaries, Westgarth by name, at Keswick
during the decade following.[9]

In November 1926, a young African experienced a moving
of his spirit at prayer. Jonathan thereafter itinerated here
and there and preached with new power. By June of 1927,
the revival became widely known, and a movement of great
strength was affecting the Ibibio Christians. It was wholly
indigenous—in fact, Westgarth appeared to be the only one
of the mission staff who encouraged it.[10]

Meetings were held three times a day, beginning at 6 a.m.
and concluding at 10 p.m. Confessions of sin on the part of
Christians were frequent, reconciliations and restitutions
followed, and praise with thanksgiving abounded. Although
there was no Pentecostal influence (missionary or national)
within hundreds of miles, there was a spontaneous outburst
of glossolalia, and there were physical manifestations re-
miniscent of the Ulster Revival of 1859.

It should be noted that the Qua Iboe Mission constituency
in the North of Ireland shared a marked antipathy towards
glossolalia, hence the critical attitudes of most workers on
the field. Westgarth himself viewed many of the manifestations with great caution; yet ten years later, he assured the
writer that he was convinced that the movement was of God,
despite its earthy accompaniments.

Mrs. Bill, the mission founder's wife, visited Uyo during
the revival, in Westgarth's absence. An Idiong headman
walked to the front and declared: 'I have been a thief and an
adulterer from my youth. I have killed men in many towns
with medicine, where people paid me for doing so. I have
worshipped idols and evil spirits all my life, and now I know
they cannot help me. Can your God help me and forgive my
sins?' Jonathan replied: 'There is no other name whereby
we must be saved except the name of Jesus.'

A year later, the Mission affirmed the reality of the work;
and in successive years[11] paid tribute to its abiding values
after the excitement had died down. But African Independency
siphoned off many thousands of the revived tribespeople.
Westgarth told the writer that the mission field rapidly became as evangelized as the better parts of England.

In the 1920s, a spirit of prayer arose among Nigerian Christians, expressed in the formation of the 'Awon Egbe Aladura' or Praying Bands. This revival movement deeply influenced the course of Christian expansion for fifty years and affected many long-established mission constituencies.

Faith Tabernacle in Philadelphia, a Pentecostal church, influenced many African Christians in Nigeria at the time of the spreading prayer movement in the 1920s. There was no dominant figure until after 1925. By 1930, Joseph Babalola of Ilesha became a leading figure in the Revival in the area around Ibadan, and the movement spread rapidly.[12] Leaders invited missioners from Wales to instruct them further, so the Apostolic Church there sent out its leading men, as a result of which arose the Apostolic Church of Nigeria, with 1200 churches and 60,000 members.

Nigerians distrustful of overseas direction seceded from the Apostolic Church and so founded the Christ Apostolic Church which by 1965 gained a hundred thousand members. This African Independent Church became quite missionary-minded, establishing congregations even in Muslim Northern Nigeria. Its base, of course, was mainly Yoruba.

The prayer movement gave birth to another denomination, the Church of the Lord. Its leading figure, Josiah Oshitelu, an ex-Anglican, became its Primate.[13] At first, polygamy was accepted without being encouraged, but afterwards an example was set by Oshitelu, who took seven wives in all. This Aladura Church of the Lord maintained only three small congregations in 1931, but it spread rapidly in Nigeria and was carried into Liberia and Sierra Leone in 1942 by a team under the direction of Adeleke Adejobi. Then in 1953 it was planted in Ghana. It is interesting to note that Adejobi later took courses of study at the Moody-founded Bible Training Institute in Glasgow, which could not fail to increase his own biblical convictions. Adejobi conducted evangelistic meetings in Britain, and founded a Church of the Lord among West African immigrants in London.

It must not be thought that all the 'Awon Egbe Aladura' or Praying Bands that arose in the Nigerian Revival of 1925 became seceders from the established missionary bodies. These praying bands by the thousands stayed within mission fellowships, and those that left did so because peculiarities made them unwelcome or suspect. Despite the controversy over polygamy, denounced by some, tolerated by others, and promoted by dissidents, the general work prospered.

The awakenings of the first decade of the twentieth century in the Niger Delta were renewed in the second and third. From 1925 onward, a great folk movement in the Isako area responded to evangelism of the Church Missionary Society, raising a hundred churches in a small but densely populated territory, some with as many as 2600 attending services.[14]

To the north, a young Yoruba prophet quit driving a steam roller and started preaching, calling for confession of sins among Christians, repentance and faith among others, and exercising a gift of healing. Hundreds abandoned witchcraft, thousands burned their idols. In the Bassa country, a folk movement resulted, overwhelming the handful of C. M. S. workers, caring for sixty new outstations begun in three weeks. Sunday morning services in one town church rose from an average of 70 to 500, 800, and more than 1000.[15]

In Ghana, where the Methodists had profited from the movement under the Prophet William Harris, another like movement began in the 1920s[16] through the ministry of an Ashanti preacher, Samson Opon, who (after a deliverance from alcoholism) saw visions and heard voices commanding him to preach repentance. One of Harris's disciples, John Nakabah, founded an African Independent Church of the Twelve Apostles.[17] The Christian Council of the Gold Coast was founded in 1929, and in the 1930s it could be said that Ghana was becoming a Christian country, with ten per cent of the population baptized. The Methodists, with 16,300 in 1912, had 110,811 members in 1929.

In the 1920s, the influence of the Prophet Harris continued potent in the Ivory Coast, and a remarkable folk movement towards the Christian faith ensued.[18] In 1924, missionaries discovered thirty thousand people in the bush, waiting for biblical instruction, and within a year scores of missionaries, national pastors and catechists were building a hundred and fifty congregations. The Methodists garnered much of the harvest, but the indigenous elements in the movements that followed sought independence, and the Eglise Harriste came into being, with a hundred thousand adherents.[19]

In the 1930s, spiritual awakenings began to occur in the vast territory of Occidental Africa. The Christian and Missionary Alliance entered Mali in 1923 and established a work at Sikasso. In 1931, three of the four resident missionaries died tragically; but shortly afterwards, a score of young men influenced by them declared their faith in Christ, the first-fruits of a spreading movement.[20]

In 1931, the Rev. Irvin Underhill, of the Nigeria field of the American Presbyterian Church,[21] called for volunteers to witness in the villages round about the Foulassi station. A hundred went forth, and others remaining spent the time in prayer. The following Sunday, May 24, so many came to church that it was necessary to hold five overflow meetings. There were 3254 people present, and 41 men, 51 women and 58 children professed faith.

As in West Africa, so also the 1930s became years of revival in Central Africa, in mission field after mission field in many denominations. Sometimes, as in West Africa, the experience of an individual became the rising up of a prophetic figure, calling the masses to repentance. Other times, the local body of believers repented of lukewarmness or backsliding, and their empowered evangelism won many hundreds, sometimes thousands, to new faith in Christ.

In 1931, thirty-five thousand communicants were enrolled in the evangelical churches of Cameroon.[22] The knowledge that countless thousands were untouched moved missionaries and believers to gather for united prayer. For three months, the area round about was reconnoitred, then visitation and preaching. Within a short space of time, 26,000 new converts were under instruction, some in hardened towns.[23]

At Bolobo, a Baptist Missionary Society station in the Congo, there were 1200 communicants, but each month 'a saddening list' of names of those suspended for serious moral lapse was read out.[24] By January 1935, relations between missionaries and members were so strained that the communion service was suspended. A Congolese carpenter entered a new life through reading the story of the Kru boy, Sammy Morris, whose hunger for God took him from Liberia to Taylor University in Indiana. He began to expose the sins that were sapping the vitality of church and community.

Opposition and ridicule were forthcoming. But people were disturbed in sleep by dreams as consciences voiced the accusations of sin. On February 24, the native pastor preached powerfully, and response was swift in coming— confessions of pilfering, reconciliations of enemies, and a stream of petitions for spiritual blessing. By March, old and hardened heathen began to repent and to seek baptism. Commented Andrew MacBeath, later Principal of the Bible Training Institute of Glasgow: 'Things we had laboured to instill into public opinion by preaching and teaching became a public possession overnight.'[25]

In the Congo in 1925, there were 9259 Protestant communicants and 108,190 in the Protestant community;[26] but by 1937, church members numbered nearly 200,000 and the Protestant community more than half a million.[27] Revivals and awakenings and folk movements were occurring with increasing frequency.

In 1933, a touch of revival was felt at Moanza, where the first resident pastor came from Banza Manteke, but where missionary supervision came from Vanga. In 1932, there had been only 226 baptisms; but the revival was followed by a folk movement among the Basuku tribe, and 1015 baptisms of believers followed.[28]

At Vanga, Lewis Brown in 1937 noted that the missionary statistics indicated a desperate need for spiritual revival. The two missionary couples decided to spend their siesta time in prayer for an outpouring of the Spirit. No adults joined them for six months, but sixty boys from the school came to show their concern. In March 1938, two teachers were reconciled, and a break followed, without classes from 7 a.m. till noon, time being devoted to confession, prayer and praise. Thefts were made right. On Easter Sunday, 67 were baptized. A blessed influence radiated outwards into the villages, and the effects of the revival were felt to the farthest corners of the Vanga field. Where in 1930 only 297 baptisms were recorded, 1337 believers publicly professed faith in 1939. 'In my opinion,' declared Lewis Brown long afterwards, 'that reviving is the greatest single factor in the growth of the churches of Vanga.'[29]

Many tribes straddle the frontier of Zaire and Angola. In 1935, a Methodist evangelist named Joaquim Bernardo experienced an anointing of the Holy Spirit which changed him from an uncertain, ineffective preacher into 'a man aflame with a passion for souls.' In 1937, Bernardo's team of workers found their ministry stymied in a certain place, pastors and people of two villages being in mutual distrust. One night, one of the pastors came under such conviction that he paddled his canoe twenty miles to seek the forgiveness of the other. A revival swept both villages in turn. A year later, Bishop John Springer was reporting that a thousand people had professed faith in Christ in this indigenous movement in Angola.[30]

Other parts of Central Africa experienced awakenings. In Malawi, about 66,000 baptized Protestants were noted in 1924; in 1936, about 174,000, more than doubling.[31]

In the 1930s, the East African Revival began, and became one of the farthest-reaching and longest-lasting movements in missionary history. It began in Rwanda, where something of a folk movement had been experienced in 1928. In 1931, there was discontent at the Gahini Hospital, which famine had swollen with refugees.[32] The doctor, Joe Church, had insisted upon hospital staff going out to preach like catechists. His senior assistant, Yosiya Kinuka, in a rebellious mood was sent to visit the recently revived Simeoni Nsibambi, brother of Blasio Kigozi, in Uganda. When Kinuka poured out his complaints, claiming that the hospital was 'rotten,' Nsibambi told him: 'The hospital is rotten, because you are rotten. You must open your heart to Jesus.' He returned to ask the forgiveness of his wife and his colleagues. Soon teams of witness began to range far and wide, earning the name 'Abaka'—'those on fire.' In October 1935, a larger team held a week's convention at Kabale, in Western Uganda, in which revival and physical phenomena occurred.[33]

Blasio Kigozi died in 1936. At this time, Joe Church was circulating among friends of the Mission a call for prayer, and from this time forward, the smouldering fires flamed up. Simultaneously, there were manifestations of conviction of sin at Gahini, Kabale, Shyira, Kigeme, Buhiga and Matana in various parts of Rwanda and Burundi, and soon revivals were occurring across the borders in Uganda, that same year; then teams visited Kenya in 1937, and from Kabete revival groups sprang up among the Kikuyu; and during the following year, the Kenya Luo were moved; African leaders in Tanganyika were revived also in 1937.[34] The revived folk were designated 'Abalokole' or 'Saved Ones.'

The East African Revival movement began in the Anglican fellowship, but it spread to many other denominations in the field. It developed peculiarities.[35] At that time, the great revival of 1927-1939 was spreading in China, completely non-partisan, thoroughly interdenominational.[36] The East African movement became thoroughly interdenominational, but it developed a somewhat partisan spirit. Its adherents were strengthened through sharing in close fellowship, but some showed a tendency to look down upon those who had not reached blessing in the same way.[37] Anglican Evangelicals were accustomed to act as a party within a wider fellowship in England—the Established Church; so the movement did not become schismatic. But it often treated other equally evangelical people as outsiders.

The movement stressed confession of sin, a 'confessing' to be maintained daily. This promoted holiness of living but it also brought about an inclination to suspect others and an attitude of 'spiritual detective,' thus inviting censoriousness. But major virtues outweighed minor vices in the movement.[38]

The East African Revival Movement itself thus became an 'ecclesiola in ecclesia' rather than a separatist movement. By staying within the organized Church, it began to provide leadership for the whole Church—in fact, in later years, in one sector at least, its opponents who organized a counter-movement within the Church found themselves outside in schism resulting in independence.[39]

A quarter of a century after the original stirrings in Rwanda, the East African Revival Movement was to pass through a fiery trial of intense persecution during the Mau Mau uprising in Kenya. When nominal Christians among the Kikuyu through fright were staying away from worship, the 'Saved Ones' maintained their witness and their composure —as the writer can testify after meeting in fellowship with them on the edge of the Aberdare Forest, where 'shoot-to-kill' orders were the rule in 1953.[40]

Furthermore, as the spiritual level among 'Saved Ones' in East Africa seemed much higher than among British and American professed Evangelicals, East African evangelists (black and white) were invited to conduct preaching missions in churches in Britain, Canada and the United States, also making a definite impact upon the Christian community in India.[41] This reverse missionary effort had few antecedents in history, Sadhu Sundar Singh of India and Andrew Gih of China being outstanding examples, though neither enlisted a following of the proportions of the Rwanda movement.

In Africa itself, the East African Revival Movement enlisted few followers among Roman or Anglo-Catholics, and after early support it met with opposition from many Africa Inland Mission leaders—perhaps due to a breakaway group, the Trumpeters, who abused opponents.[42] Few observers expected the revival to last a generation, yet, in the 1950s, it triggered awakenings in a wider circle than ever, stirring communities in the Sudan, the Congo, and the trio of East African nations, Kenya, Tanganyika and Uganda.[43] It did not affect the non-Bantu nations of West Africa, nor did it have effect upon Bantu-speaking Christians south of the Zambesi or upon Europeans in South Africa and Rhodesia isolated by apartheid, East African evangelists refused visas.[44]

BETWEEN WARS AWAKENINGS   167

Political events produced a profound effect on Ethiopian evangelization. The regent, Ras Tafari, became 'King of Kings' in 1930. Five years later, his country was invaded by the forces of Mussolini, and the Emperor was driven into exile—where, it may be noted—he cherished a friendship with Rees Howells, the Welsh evangelist who had performed signal service in the southern African awakenings during the second decade of the century.[45]

In some ways, the Italian occupation helped modernize Ethiopia, through the building of roads, development of the country, and the like. But the Italians naturally supported Roman Catholic missions, and discouraged the Protestant churches, whose missionaries had been compelled to leave.

The converts of the Protestant missions were left to their own devices. When missionaries of the Sudan Interior Mission had arrived in Wallamo Province, there was not one Wallamo believer, and not one word of the Scriptures in their language. Nine years later, there were only forty-eight believers, and only a little of the Bible translated for the few who could read. Much the same condition prevailed in other areas when the missionaries were evacuated.

The Coptic and the Muslim priesthoods fitted usefully into the Italian project of 'divide and conquer,' but the existence of indigenous Evangelical churches disturbed them. The Italians set about a policy of repression, arresting and imprisoning both evangelists and church leaders.

When the missionaries returned, it was to find that the Wallamo believers had multiplied beyond imagination— where there were 48, now there were 10,000.[46] Where there was only one church, now there were a hundred assemblies. And the Wallamo churches had become self-governing and self-supporting and self-propagating. The persecution that the believers had to suffer from the Italians refined the tiny church, and its revival thrust forth evangelists who met the needs of a whole tribe hungry for God.

The awakening among the Wallamo followed immediately on the departure of the missionaries.[47] In Kambatta, two elders spent the month of August 1937 preaching and teaching their new found faith. The early converts spent much of their time itinerating, preaching around a circuit, unpaid. New converts were encouraged to learn to read, and soon they too were using their limited knowledge of the Word to win others. The work of evangelization was accelerated by miraculous healings.

Before long, the work began to spill over the bounds of the areas being evangelized into districts farther away which called for resident preachers and teachers. In 1940, the Ocholo district was entered by evangelists from Wallamo. Refugees from Kullo, where a dialect of Wallaminya was spoken, were evangelized by Wallamo preachers also.[48]

After the defeat of the Italians and the reinstatement of the Ethiopian Emperor, persecution of the Evangelicals did not cease; rather, the Orthodox Church provided most of the persecution.[49] The conversion of many other people in jail through the witness of the believers often precipitated their release. The police tired of acting as unpaid hosts of the evangelists. Yet a severe penalty was paid by the Evangelicals. In 1951, twelve believers were arrested in Chencha, and three died in prison. Persecution marked the growth of the Church in Sidamo, but in a few years there were fifty churches in the area. Most of the persecution was local, and the Government at Addis Ababa punished the persecutors when evidence was submitted to them.

In 1942, there were eighty churches in Wallamo; in 1945, 150; in 1950, 200; in 1955, 250; in 1960, 334; in 1965, 340; in 1970, 493; in Kambatta, there were seventy churches in 1942; in 1945, 100; in 1950, 145; in 1955, 170; in 1960, 216; in 1965, 312; in 1970, 333. In 1950, there were only three churches in Sidamo, but by 1970 there were 191; in Darassa, eighteen churches in 1955 became 141 in 1970; and similar growth was reported in other fields.[50]

The Sudan Interior Mission's statistics indicated that a hundred and fifty churches in 1942 became 250 in 1945, 800 in 1960, and more than 1500 in 1970.[51] The average church membership was small, 100-120. Out of seeming defeat came one of the greatest triumphs of church expansion in the history of Ethiopia. The same kind of reports were given by other missionary societies sharing in the general awakening among the non-Coptic, non-Muslim peoples.

The Hermannsburg Mission found that the Spirit of God had moved mightily among the Galla tribespeople, a folk movement developing. The converts of the Swedish Mission and of the United Presbyterians also multiplied vastly, and the awakenings spread throughout sectors of Ethiopia, in all non-Coptic and non-Muslim areas.[52] Missionaries believed that a new day had dawned in Ethiopia.

19

EVANGELISM IN TENSION

In the quarter of a century after the establishment of the Union of South Africa, the population of the country nearly doubled, European and non- European alike. The proportion of church membership and adherence remained much the same among Europeans—54% adhering to the three Dutch Reformed Churches, Anglicans decreasing from 20% to 17%, while Baptists, Congregationalists, Lutherans, Methodists, and Presbyterians and other Protestants accounted for 15%, more or less, only the Methodists gaining (6% to 7%).[1] The Roman Catholic Church remained less than 5%.

In South Africa, less than 1% of the European population maintained no church loyalty, as compared with 13% in the 1930s in the Commonwealth of Australia.[2] It could be said that European church membership and adherence was holding its position. But, in the same quarter of a century, among the Bantu peoples of South Africa, Christian loyalty rose from a third to a half of the total population. Of these, the Dutch Reformed affiliation rose to 5%, the Anglican (which included a vigorous evangelical missionary element) to 7%, the other Protestants from 19% to 22%, of which Methodism accounted for exactly half, while African Independent bodies rose to 14% of the total non-European population, or about a million adherents. Only 3% of the non-Europeans held to Islam, Hinduism and the like.[3] It seemed obvious that the native Bantu animism was capitulating to Christianity of some form or other.

In South Africa, there was tension between the two major European elements; there was tension between Coloured in the Cape or Indians in Natal and the white population; there was tension between the Bantu peoples and the others. Yet, despite these tensions or because of them, the Christian cause maintained itself in the dominant culture and rapidly advanced in the others. One of the major factors seemed to be evangelism, whether that of the historic Protestant Churches or of the emerging African Independent bodies. Neither hindering nationalism nor racism prevented it.

Of the Dutch Reformed bodies, the historic Nederduits Gereformeerde Kerk manifested the greatest concern for evangelism, a legacy of the great revival of 1860 which was celebrated each year with a week of evangelistic and revival services at the season of Pentecost.[4] In every generation, the Dutch Reformed Church (N.G.K.) raised up an outstanding minister to carry on the tradition of the younger Andrew Murray, who combined an advocacy of holy living with a zeal for evangelism, set in a practice of loyal churchmanship.[5]

Alone of the three Dutch Reformed bodies, the Nederduits Gereformeerde Kerk possessed a large body of clergy and people willing to cooperate with like-minded English-speaking people in the other denominations. True, some of the N. G. K. dominies disdained cooperation with English-speaking churches in evangelism, generally because of an antipathy of political origin. But in every interdenominational effort in evangelism, the Dutch Reformed Church (N. G. K.) was likely to supply half the support, even though most of the visiting evangelists were English-speaking.[6]

Support was given by the minority Church of England in South Africa, an autonomous body in opposition to the Church of the Province of South Africa.[7] There were occasions on which Anglican clergy of the larger, more Anglo-Catholic organization cooperated in interdenominational efforts — the present writer, for instance, enjoyed the support in the 'chair' of such Anglican leaders as the Archbishop of Cape Town and the Bishop of Johannesburg.[8] But, in most cases, interdenominational evangelism lacked Anglican support.

The Methodists inherited a legacy of evangelism from the nineteenth century, and although anti-evangelistic attitudes developed with the rise of liberal theology, Methodist participation in mass evangelism was usually forthcoming. That of the Baptists and the minority Church of England in South Africa was automatic.[9] Presbyterians cooperated on many occasions, Congregationalists less so.

After World War I, Pentecostalism provided a new force in evangelism in South Africa, the Apostolic Faith Mission attracting quite a following of Afrikaners, the Assemblies of God reaching many of other tongues. Neither body was made very welcome in interdenominational campaigns, for fear of proselytism, but both practised ardent evangelism. The Assemblies of God developed a considerable Bantu ministry, while the Apostolic influence (like that of the Zion mission of John Dowie) shaped African Independency.[10]

In the early 1930s, Lionel B. Fletcher, an Australian pastor-evangelist with considerable experience in Great Britain, Australia and New Zealand, became confident that 'a wave of religious revival was on the point of gathering to sweep the world.'[11] The Movement for World Evangelization based at Mildmay (London) appointed him Empire Evangelist and sponsored him around the world. He seemed not to make an impression in Canada and the United States,[12] but he soon became the best-known evangelist in the rest of the British Commonwealth.[13]

While revivals and awakenings were occurring up north in black Africa, there was a rising tide of interest in South Africa. Fletcher made three visits to the Union, in 1934, 1936, and 1938. He added many thousands of converts to the South African Churches.[14]

Fletcher conducted evangelistic campaigns with widest support in Pretoria, then Johannesburg, Pietermaritzburg, Durban, East London, Port Elizabeth, Wynberg and Cape Town during the middle months of 1934.[15] He regarded the response to the evangelistic appeal the greatest he had ever known. From Cape Town, his messages were relayed to points near and far, even to Bloemfontein and Kimberley. Enormous crowds filled available accommodation. Fully 25% of the inquirers were of Dutch Reformed background, Methodist 23%, Presbyterian and Congregational much in proportion to strength, Baptist far higher, Church of the Province far lower, though there was a high percentage of other Anglicans. More than seven thousand inquirers were registered. Most encouraging was the cordial cooperation of Dutch Reformed churches in many cities, often the biggest church being used for the interdenominational meetings. It remained to integrate the inquirers into church life.[16]

Lionel Fletcher returned in 1936.[17] He campaigned with significant success in Stellenbosch, Grahamstown, King-William's-Town, Uitenhage, Kimberley, Germiston, and Bloemfontein, with visits to Salisbury and Bulawayo in Rhodesia. Again there was a great response, smaller but in proportion to population. Again the emphasis was one of evangelism. In 1938, Fletcher visited South Africa for a last time, ministering in Dundee, Umtata, Queenstown, Beaufort West, Oudtshoorn, Graff-Reinet, Cradock, and Wellington.[18] These were smaller towns, but strategic. It was said that 18,000 in all registered as inquirers in the Fletcher campaigns, in fourteen months of ministry.[19]

In July 1936, Fletcher's South African sponsors invited a
young Irish-born evangelist for revival ministry in the larger
cities.[20] A scholarly bishop reviewed it thus:[21]

> Meetings in Central Baptist Church (Durban) became over-
> crowded, with people standing in doorways and vestibules, in
> overflow meetings and outside the church windows. Hundreds
> of people professed conversion in five week-night services,
> though the various topics chosen for preaching were meant
> for the Christians. Two thousand people gathered in the
> City Hall on Sunday afternoon and an even larger crowd in
> the Princes Theatre on Sunday evening with a tenth of those
> attending making public profession of faith. In Bloemfontein,
> the Orr Campaign packed the Town Hall and brought a
> thousand inquirers. The Johannesburg meetings were spon-
> sored by the Witwatersrand Church Council, and began with
> noonday meetings in Wesley Hall, evening meetings in Cen-
> tenary Hall in De Villiers Street, both series being trans-
> ferred to the larger Central Hall to accommodate the crowds.
> The final meetings on Sunday were held in the Bijou Theatre,
> with more than 2000 people present in each service. Again
> there were more than 1000 inquirers in the campaign, 55%
> Dutch Reformed, 15% Methodist, 8% Anglican, 4% Baptist,
> and 3% Presbyterian. After meetings in Eastern Province
> cities, Edwin Orr was welcomed by the Cape Peninsula
> Church Council to Cape Town where the Evangelical Fellow-
> ship organized the mission in the historic Groote Kerk, South
> Africa's oldest and biggest church . . . Orr completed his
> tour in South Africa. He travelled 12,000 miles in eight
> weeks, and spoke in 120 meetings. Over 100,000 people had
> listened to his addresses, given generally in town halls or
> large churches. Over fifty per cent of the people to whom
> Orr preached belonged to the Dutch Reformed Church.
> There were different degrees of revival in various places
> according to the readiness of the people. Several thousand
> persons made public profession of faith in Christ. One of
> the converts who became a Methodist minister wrote that
> hundreds of these converts . . . included pastors, evangelists,
> teachers and missionaries (who) formed a committee of
> converts to sponsor the 1953 Orr series. Their chairman
> was a Methodist minister, their secretary an evangelist
> who served ably as President of the national Youth for Christ
> work. The 1953 campaigns were supported by the Archbishop
> of Capetown, Anglican and Lutheran bishops, the Moderators
> of the Dutch Reformed and Presbyterian Churches, and the
> Presidents of the Methodist, Baptist, Congregational, and
> Disciples connections in South Africa.[22]

At the same time, in 1936, there was a spirit of revival
manifested among the Bantu peoples in South Africa.

One of the more exotic fringe groups of Evangelicalism in America was the Christian Catholic Church, founded by an Australian, John Alexander Dowie, and based at the city of Zion, Illinois, a wholly religious foundation. Dowie proclaimed himself the Prophet Elijah, the restorer, and soon suffered delusions of grandeur followed by disgrace.[23]

In 1904, Dowie sent a missionary, Daniel Bryant, to South Africa, where he baptized a score or more Africans and formed the Apostolic Faith Church in Johannesburg, an arm of the Christian Catholic Church in Zion.[24] This designation 'Zion' provided the clue to the origin of so many African Independent Churches which readily adopted the name Zion, and many of their founders seemed influenced by Dowie's adoption of the role of prophet and his delusions of grandeur.

In 1908, certain Pentecostal missionaries persuaded the Zion disciples that they lacked the pentecostal baptism, so the Apostolic Faith Mission was founded in 1910, chiefly by Zion leaders who had adopted pentecostal doctrine.[25] This Apostolic Faith Mission spread rapidly among Afrikaners, whose inhibitions about race soon directed the Church into a segregated fellowship. Members of the Apostolic Faith Mission rose to high positions in South African government, and one well-known to the writer became a world figure in the Charismatic Movement of the latter half of the twentieth century—Dr. David du Plessis.[26]

The Bantu pastors of the Apostolic Faith constituency drifted into independency. From this Apostolic-Pentecostal-Zionist tradition, a host of African Independent bodies soon developed. Scholars, following Bengt Sundkler, have divided the African Independent Churches into three categories: (1) Ethiopian, representing reaction against racial domination of Bantu by European; (2) Zionist, influenced by the prophetic notions of the Zion missionaries; and (3) Messianic, where the leader claims the place of a Saviour.[27] The latter groups are regarded as non-Christian.

The Bantu Independent Churches, appealing to feelings of race, rapidly multiplied their following, two-thirds of their folk being converts from paganism, according to some. By 1967, they numbered three million in South Africa.[28] They had few links with historic Protestantism, but a farseeing missionary of the Assemblies of God, Fred Burke, set up a diploma-granting Bible School for their new leaders, thus influencing hundreds of students and thousands of correspondents in key positions by elementary Bible teaching.[29]

The Assemblies of God in South Africa developed from the work of R. M. Turney and his friends, and became an independent organization in 1932. The polarization of South African society separated this missionary body into African and European divisions, the white congregations operating as European Pentecostal churches, the black as African, sharing the same body of doctrine and practice.[30]

From the background of the Assemblies of God arose a Bantu evangelist of the stature of Charles Pamla.[31] Son of a Lutheran pastor, Nicholas Bhengu was born in Zululand in 1909, but ran away to Kimberley and joined the Communist party. He broke off his connection therewith as a result of being converted in a Pentecostal church maintained by two young Americans. In 1936, Bhengu completed his studies at the South Africa General Mission Bible School. Working as a court interpreter, he became perfect in English and proficient in Afrikaans, speaking exquisite Zulu and fluent Xhosa, managing also in Seswati, Shangaan and Sotho. (He interpreted the present writer's address into Xhosa in East London, and it was as effective as the best of his experience.)

Nicholas Bhengu preached all over South Africa, with huge success, but it was in East London that his most start-ling work was done. In the break-up of Bantu tribal society through the migration from the kraals to the locations near the cities, restraint gave way to crime, drunkenness and immorality. Bhengu declared war on crime. His preaching provoked hearers to confess murder, robbery and the like. Attempts have been made by 'tsotsis' (hooligans) to kill the evangelist. Surprising to some, but not to others equally concerned for social justice, Bhengu supports the idea of parallel development rather than integration, insisting that only thus can the black man achieve a status which will gain social recognition.[32] Chief Albert Luthuli, president of the African National Congress, respected Bhengu as a sincere and honest man; and Bhengu regarded Luthuli as 'one of the best' Bantu Christians— though each had reservations about the other's political attitudes.[33] But Manilal Gandhi branded Bhengu as a traitor.

The writer visited Bhengu in his East London assembly. It was a dynamic service. Shortly before the visit, Bhengu baptized thirteen hundred converts upon profession of faith before 7000 witnesses at Eastertime.[34] Such was the impact against violent crime that the Government noted Bhengu as a constructive force in society.

Consequently, Nicholas Bhengu has been able to travel freely. (The writer has met him twelve thousand miles from home). He has journeyed through other African states as far as Kenya; he has visited Japan; he has ministered in Britain, Canada and the United States; he was an adviser to the World Pentecostal Conference in Toronto; and yet he is not a narrow Pentecostal, feeling fellowship as much with the Baptists, preaching for all denominations, referring converts to Anglican churches on occasion.

It is interesting that the most effective ministry among the Natal Indians is carried on by another very moderate Pentecostal, Pastor Rowlands, an Englishman.[35] The Natal Indians have become almost completely Anglicized, giving up their mother tongues for use of the lingua franca. They have developed many churches of various denominational affiliation, but support their own congregations as part of a tightly knit, hard working and prosperous community.

The number of domestic servants, male and female, in the great cities of South Africa exceeded quarter of a million when a former Pretoria postmaster extended his family worship with the servants into a Garage and Kitchen Mission. Many Bantu folk, seeking work in town, found a faith.[36]

Hans von Staden was born in the year 1905 and 'born again' twenty-one years later. He experienced an initial filling of the Spirit during a time of refreshing at the University of Stellenbosch. In 1942, his heart was touched by a sense of the need of the Bantu-speaking masses in the 'locations' in which they were settling around South Africa's great cities.

In the 1950s, Mr. and Mrs. Hans von Staden decided to devote themselves to the evangelization of the locations. Von Staden was especially struck by the declaration of an overseas evangelist that the future of Bantu folk would be decided in the locations rather than the kraals.[37] Since that time, the Dorothea Mission has spread to the major locations of South Africa, to Rhodesia, and to farther afield, missions being successfully carried through in Zambia and Kenya.

The Dorothea Mission evangelists used tents to reach the inhabitants of the locations.[38] Many were their adventures and deliverances. In Moroka, near Johannesburg, African evangelists were sleeping as usual in the tent when a group of men with incendiary torches approached, intending to burn it down. They fled at the sight—as they thought—of armed soldiers guarding the tent, but the evangelists gave thanks for the protection of angels, they insisted.[39]

The Nationalist Government of South Africa embarked on a policy of relocating to self-contained townships the non-European populations squatting near the cities—townships in which conditions were much better than in the shanty-towns hitherto occupied by the work force. Being detached from traditional relations, the people of the townships were much more responsive than were their kinsfolk back in the kraals of the Bantu territories. Evangelism in the locations therefore proved most opportune.

Unlike other missions, the Dorothea Mission performed its evangelistic ministry as a service auxiliary, urging its converts to join existing churches but offering Bible study correspondence courses.[40] The Mission developed Bible School facilities outside the Republic also.

In 1959, the missionaries of the Dorothea Mission met during the season of Pentecost, when many churches in the country were commemorating the Awakening of 1860.[41] A spirit of revival entered into the intercessors, mealtimes and sleep forgotten in a round of prayer meetings. Revival proved to be the precursor to advance.

Next year, the Dorothea Mission extended operations to Zambia, actually beginning at mid-year. Just one convert was registered in the tent on the first day, two on the second, and three on the third; but a hundred had made professions of faith by the end of July.[42]

A call from Ds. Marthinus Daneel of Salisbury, Rhodesia, encouraged the Dorothea missionaries to aim for a thousand converts in the locations nearby. Despite attacks by a mob, about five hundred people made public profession of faith in the ministry in the Salisbury townships.[43]

All the while, the historic denominations of South Africa have been increasing their Bantu-directed activities. The Dutch Reformed Church in every province increased its missionary contribution in men and money.[44] The Methodists maintained their lead as a Bantu-winning denomination. The Presbyterians, both South African churches and Scottish missions, extended their ministry in South Africa and the countries to the north.[45] The Baptists developed their work in the eastern part of the Union,[46] and in Lambaland (Zambia). The Congregational Union,[47] and the London Missionary Society, maintained their work among Coloured and Bantu. The Church of England in South Africa attracted more than 30,000 Bantu to membership;[48] the Church of the Province served quarter of a million Coloured, half a million Bantu.

The ever-increasing activity of South African Churches among the non-European peoples within their own borders has caused surprise among overseas critics who have been inclined to credit them with neglect or indifference.[49] Added to their efforts have been the work of overseas missionary societies representing denominations with related European Churches in South Africa, and the work of interdenominational societies such as the Africa Evangelical Fellowship (South Africa General Mission) and Evangelical Alliance Mission (Scandinavian Alliance Mission).[50] The missionaries of most of these societies working with Bantu people nevertheless maintained fellowship with South African congregational life. It is of great significance that most of the education of the non-European children, until the transfer of the schools to the national government, was carried on by these missions, South African and overseas. That was the year 1953, when the National Party consolidated its power in parliament.

The writer happened to be in South Africa that year, in interdenominational campaigns, ten weeks in the Cape area with much revival and hundreds of inquirers; ten weeks in the Pretoria-Johannesburg-Rand complex, filling Central Baptist and Wesley Churches and overflowing Groot Kerk in Pretoria, 700 inquirers in the area; ten weeks in the coastal cities of Port Elizabeth, East London, and Durban, the Anglican, Dutch Reformed and Interdenominational Ministers' Fraternal supporting the Port Elizabeth effort which filled St. John's and the Moederkerk; and ten weeks in interior cities, Bloemfontein, Kimberley and faraway Windhoek.[51] At the same time, an apologetics evangelism was carried on in the universities and high schools, and in the latter there were 10,000 inquirers—recommitment of luke-warm, claiming of assurance, first public profession of faith, and outright conversion.[52] In 1958, the President of the Methodist Conference, Edgar Wilkinson, commented: 'The ministry met with remarkable response, and there are many young people throughout South Africa (some still meeting regularly in Bible class) who made their decision for Christ as a result of (the) appeal to their mind and heart and will.'[53] The work was effective in Afrikaans and English medium. Principal Stan Edkins reported in 1958 that the great major-ity of the inquirers at Rondebosch High—where 115 lads responded and 100 attended a weekly instruction class—had continued in the faith, and that a number of these commenced to study for the ministry of the churches.[54]

The post-war period produced an outstanding evangelist in South Africa, an able preacher and capable musician— Denis G. Clark. Clark had been converted during the Orr campaign in Johannesburg in 1936. He was of Brethren background, but had drifted a long way from his family faith, threatened with expulsion from school, addicted to profanity. His musical talent found an outlet in the entertainment field, and he became a dance band leader. Curiosity drew him to the campaign meetings, where someone asked him to usher. He was converted with song-sheets still in his hands, and he realized that he had been delivered from swearing.

In 1952, Denis Clark resigned a directorship in business and a career in accountancy.[55] He was appointed director of Youth for Christ in South Africa and engaged in a fruitful ministry of evangelism and renewal, interdenominational and international. He left the South African Youth for Christ work in the capable hands of Jim Ferguson, afterwards a missionary in Chile. Clark became European Director of Youth for Christ, a key leader in the Copenhagen Youth for Christ World Congress. His ministry became popular in Scandinavia, but he made his base in Britain, more and more becoming an advocate of renewal as well as an evangelist.

The same years produced a capable Dutch Reformed evangelist, Wilhelm Marais, who campaigned with Afrikaans and English-speaking cooperation.[56] Becoming a pastoral evangelist, Marais engaged in significant ministry in the goldfields of the Orange Free State at Welkom. He became a doctoral graduate of the University of South Africa. Able pastoral evangelists were not rare in that denomination.

Meanwhile, during the mid-1950s, the Student Christian Association (C. S. V.) was finally divided into independent associations along linguistic lines. The English-speaking Student Christian Association was further rent by liberal-conservative tensions, reducing the general effectiveness of united student evangelism in the growing universities. In general, South African universities escaped the debauchery which accompanied worldwide student unrest, though unrest occurred in various academic communities.

Across the South Atlantic, in Latin America, a movement mobilizing the churches for renewal and evangelism had begun in the 1960s. Evangelism-in-Depth was paralleled in South Africa by Project Evangelism, a practical outworking of the ministry of a South African layman, Ken Terhoven, and his associates.

Ken Terhoven, of Netherlands parentage, became an interdenominational evangelist through Youth for Christ, and an international one by reason of a remarkable work done among hippie troglodytes in the caves of Derbyshire in England. Returning to South Africa in 1967, Terhoven sought to enlist Afrikaans and English-speaking support for city-wide project evangelism, training and mobilizing the churches and their members for outreach, and engaging in both conventional and unconventional evangelism.

A score or more churches supported an East London area project that involved ten ordained evangelists and many lay workers.[57] The City Hall was overcrowded, many inquirers being given counsel. Similarly, a project campaign was held in Cape Town; a Port Elizabeth project filled Feathermarket Hall besides crowding meetings in a large Dutch Reformed church there.

Project campaigns were undertaken in Worcester, Parow, Ladysmith, Newcastle, Hillary, Cathcart, Beaufort West, Knysna and Port Shepstone. The efforts were continued in the 1970s, a cooperative simultaneous campaign in Benoni concluding in a 3000-capacity tent. Project evangelism also included missionary safaris in areas of Bantu population.

A white South African, born in Lesotho, educated in Natal, was converted at Cambridge University and completed his graduate work at Fuller Theological Seminary in California where he laid plans for African Enterprise, team evangelism. Michael Cassidy and his colleagues tackled various towns and universities in South Africa, handicapped unfortunately by a paucity of Dutch Reformed support. African Enterprise in 1967 held a mission to youth in the Cape Town suburbs, followed by a series of lectures and discussions in the great University of the Witwatersrand, the main lectures drawing five hundred students daily.[58] In 1969, the team conducted a mission to the University of Cape Town, attracting 1500 or so to midday symposia, half that number at night.

In March of 1973, African Enterprise helped sponsor an all-Africa Congress on Evangelism, with Dr. Billy Graham as the main speaker. The congress meetings were interracial, 720 delegates coming from thirty denominations and as many service organizations, the South African Council of Churches co-sponsoring the rally, for which Durban was chosen as the venue. On St. Patrick's Day, 45,000 people gathered at the King's Park Stadium, and 3500 inquirers responded to Graham's invitation.[59]

On Sunday 25th March, the same evangelist addressed a rally in Wanderers Stadium in Johannesburg, 60,000 people of all races and denominations attending. Contingents came in by train and bus and plane from a wide radius in South Africa, principally from the towns and locations of the great Gold Reef. The rally was sponsored by Youth for Christ. The 4000 inquirers were instructed in a dozen languages and dialects by 2000 volunteers.[60]

The major work of evangelism in South Africa has been done in hundreds of churches and in auxiliary organizations of evangelical conviction. The great rallies served their purpose as occasions of celebration and harvesting.

Thus evangelism continued through the years of tension. The conclusion is inescapable that despite—or because of —the tensions with which South Africa has been beset, the things which Churches in other countries covet, encouraging church attendance, interest in matters spiritual, generosity to spiritual causes, desire for betterment, evangelism at home and missionary interest farther afield, all have been experienced in higher degree among all races than in any similar commonwealth. That South Africa's problems loom so large must be viewed in perspective with the observation that no other country in the world faces the same problems in such magnitude. The South African Churches appear to be far from dead.

20

THE WINDS OF CHANGE

The writer spent a year in Africa in 1953, having visited more than thirty of its countries south of the Sahara and observing a quickening tempo in the forces for change. The year concluded with experiences in Mau Mau territory. In 1960, the British Prime Minister, Harold MacMillan, coined a new phrase in addressing the South African Parliament on the African situation—'the winds of change.'

Before the seven years had passed, the Gold Coast was granted independence, and became a sovereign state within the British Commonwealth as Ghana. Soon the 'winds of change' reached gale force, and country after country in black Africa was granted freedom by France or Britain—and South Africa became a republic.

There were some observers who felt that these winds blew too soon in some places, some who wished that some kind of consortium of developed nations could have prepared the backward states for self-government, but the 'cold war' between western democracies and communist dictatorships made any such arrangement unworkable, and independence was granted country after country, whether ready for it or otherwise.

Despite the preoccupation of the African elite with their agitation for independence and the turmoil and unrest among the masses, the growth of Christianity went on by leaps and bounds, by steady growth and by great awakenings.

The 1950s brought about no diminishing of the revival in Rwanda-Burundi, nor in nearby Uganda. Teams began to go forth from East Africa, European-African in composition, travelling far afield to India and Pakistan, Australia and New Guinea, Canada and United States, Great Britain and Europe, even to Brazil.[1] African teams overflowed into the nearby countries, the Sudan, Congo, Tanganyika and Kenya. There was a gathering storm in Kenya, but the East African Revival not only weathered it, but drew strength in reverse from it, for by 1957, Protestant membership had increased to 291,118 from 134,037, community to 610,561 from 330,666.[2]

The Mau Mau were a secret society, bound by horrifying oaths, committed to driving the Europeans and Asians out of East Africa, by extermination if need be. Their methods became more and more ruthless, directed not only against the government but against the settlers, their children, and against all Africans who would not support the terror.

There were several factors in the rise of the Mau Mau. Resentment of missionary opposition to various uncouth native practices, such as female circumcision, helped to develop a system of Kikuyu schools from which the mission influence was excluded; discontent with the dominance of white settlers who had flocked to Kenya from World War I onwards, purchasing the best land in the highlands; and the support for nationalism by forces opposed to democracy in even the western countries.

Eighteen hundred people had attended a convention for the deepening of the spiritual life sponsored by the Kenya leaders of the revival movement in August 1948. In 1949, five thousand attended.[3] In 1950, the convention grew, but the Mau Mau terror was beginning. Vernacular newspapers contained columns of direct attack on the Christian message and on the holding of such conventions.

Leonard Beecher, Anglican Archbishop, studied closely the Revival in Kenya, and validated it as an authentic movement of the Spirit by its spontaneity and by its close relevance to the needs of the hour.[4] He agreed that there had been extravagances that tended to mar the effectiveness of the Revival. In its earlier stages, there was uncontrolled dancing and singing, over-emphasized confessionalism and unwise leadership; but he insisted that, despite the use of a theological jargon, the revival leaders were maturing and in necessary ways the movement was disciplining itself.

In Nairobi, the 'Saved Ones' conducted a convention in the heart of the worst of the Mau Mau dominated districts. Two thousand Kikuyu Christians sat in orderly fashion in an open air arena, led by a team of Kikuyu revivalists, every one of whom was a marked man.[5] The Europeans attending took their lives into their own hands. The speaker was a Kikuyu clergyman, face scarred, partly paralysed from a slashing received for refusing to deny Christ. His was a message of freedom, freedom from hatred of other tribes and races, freedom from fear. It was the same in a little gathering on the edge of the Aberdare Forest, addressed by the writer, the meeting concluded with singing 'Tukutendereza Yesu.'[6]

There were two reasons for the special attack upon the Revival partisans: the revivalists boldly preached Jesus, whom the Mau Mau affirmed was a cunning European or Asian, incredible blasphemies being uttered against Him; the Revival broke down racial distrust and separation, and called every believer 'brother' regardless of tribe or race.[7]

The Archbishop of East Africa assured the writer that, when a great falling-away occurred in Kenya, due to fear of Mau Mau terror, the bulk of those who maintained their witness cheerfully and fearlessly were the revived people. Many were tortured, and some were killed. It took British forces seven years to stamp out the uprising, but the East African colonial authorities initiated a plan for the eventual independence of the territories.

Ten thousand Mau Mau terrorists were killed; thousands were taken prisoner and thousands gave themselves up. In the detention camps, the missionaries tackled the matter of the evangelization of the prisoners, and a great ingathering followed, adding to the strength of evangelical faith when peace was re-established.

The revival movement affected Tanganyika in due course. Australian Evangelical Anglicans took over the diocese of Central Tanganyika in 1927.[8] The work of evangelizing the Wagogo proved particularly difficult. In the 1930s, there was a decided impact made by revived Africans from the west (Uganda), but resistance rose partly because of a tone of forthrightness manifested by revivalists. In the 1950s, a team of Africans held a convention at Mvumi, with striking results. In 1951, another convention was held at Kilimatinde and a spirit of repentance, confession and conversion was poured out. Evangelistic missions were held here and there, including one in the cathedral at Dodoma. The movement was primarily one of the revival of the body of believers, but resulted in winning outsiders as well.   Not only were the Anglican churches moved, but Lutherans, Mennonites, Methodists, Moravians and Presbyterians and others.[9] In 1936, there were 133,000 baptized Protestants; within twenty years, the number of communicants had reached 263,000. Independence came to Tanganyika in 1961 without bloodshed, and Julius Nyerere, a Christian of strong convictions, a former teacher in a Roman Catholic school, became premier. It was otherwise in Zanzibar, where the wrath of oppressed Africans, abetted by revolutionary forces from outside, was directed against the Arab elite.

In the Sudan, the impact of the Revival resulted in Kuku, Kakwa and other tribal movements seceding from Anglican fellowship,[10] maintaining worship in forms of praise, then being re-absorbed into the Episcopal Church of the Sudan. Christians in the Sudan were to enter a bloodbath in the 1960s as the Muslim North sought to dominate the Christian South. Missionaries were driven out, and black Christians took to the bush, churches burned and homes destroyed.

Kenneth Kaunda, 1964 president of the emergent nation of Zambia, was born into a pastor's family, and maintained a friendly attitude towards evangelical Christianity. By 1957, membership in Zambian Protestant churches had risen to seventy thousand, with a community of quarter of a million. The largest Protestant denomination was that founded by the Dutch Reformed Church of South Africa.[11] Alice Lenshina drew a hundred thousand people out of Roman Catholic and Protestant communities, forming the exotic Lumpa Church, which the Zambian armed forces crushed, killing 700 people. In Malawi, where the president of the emergent nation, Hastings Banda, was also a product of evangelical missions, nearly a quarter of a million were members of Protestant Churches, half a million or more in their community.[12]

In the 1950s, tribal response to the message of the Word proclaimed by Methodists and Free Methodist workers in Mozambique, or among Mozambique miners on the Rand, began to increase rapidly.[13] The whole Protestant membership (including Anglicans) gained more than 20% in five years. Apart from transplantings of Zionism from Johannesburg, there were few secessions in Mozambique. News of the revolt in Angola caused unrest up and down the country.

Kongo tribespeople populated northern Angola as well as western Congo, and movements of revival were shared, as well as political uprisings. The Kimbanguist movement had a profound effect in Angola also; and, in the 1950s, Simao Toco[14] organized an independent church of the same sort. He was deported, but Portuguese persecution augmented his following; when permitted to return, he was welcomed 'as risen from the dead' by great crowds. The rebellion of 1961 added to the growth of his Church of Jesus Christ. During the revolt, the Portuguese authorities blamed Protestantism for the troubles, and many churches suffered persecution. Bloody was the rebellion against white rule, and bloody was the repression.[15] Evangelical Christianity did not lose its appeal either in Angola or among its refugees.

In 1914, C. T. Studd and Alfred Buxton founded in Ituri
the Heart of Africa Mission which developed into the international Worldwide Evangelization Crusade.[16] Within forty
years time, a worshipping community of many thousands had
been gathered into several hundred village churches, served
by literate elders, trained evangelists, and itinerant pastors.
In 1935, an extraordinary revival began at Imbai when Jack
Roberts preached thrice on 'God commandeth all men everywhere to repent.' Confessions of sin and powerful praying
preceded 'floods on the dry ground' and a harvest of souls.

In 1953, at Lubutu (Ituri Forest), a workers' conference
was held, missionaries and nationals speaking on aspects
of the work of the Holy Spirit.[17] Church business lasted all
of one day, and in the evening the missionaries were holding
their usual prayer meeting, the Africans gathering in the
school house for theirs, when suddenly strange loud cryings
were heard. The missionaries found people overcome with
a violent shaking, quite uncontrollable. After a time, they
sought to close the meeting, but it went on for hours, many
standing with their hands upraised, others confessing hidden
sins not to the missionaries or leaders but to some unseen
Power. After the missionaries retired, one was awakened
by his house servant, still shaking, wishing to confess petty
pilfering. The movement proved to be genuine, resulting in
a renewal of the life of the congregation.

At Opienge, to the north, a spirit of conviction had fallen
upon some of the elders.[18] In May, one of them in temper
struck his wife, and was immediately overcome with fearful
remorse. He trembled as he cried to God for forgiveness.
Then a godly woman from Lubutu visited the church, and in
the course of the service jerked and trembled. The people
thought that she was ill, physically or mentally. That night,
she claimed a vision of the Lord, Who told her to clear away
the ashes so that He could light a fire. Strange to relate, a
missionary on trek also had a vision of the people shouting
and shaking and confessing their sins, which filled him with
fear. When the missionary returned, the woman spoke to
the women of the village, the missionary to the men. The
whole place seemed as if charged with an electric current.
Men were falling, jumping, laughing, crying, singing, confessing, and some shaking uncontrollably. 'It was a terrible
sight,' said the missionary, who described it as a spiritual
tornado. The movement next affected the women, then the
younger people in turn. The power was irresistible.

At the week-end, people began arriving from far away, some walking nearly a hundred miles. The meetings that followed were indescribable, some overcome with 'savage joy,' others in an agony of conviction, some jumping and dancing, others staggering or prostrate. Confessions were made of breaking the moral commandments, but also of petty faults. Hardened sinners were converted.

Bomili, also in the Ituri Forest, was next visited by the strange manifestations.[19] A praying missionary began to tremble, feeling even to the fingertips a contact with power. Then the movement swept the compound. Spurgeon's prayer, 'Lord, send us a season of glorious disorder,' was fulfilled at Wamba.[20] People far from the meeting were prostrated, and many spoke of 'the whip of the Holy Spirit' compelling them. To some, it meant an experience of regeneration; to others, it was a filling of the Holy Spirit.

At Ibambi, headquarters of the Mission, the manifestation of revival produced the same agony of conviction, the same joy of forgiveness. Prostration was followed by praising, praying by preaching, resulting in confession by believers and conversion of sinners.[21] At Egbita, the most difficult of the stations, the first meeting went on till 2.30 a.m. with 'frightening' results, the whole company rising to its feet as one man to cry for mercy. Tribe after tribe was moved, and the awakening was felt throughout the area.

Although news of the Rwanda Revival had helped stir up missionaries in the Congo, and through them the Congolese, there were significant differences in the outbreaks. In the movement in the Congo, there was a greater awareness of the Holy Spirit, and the physical manifestations recalled the extravagances of the American frontier 150 years before.

The largest of the Congo mission-related denominations, the Baptists, reported great ingatherings during the years of turmoil, 'evidence of the work of the Holy Spirit even amid tensions and uncertainties,' as the American Baptists saw it.[22] Of the 11,326 baptisms in their fields, three-fourths occurred in the Vanga area in 1960, and in 1964 the Vanga and Busala churches reported one half the 8000 baptisms.

It is impossible to chronicle all the awakenings occurring in the Congo in the 1950s. Communicant membership rose thirty per cent in five years,[23] the community one per cent— which seemed to suggest that the movements made for a deepening of the spiritual life rather than actual evangelism, before the storm of the 1960s broke upon the country.

The Belgian Congo became the Republic of the Congo in mid-1960. Few Congolese possessed secondary, let alone higher education, and the country was plunged into disorder, tribal, factional and regional civil war ensuing, fanned by the intervention of revolutionary and counter-revolutionary forces. The resentment of the population against Belgians flared into attacks upon residents, murder and rape. Tribe attacked tribe, and Tshombe proclaimed the independence of Katanga. Lumumba was murdered. The situation became so chaotic that the United Nations intervened. Bloodletting continued in the various provinces. Tshombe was driven out of Katanga, but in a surprising switch around became prime minister of the Republic. Revolutionary forces set up a rebel republic in Stanleyville, their followers becoming militantly anti-Christian as well as anti-democratic. Missionaries were murdered, nuns were raped, native Christians killed. The Belgians landed paratroopers to rescue hostages and to assist the Congolese Army in crushing the rebellion. White mercenaries remorselessly destroyed the Simba rebellion, and the Congolese Army cleared up after them. Mobutu, a military man, assumed power, dismissing Tshombe, who was later kidnapped to Algeria.[24] In 1967, a handful of white mercenaries and a thousand Katanganese gendarmes defeated Congolese Army forces at Bukavu. When the Congolese re-entered Bukavu, they killed civilians and brutally abused European women innocent of any mischief—the writer was then ministering to refugees across the Rwanda border, so gaining an insight into the brutal cruelty endured by Congo Christians and missionaries during the long decade of civil war and tribal strife.

The years of revival in the 1950s had prepared Congolese Christians for the fiery trial in the decade following. Tales of diabolical cruelty to missionaries were matched by stories of incredible bravery of the Christians. The upsurge of tribal and national feelings aided independent movements, which soon numbered hundreds, making inroads especially into the Roman Catholic Church. Kimbanguism, which had arisen from the Baptist constituency, increased until it became by 1966 the largest independent Church on the African continent. The Baptists, Disciples and Presbyterians were the three largest Protestant denominations. Revival movements were felt in Evangelical congregations of various missions, as (for example) the large-scale awakening in the Tetela tribe served by American Methodist missionaries.[25]

Before 1960, trouble began in Rwanda, the land in which the East African Revival began three decades before. The Bahutu, a Bantu people in feudal servitude to the Batutsi (the tall, aristocratic overlords of Rwanda) overthrew the monarchy and established a republic. Undoubtedly, although the missions were welcomed by the Batutsi, and the White Fathers in particular gained influence by educating the sons of chiefs, the Christian message reached the Bahutu also, and kindled a desire for freedom. The Bahutu rose en masse against their overlords, burning their huts, killing their cattle, beating any who stood in their way. Tutsi believers fled to the mission stations for refuge, which caused more than one incident with the revolting tribesmen. Joe Church, a friend of royalty, became a marked man, and retired to Uganda. Refugees poured into Burundi and Uganda, giving the missionaries an opportunity to evangelize them in their camps. The believers in Rwanda held true to their faith, but irreparable damage was done to the country, bitterness and hatred poisoning the relationship of the masses. The younger generation, unmoved by the Revival, grew up into apathy or antagonism. The ongoing Rwanda Revival, twenty-five years effective, suffered its worst setback.[26]

The Batutsi managed to maintain their position in nearby Burundi, where the tribal bloodletting was postponed until the 1970s. In 1962, a secession of 20,000 from the Anglican Church in southern Burundi occurred but becoming involved in politics it was later suppressed by the government, and a majority returned to the fold. In the meantime, a revival-awakening of great strength occurred in the Danish Baptist mission field.[27] In the 1970s, many of the Bahutu pastors and people were to lose their lives in the tribal slaughter that burst upon Burundi.

On 1st January 1960, Cameroon became a republic and was joined by the British territory of the same name. The coming of independence was heralded by tribal bloodletting as well as armed uprising.[28] In one district, 1% of the total population was slaughtered, and three quarters of all their schools, manses and churches were destroyed. Ten per cent of the population professed a Protestant faith, and they inherited a revival tradition from past movements among American Presbyterian converts. The Cameroon Baptist body, an African establishment, accounted for half the Duala tribe of 70,000 in 1965. A folk movement among Bamileke tribesmen won many thousands a year in the 1960s.[29]

Successive awakenings had greatly augmented the strength of Nigerian Anglicans built by the Church Missionary Society into a community of a million, with a hundred thousand in communicant relationship in 1957.[30] Next in size were the Apostolic Churches, followed by the Baptists, Methodists and the Qua Iboe Mission, raising communicant membership to more than a quarter of a million, community to 1,370,000. In the 1950s, spontaneous revival movements occurred in various parts of Nigeria. In 1956, a missionary reported that 'God did the impossible in reviving the dry bones of the Angwa Takwa territory, 125 miles southeast of Jos.'[31] In 1964, the Bible was published in the Tiv tribal language, feeding into an indigenous Bible school movement which had multiplied to a thousand schools, thanks to a folk movement begun even before the Dutch Reformed Church of South Africa transferred its interests to the Christian Reformed Church of the U.S.A. In 1957, there were 1500 Tiv church members, 11,000 within ten years, while church attenders increased from ten thousand to two hundred thousand.[32]

The writer was in Lagos, Nigeria's capital, the very day that Nigerian federal troops marched against the seceding Ibo territory, Biafra.[33] The tribal bloodletting had begun earlier with the slaughter of Ibos in the Hausa North, and a sanguine civil war erupted. Roman Catholicism dominated the Ibo territory, just as Protestantism (also Irish— Qua Iboe Mission) influenced the Ibibios.

In independent Ghana, the Methodists had fifty thousand or more communicants, a hundred and fifty thousand related community.[34] The Presbyterians claimed thirty-six thousand communicants, and a hundred and ten thousand community! An Apostolic offshoot among the Ga tribe claimed twenty-five thousand communicants, a hundred thousand adherents. The founding president of Ghana, Kwame Nkrumah, professed a Christian faith but showed alarming signs of apostasizing from it. The 'Osagyefo' (Saviour) plunged Ghana into crisis.

Various revival movements were reported in Ivory Coast, working within the Churches. A Methodist prophet, Josue Edjro,[35] engaged in a healing-evangelistic ministry in 1965. In Upper Volta, a movement began among Mossi tribesmen, served by the Christian and Missionary Alliance, and spread across the border into Mali, among the Dogon people.[36] A revival began in 1965 in the Assemblies of God at the capital, Ouagoudougou, and stayed within the fellowship, unlike a previous movement in 1959.[37]

In 1960, Billy Graham embarked upon a 'safari for souls' across the breadth of Africa, obviously more of a harvesting mission than a revival movement. The evangelist received a great welcome from his friends in Liberia. In Ghana, the attendance in three cities numbered 45,000. In Nigeria, the top attendance in Lagos was a hundred thousand. In Rhodesia, attendances ranged from 10,000 to 20,000 in Bulawayo, and 15,000 came out in the rain in Salisbury, with more than a hundred thousand aggregate attendance of all races, 6000 inquirers being counselled. Joe Blinco preceded Graham in Nairobi, drawing fourteen thousand aggregate, and 9000 attended the Graham rally; there were twelve hundred in inquiry sessions. Ethiopian Evangelicals arranged a series in Addis Ababa, 12,000 attending the first Graham rally. It proved a great encouragement to faithful workers.[38]

The 1960s were years of spiritual decline in the English-speaking world, marked by student rioting, permissiveness in sexual relations, an epidemic of venereal disease, an increase of illegitimacy and abortion, and an upsurge of crime. Yet two new movements for the evangelization of Africa rose at this time from the concern of individual English-speaking missioners of transatlantic experience.

In 1951, Dr. R. Kenneth Strachan accompanied the writer and interpreted his messages around South America.[39] As director of the Latin American Mission, the former was much concerned about reaching the masses by some new method or adaptation of methods. In the 1960s, his mission sponsored Evangelism-in-Depth, mobilizing the prayer life of the churches, training personnel, ministerial and lay, engaging in visitation, conducting campaigns of local and regional and national scope, and following up the converts. Strachan was unaware that the same sort of plan had been put into operation in Japan half a century earlier, called Taikyo Dendo.[40] This saturation evangelism proved highly effective, though without provoking a spontaneous revival or significantly adding to long-term church growth.

Saturation evangelism made its appeal to a Sudan Interior missionary, Gerald O. Swank, who adopted some of the methods of Evangelism-in-Depth, but studied carefully the West African conditions of operation. In 1963, he found support among Anglicans, Baptists, Methodists and inter-denominational missions in Nigeria. New Life for All soon developed into an indigenous Nigerian evangelistic movement effective across the country, and farther afield.[41]

Ten thousand people, anxious to witness to the multitudes, were mobilized in the city of Kaduna.[42] They marched six-abreast to the Ahmadu Bello Stadium for a final meeting which climaxed the week of ministry of the American negro evangelist, Howard Jones, of the Graham Association. The message was interpreted into Hausa by Malam Dalhatu, and six hundred of the 16,000 present were counselled.

Teams tackled smaller towns, reaping a harvest. Some churches increased by 25% to 50% in attendance, baptisms by 15% to 35%. The Evangelical Churches of West Africa, numbering nine hundred, grew to eleven hundred in three years, membership increasing from 21,000 to 42,000, with a third of a million people attending their services. The Church of Christ in the Sudan reported similar growth. These denominations, related to the Sudan Interior Mission and the Sudan United Mission respectively, seemed to draw the greatest benefits from the movement, which was backed by the prayers of fifty thousand people meeting daily.

Leaders of New Life for All conducted conferences on evangelism and renewal in Sierra Leone, Ivory Coast, Upper Volta, Mali and Niger, as the movement spread to West African communities. In 1968, a West African Congress on Evangelism was held in Ibadan, drawing five hundred or so delegates from about twenty-five African countries to discuss missionary outreach and strategy.[43] Contact was thus made between West African movements and those in East Africa and countries farther to the south, where another saturation-evangelism movement had been organized.

During the first five months of 1966, Michael Cassidy and his African Enterprise team tackled the land-locked country of Lesotho, completely surrounded by South Africa. The main meetings, lasting fifteen days, drew a thousand to twenty-five hundred nightly in Maseru, the Sotho capital but a small town with five thousand population. There were more than six hundred inquirers.[44]

Preparations for a sustained African Enterprise mission in Nairobi began in October 1969.[45] The various churches of Nairobi cooperated, and more than thirty thousand attended the main rallies, of whom one in ten became inquirers. The major ministry was shared by Michael Cassidy and Festo Kivengere, a Muganda Anglican well-known around the world as an East African Revival evangelist. Follow-up meetings were held in the Anglican Cathedral. Saturation evangelism following recent revival proved much more fruitful.

In 1970, the African Enterprise team moved to the city of Johannesburg, where evangelistic meetings were held in Soweto, the vast African township southwest of the city, led by Ebenezer Sikakane, climaxing at Mofolo Park with 2500 attending, and in Ellis Park, where Europeans gathered to hear Michael Cassidy, the largest attendance being 3000, with 250 inquirers in follow-up.[46]

Festo Kivengere became the evangelist of an East African team, and continued his worldwide ministry under the aegis of African Enterprise, with Zebuloni Kabaza as colleague. A successful simultaneous campaign was held in Dar-es-Salaam in Tanganyika, climaxed in the local stadium. The Anglican Church in Uganda reached a crisis situation in late 1971, with one diocese threatening to secede. A moving of the Holy Spirit in an inter-diocesan council summoned to Kampala brought about a reconciliation.[47] Then, in 1972, Festo Kivengere was appointed Bishop of Kigezi in Uganda, at a time when the outlook for Christians in that country became threatening. Burundi was already distressed with tribal bloodletting, and Uganda was at loggerheads with its neighbours. At this critical juncture, World Vision and African Enterprise convened a pastors' conference in the Makerere University in Kampala, attended by more than 600 ministers from Uganda, Rwanda and Burundi.[48] Never was the ministry of reconciliation more needed. In 1972, the East African team had been invited to take part in an all-Zambia Crusade, organized by New Life for All, but last-minute political interference ruled out the visit.

Conditions in Burundi rapidly deteriorated, the slaughter of Bahutu by dominant Batutsi being described as systematic genocide by some observers.[49] The singling out of educated Bahutu for liquidation inflicted terrible losses on the pastors of the churches, teachers also suffering decimation.

In Africa, south of the Sahara, the winds of change shook the foundations of national and tribal life, stability nowhere in evidence. Yet the preaching of the Good News continued and evangelism demonstrated surprising vitality, seeming to encourage the hopes of Africa becoming in the main a Christian continent.[50]

CONCLUSION

The past two hundred years have been crucial in the relationship between the peoples of Africa and the rest of the world. The challenge of the American Declaration of Independence and of the French Revolution had immediate effects upon South Africa; the extension of British and French imperialism and the European Scramble for Africa affected the whole continent; the industrialization of the developing countries led to the exploitation, for better and for worse, of the undeveloped territories; the rise of the working classes in Europe and North America, the education of the masses, the extension of the franchise, and the organization of trade unions immediately affected South Africa and produced a slow movement for betterment elsewhere.

Since the time of the American and French Revolutions, there have occurred at least seven great worldwide revivals of Evangelical Christianity: first, the revival at the turn of the nineteenth century; second, that of the 1820s and 1830s; third, the one that began immediately before 1860 and continued for a decade; fourth, that of the 1880s and 1890s; fifth, the awakening in the first decade of the twentieth century; sixth, the revivals of the 1920s and 1930s; and seventh, the mid-twentieth century awakening. Some of these movements were major; some were minor; some were more effective on certain continents than others. All of these great awakenings immediately affected the Christian community in South Africa, and within a decade were effective in the rest of Africa, the mission fields.

Evangelical Christendom, when John Wesley died, was confined to Great Britain, Scandinavia, and majorities in Germany, Holland and Switzerland, minorities in France and Hungary, and populations east of the Alleghenies in North America, but Latin America was closed by the intransigent governments of Spain and Portugal, Islam was hostile to the Gospel, the East India Company made missionaries unwelcome in India, and none resided in China, Japan and Korea. The South Seas islanders were savages, as were most of the tribes in unexplored Africa, at whose tip existed a colony of about twenty thousand heedless Europeans.

Throughout the western world were churches assaulted by a revolutionary scepticism. The evangelical denominations were without Sunday Schools, Bible Societies, Home Missions and Foreign Missions—apart from the Moravians and the overseas chaplaincy of the Anglican S. P. G.

A thoroughgoing renewal of numerical strength occurred in the dormant churches in the homelands, and even in the unsettled Cape Colony. The 'turn of the century' awakenings sent off pioneer missionaries to the South Seas, to Latin America, to India and China, and through South Africa to aboriginal Hottentots and immigrant Bantu. Denominational mission societies were founded, Sunday Schools were formed and Bible Societies started their work of distributing the Scriptures, reaching Africa from overseas and rising also among South Africans themselves.

The early nineteenth century awakenings equipped South African churches using both languages with ministers of decided evangelical convictions, with Sunday Schools, and with a host of evangelistic and philanthropic agencies. Thus in South Africa itself, not only missionaries from overseas engaged in the evangelization of the heathen but local revivals stirred up stalwart residents of the country to reach their neighbours of alien race and lesser civilization.

Then a second wave of revival reinforced the foreign missionary invasion of all the continents, and continued its social impact upon the sending countries. Captain Allen Gardiner who reached the Zulus of Natal with the Gospel pioneered in the wilds of South America and died tragically. Missionaries reconnoitred the citadels of Islam. William Carey was followed by societies ready to evangelize India. Robert Morrison opened a way for missionaries to settle in the treaty ports of China. Evangelism in Oceania preceded extensive awakenings in Hawaii and the other Polynesian kingdoms. Missionaries pushed north, using South Africa as a base, and pioneers like David Livingstone explored the African hinterlands.

The epic Great Trek of the Cape Boers brought a hardworking, God-fearing people into the wilderness, carrying with them the daily practice of the faith of Calvin and Knox. They helped to set high standards of community integrity. The English-speaking settlers of 1820, sharing in the expansion of the South African nation, also owed much to the revivals of Napoleonic times. In their newly-founded towns there was no lack of true religion.

The people of other races, Hottentot aboriginal and Bantu immigrant, with whom the Boers and Britons came into contact, were regarded as uncivilized and uncultured heathen. The vigorous life that some enjoyed in a delightful climate was matched by death which carried away too many infants and adults. Warfare was continuous and savage—kill and be killed—and religion was witchcraft lacking in mercy but abounding in cruelty. No writings taught the wisdom of the past and no laws maintained the rights of human beings. Christianity brought them life and peace and prosperity.

The nineteenth century Awakenings had already led to the founding of numerous schools, high schools and colleges in the United States and Europe and elsewhere— extending education until the State took over a fully-fledged system. In South Africa, the missionaries undertook the same tasks of educating the ignorant; they extended their projects into country after country northward until fully-fledged education systems became part of the life of African states.

Inevitably there came about a decline in the spirituality of the churches affected by the post-1800 Awakenings. Not only was the attack of unbelievers renewed, but anti-evangelical notions claimed a following in the Anglican, Lutheran, and Reformed constituencies, even among Baptists, taking a form of non-cooperation with other Christian denominations and resulting in hyper-Anglicanism, hyper-Lutheranism and hyper-Calvinism, and even a hyper-Baptist faction.

In the autumn of 1857, there were signs of an awakening— success in revival and evangelism in Canada, and an extraordinary movement of men to prayer in New York City which spread from city to city throughout the United States and over the world. Churches, halls, and theatres were filled at noon for prayer, and the overflow filled churches of all the denominations at night in a truly remarkable turning of a whole nation toward God.

The same movement also affected the United Kingdom, beginning in 1859 in Ulster, the most northerly province in Ireland. Approximately ten percent of the population professed conversion in Wales and Scotland as well and a great awakening continued in England for years. Repercussions were felt in many other European countries.

The phenomena of revival were reported in countries all around the world, and in South Africa in Bantu, Dutch and English churches during the decade that followed the revival in the homelands and sending countries.

A phenomenal outbreak occurred in 1860 at Worcester in the Cape, with simultaneous audible prayer, confession of sins and outright conversions. This great movement spread throughout Dutch Reformed churches and was followed by revival in English-speaking churches. The evangelical spirit was renewed and evangelistic practices sustained.

The 1858-59 Awakenings extended the working forces of evangelical Christendom. Not only were a million converted in both the United States and the United Kingdom, but existing evangelistic and philanthropic organizations were revived and new vehicles of endeavour created. The Bible Societies flourished as never before, Home Missions and the Salvation Army were founded to extend thus the evangelistic-social ministry of revival in a worldwide operation. The impact upon the youthful Y. M. C. A. organization was noteworthy.

These mid-century Awakenings revived all the existing missionary societies and enabled them to enter other fields. The practical evangelical ecumenism of the Revival was embodied in the China Inland Mission founded by Hudson Taylor in the aftermath of the British Awakening, the first of the interdenominational 'faith missions'—the South Africa General Mission being one. As in the first half of the century, practically every missionary invasion was launched by men revived or converted in these Awakenings in the various sending countries, including South Africa.

The Awakening of 1860 developed a missionary concern among both Dutch Reformed and English-speaking churches in South Africa, a missionary thrust being made immediately. Not only did the European churches experience the phenomena of revival but also churches among Bantu and mixed bloods. The immediate effect of the Awakening upon South African Christians of European stock was to replace racial antipathy by a social sympathy which was reciprocated by the converts.

The 1860 Awakening and Livingstone's explorations in Africa were followed up by societies of eager missionaries, entering opening countries. Most of the work thus begun among the pagan tribes was elementary evangelism, but even so the greatest advances were made wherever outbreaks of the phenomena of revival occurred in the infant churches.

Yet many missionaries who had seen the power of God in revival in the homeland waited in vain for the same in the land of their service. Theirs was the prospecting, the ploughing, the removal of obstacles, and sometimes the planting, leaving the harvesting to their successors.

Others who had not seen revival phenomena in the homeland witnessed its advent on the mission field. Theirs was the satisfaction of knowing that such awakenings could occur among peoples in any stage of civilization.

The Revival had evangelistic and missionary extensions. In the 1870s, Dwight L. Moody rose to fame as a world-evangelist. Beginning modestly in York in 1873, Moody progressed through Sunderland, Newcastle, Edinburgh, Dundee, Glasgow, Belfast, Dublin, Manchester, Sheffield, Liverpool, and Birmingham, using the methods of the 1858 Awakening. In 1875, Moody returned to his native land a national figure, campaigning equally successfully in Brooklyn, Philadelphia, New York, Chicago, Boston and other cities. From then on, he ministered in cities on both sides of the Atlantic. His influence was worldwide, although he never visit any part of Africa.

A world evangelist of Moody's rank, William Taylor of California, visited South Africa in the wake of the 1860 Revival and reaped a harvest among Europeans and Bantu-speaking tribesmen, his ardent evangelism accompanied by widespread revival. Andrew Murray, a leader in the 1860 Revival, became a pastoral evangelist, ministering chiefly to people of European stock. Several evangelists, such as Spencer Walton and George Grubb, made an evangelistic impression upon South Africa. The outstanding African evangelist of the latter half of the nineteenth century was Charles Pamla, a Fingo chief. Not until the early twentieth century did evangelists of note emerge in other sectors of Africa, where missionaries were still pioneering, although occasional revival-awakenings and folk movements erupted.

The evangelization of Africa received a powerful impetus from an unexpected source, the world of higher education. Controversy had arisen between theologians and scientists in the wake of Darwin's publication of his innovative theses. Yet far from antagonizing the academic world, the Great Awakening resulted in the most extraordinary invasion of the universities and colleges by the Christian message and the most successful recruitment of university-trained personnel in the history of higher education and evangelism. No less than six hundred student volunteers came from American universities alone to the African missions in thirty years, a like contingent from British and European universities. The lasting impact of this movement upon the life of Africa may be deemed incalculable.

The effects of evangelical Christianity upon African folk may be gauged by comparing region with region in the vast continent. Throughout East Africa, a more evangelical Anglicanism prevailed and became a dominant force in the Christian life of the tribes and nations there. A less evangelical Anglicanism prevailed in South Africa, and lagged behind other denominations for many years, allowing a very virile Methodism to surge ahead. In Central Africa, Baptists and Presbyterians pioneered, and were moved by evangelical revival at home and abroad. In West Africa, denominational emphases were largely evangelical.

Evangelical missionaries in Africa shared the field with Roman Catholic and other traditionalist forces engaged in winning Africans to Christianity and Christianizing society. What were the effects of the missionary impact on living? African citizens of the emergent nations possess a readily understandable eagerness to claim from the past some tokens of indigenous civilization. The fact remains that in no part of their area was there a native literature or native law.

Missionaries reduced the languages of the Africans to writing, prepared translations of the Scriptures, taught the people to read and write, opened schools for the children, established hospitals for the sick, introduced arts and crafts, and built up law-abiding Christian communities.

Missionaries hastened the disintegration of the native cultures. Polygamy was discouraged by most, marriage purchase by many, and initiation rites at puberty were discountenanced as being breeders of immorality. Missionaries struggled against murder and ritual killing, and opposed witch doctors, ancestor worship and animism.

Missionaries often fought exploitation of the natives by Europeans and adamantly opposed slavery and the slave trade, Evangelicals being the leaders in that opposition. They also encouraged their native charges to become self-reliant, in this way preparing for self-government to come. Emergent nations, in Africa south of the Sahara, owed their existence to the pervading influence of Christianity, direct or indirect.

Apart from the struggle of tribal tyrannies against fate, the first signs of a developing maturity among African folk came in the spiritual rather than the political realm. Long before the African masses aspired to self-government in matters political, they demonstrated a desire for autonomy in their churches, as the rise of Ethiopianism demonstrated both in South Africa and West Africa around 1900.

At the turn of the twentieth century, the white man in South Africa was preoccupied with a kind of civil war. For a while, it seemed as if 'two nations' and 'two manner of people' were struggling in the womb of white South Africa. But, when the pains of travail ended, the offspring was one, a new nation with the languages and characteristics of both its European motherlands and its African home, inheriting a responsibility for other peoples within its boundaries.

The troubles of the South Africans were by no means over, but the 'union of provinces' was preceded by yet another spiritual reviving that blessed both sections of the population. And as before, the revival among South Africans was followed by an outreach to Bantu folk and by revival in Bantu Christian churches throughout southern Africa. Awakenings occurred in East Africa and West Africa also. In the new century, when movements in the wake of the Welsh Revival swept the world, two new forces were introduced to African churches, Zionism with its somewhat exotic exaggeration of the role of a prophetic leader, and Pentecostalism with its stress upon emotional experience, both appealing to Africans.

While Europeans fought to exhaustion the First World War, evangelical awakenings swept many of the African mission fields. During the post-war recovery and the great Depression, there were renewed outbreaks of revival in East Africa and West Africa and in the Congo. The rapid growth of Independent African Churches owed much to these indigenous awakenings, the adherence to or secession from the established Churches often depending upon the reaction of the revived Africans to missionary policies. Where the mission-related Churches were unsympathetic to revival or opposed to native autonomy, secessions followed.

The rapid westernization of Africa south of the Sahara raised an African elite which tried in vain to penetrate the European power structure in the various colonies. Failing, the elite began to agitate for increasing autonomy and finally for independence. Often, the leaders of the African movements were mission-trained. The involvement of colonial nations in the Second World War accelerated the process of Africanization, and made inevitable the widespread changes of the 1950s and 1960s.

As in other parts of the world, evangelical awakenings often preceded political turmoil. Just as the 1858 Revival preceded the American Civil War, so many African revivals preceded the power struggles and bloodlettings.

Christianity has encountered three major rivals for the soul of Africa south of the Sahara. The first confronted was animism, sometimes congenial to monotheism, sometimes antipathetic; but animism has been unable to withstand the missionary onslaught of logical persuasion and superior service. The second rival, solidly resistant in its Middle Eastern and North African homelands, is Islam, which for many years was growing rapidly in trans-Saharan societies but now has seemingly slowed down to 'biological growth' rates, lagging behind indigenous Christian increase. The third great opponent is atheism, the basic philosophy of Leninist and Maoist Communism. While socialism of some sort makes its appeal to the African elite as a solution to African problems of economic backwardness, and leaders seem willing to play one power against another for foreign aid, atheism has made little appeal and is unlikely to be established anywhere except by military imposition.

David Barrett has insisted that the rate of Christian growth since 1910 has been twice that of population growth, and Bishop Stephen Neill has affirmed, on the most sober estimate, that the Christian is reasonably entitled to think that by the end of the twentieth century Africa south of the Sahara will be in the main a Christian continent.

There are three main forms of Christian faith in friendly but real competition. Roman Catholics outnumber members of Protestant Churches in many African countries, but the rise in literacy and the increased availability of Scripture in the vernacular has encouraged secessions into Independent Churches, whose position is closer to Evangelicalism. The signs are not lacking that African Independents of the second and third generations, after the death of their prophet, turn towards Scripture for reorientation. In Protestant mission fields, it can be affirmed that wherever evangelical revival or evangelism is prayed for or proclaimed, the increase of active membership has been very gratifying. Anglicans in West Africa or East Africa, Presbyterians in Malawi or Cameroon, Methodists or Baptists in the Congo or Nigeria, all witness to this fact. And even the Dutch Reformed Church of South Africa, with an obvious political handicap, has enjoyed great ingatherings from Zambia southwards.

Evangelical awakenings, in all this, have been one of the major factors, perhaps the greatest, in the winning of South Africa and all Africa to faith in the Good News of Christ as revealed once for all in the New Testament.

Notes on Chapter 1: THE SECOND GENERAL AWAKENING

1 See J. Edwin Orr, THE EAGER FEET, Chapters 1-12, for an account of the Second General Awakening and fuller documentation of the details.
2 Robert P. Evans, 'The Contribution of Foreigners to the French Protestant Reveil, 1815-1850,' Ph.D. Dissertation, University of Manchester, 1971; B. C. Poland, FRENCH PROTESTANTISM AND THE FRENCH REVOLUTION, appendices detailing French Huguenot abjurations.
3 On the Union of Prayer in the 1780s in Britain, and the Concert of Prayer in the United States in the 1790s, see J. Edwin Orr, THE EAGER FEET, pp. 14-15; pp. 52-53; also documented notes by E. A. Payne, 'The Evangelical Revival and the Beginning of the Modern Missionary Movement,' CONGREGATIONAL QUARTERLY, 1943, XXI, pp. 223ff; and by R. P. Beaver, 'The Concert of Prayer for Missions,' ECUMENICAL REVIEW, 1957-1958, X, pp. 420ff.
4 See G. M. Trevelyan, ENGLISH SOCIAL HISTORY, p. 468, for reaction in Britain.
5 James Sigston, A MEMOIR OF THE LIFE AND MINISTRY OF WILLIAM BRAMWELL, pp. 65ff.
6 D. E. Jenkins, THE LIFE OF THOMAS CHARLES OF BALA, Volume II, pp. 89-94.
7 See Alexander Haldane, THE LIVES OF ROBERT AND JAMES HALDANE; Hugh Watt, THOMAS CHALMERS AND THE DISRUPTION; John Kennedy, THE APOSTLE OF THE NORTH (Dr. John MacDonald).
8 C. H. Crookshank, HISTORY OF METHODISM IN IRELAND, Volume II, passim.
9 Heman Humphrey, REVIVAL SKETCHES, pp. 286-287.
10 See Sverre Norborg, HANS NIELSEN HAUGE.
11 See Bengt Jonzon, STUDIER I PAAVO RUOTSALAINEN.
12 Gunnar Westin, GEORGE SCOTT OCH HANS VERKSSAMHET I SVERIGE.
13 Alexander Haldane, THE LIVES OF ROBERT AND JAMES HALDANE, pp. 401ff.
14 See Paulus Scharpff, GESCHICHTE DER EVANGELISATION, pp. 114ff.
15 A. B. Strickland, THE GREAT AMERICAN REVIVAL, pp. 43ff.
16 See Heman Humphrey, REVIVAL SKETCHES; W. B. Sprague, LECTURES ON REVIVALS OF RELIGION, appendices.
17 William Speer, THE GREAT REVIVAL OF 1800, passim.
18 NEW YORK MISSIONARY MAGAZINE, 1802, p. 87.
19 See J. Edwin Orr, THE EAGER FEET, Chapter 10.
20 C. P. Shedd, TWO CENTURIES OF STUDENT CHRISTIAN MOVEMENTS, pp. 37ff.
21 See J. Edwin Orr, THE EAGER FEET, pp. 93ff.
22 Details in chapter 2: 'Quickening at the Cape,' following.
23 W. Canton, HISTORY OF THE BRITISH AND FOREIGN BIBLE SOCIETY, Volume I, pp. 1ff.
24 See J. Edwin Orr, THE EAGER FEET, Chapter 13.
25 The volume, THE EAGER FEET, Chapters 2-5, provides the details of the British response.

Notes on Chapter 2: QUICKENING AT THE CAPE

1 J. du Plessis, THE LIFE OF ANDREW MURRAY OF SOUTH AFRICA, pp. 63ff.
2 See T. N. Hanekom, HELPERUS RITZEMA VAN LIER, a fully documented biography in Afrikaans.
3 H. R. van Lier, Ph. D., University of Groningen, May 1783.
4 See W. Cowper, THE POWER OF GRACE ILLUSTRATED, (the biography of an unnamed minister, actually H. R. van Lier).
5 T. N. Hanekom, VAN LIER, pp. 135ff, pp. 189ff.
6 See M. C. Vos, MERKWAARDIG VERHAAL.
7 W. J. van der Merwe, THE DEVELOPMENT OF MISSIONARY ATTITUDES IN THE DUTCH REFORMED CHURCH IN SOUTH AFRICA, pp. 73ff.
8 baptized Machtelt Combrink, 17 August 1749.
9 See John Philip, MEMOIR OF MRS. MATHILDA SMITH.
10 K. S. Latourette, A HISTORY OF THE EXPANSION OF CHRISTIANITY, Volume V, p. 339.
11 P. J. Blok, GESCHIEDENIS VAN HET NEDERLANDSCHE VOLK, Volume VI, pp. 501ff.
12 John Kendrick, MS Letter, 29 November 1810, at Cape Town, to Thomas Blanshard; in Archives of the Methodist Church of South Africa, Cory Library, Grahamstown.
13 WESLEYAN METHODIST MAGAZINE, 1810, p. 207.
14 George Middlemiss, Letter in the WESLEYAN METHODIST MAGAZINE, 1810, p. 446.
15 John Kendrick, Letter, 20 November 1810; also his journal, in JOURNAL OF THE METHODIST HISTORICAL SOCIETY OF SOUTH AFRICA, Volume II, Number 4, p. 84.
16 J. Whiteside, HISTORY OF THE WESLEYAN METHODIST CHURCH IN SOUTH AFRICA, pp. 35ff; see also W. C. Holden, A BRIEF HISTORY OF METHODISM IN SOUTH AFRICA.
17 R. Godlonton, MEMORIALS OF THE BRITISH SETTLERS OF SOUTH AFRICA, (1954 edition).
18 See P. Hinchliff, THE ANGLICAN CHURCH IN SOUTH AFRICA: The Church of the Province of South Africa.
19 William Shaw, THE JOURNAL OF THE REV. WILLIAM SHAW, Cory Library, Grahamstown.
20 William Shaw, Letter of 12 July 1822, printed in WESLEYAN METHODIST MAGAZINE, 1822, p. 801.
21 G. E. Cory, THE RISE OF SOUTH AFRICA, Volume II, pp. 96ff.
22 William Shaw, Letter of 19 December 1831, in the Archives of the Methodist Missionary Society, London; WESLEYAN METHODIST MAGAZINE, 1832, p. 525.
23 Samuel Young, Letter of 24 July 1831, in the Archives of the Methodist Missionary Society, London.
24 Letter of Samuel Young, 24 July 1831, Methodist Archives.
25 Minutes of the Methodist District Meeting, in Grahamstown, 1831, Cory Library, Rhodes University.
26 Additions to the South African Methodists in 1832 or 1833 exceeded those of 1831 or 1834 by 300%.
27 The writer was well-acquainted with Afrikaner folk named Murray or MacDonald, some without knowledge of English.
28 J. du Plessis, LIFE OF ANDREW MURRAY, pp. 210-212.
29 W. M. Douglas, ANDREW MURRAY AND HIS MESSAGE, p. 15.
30 J. du Plessis, LIFE OF ANDREW MURRAY, pp. 34ff, 55ff.

31 See M. E. Kluit, HET REVEIL IN NEDERLAND.
32 E. A. Walker, A HISTORY OF SOUTHERN AFRICA, Third Edition, p. 150.
33 G. E. Cory, THE DIARY OF THE REV. FRANCIS OWEN, p. 4. (The first Anglican missionaries in South Africa were Evangelical, of the Church Missionary Society constituency.
34 See I. Schapera, THE BANTU-SPEAKING TRIBES OF SOUTH AFRICA; also THE KHOISAN PEOPLES OF SOUTH AFRICA, BUSHMEN AND HOTTENTOTS; Wilson & Thompson, OXFORD HISTORY OF SOUTH AFRICA, Volume I, Chapter II (Wilson).
35 J. McCarter, THE DUTCH REFORMED CHURCH IN SOUTH AFRICA, pp. 7-14.
36 See J. du Plessis, A HISTORY OF CHRISTIAN MISSIONS IN SOUTH AFRICA, pp. 50ff.
37 J. du Plessis, CHRISTIAN MISSIONS IN SOUTH AFRICA, p. 73.
38 See A. D. Martin, DOCTOR VAN DER KEMP; & D. C. van der Kemp, LEVENSGESCHIEDENIS VAN DR. VAN DER KEMP, in Nederlands.
39 J. du Plessis, CHRISTIAN MISSIONS IN SOUTH AFRICA, p. 81.
40 See C. Anshelm, BISKOP HANS PETER HALLBECK, den Förste Svenska Missionåren i Afrika, passim.
41 R. Philip, THE ELIJAH OF SOUTH AFRICA: REV. JOHN PHILIP; see also R. Lovett, A HISTORY OF THE LONDON MISSIONARY SOCIETY, Volume I, p. 539.
42 D. J. Kotze, LETTERS OF THE AMERICAN MISSIONARIES, 1835-1838, p. 33.
43 D. J. Kotze, LETTERS, 1835-1838, p. 35.
44 TRANSACTIONS OF THE LONDON MISSIONARY SOCIETY, Volume IV, pp. 28-29.
45 TRANSACTIONS, Volume IV, pp. 164ff.
46 Cf. London Missionary Society, QUARTERLY CHRONICLE, & TRANSACTIONS OF THE LONDON MISSIONARY SOCIETY.
47 TRANSACTIONS OF THE LONDON MISSIONARY SOCIETY, Volume IV, pp. 164ff.
48 Cf. London Missionary Society, QUARTERLY CHRONICLE, & TRANSACTIONS OF THE LONDON MISSIONARY SOCIETY.
49 London Missionary Society, THE QUARTERLY CHRONICLE, Volume I, p. 197.
50 THE QUARTERLY CHRONICLE, Volume I, p. 197.
51 See Robert Moffat, MISSIONARY LABOURS AND SCENES IN SOUTH AFRICA, pp. 200ff.
52 A. T. Pierson, SEVEN YEARS IN SIERRA LEONE: the Story of the Work of W. A. B. Johnson, London, 1897, pp. 34-35.
53 Anonymous, MEMOIR OF WILLIAM A. B. JOHNSON, London, 1852; see also A. T. Pierson, p. 8.
54 See D. Salmon, THE PRACTICAL PARTS OF LANCASTER'S IMPROVEMENTS AND BELL'S EXPERIMENT: Johnson made use of monitorial methods, preferring Bell's.
55 A. T. Pierson, SEVEN YEARS IN SIERRA LEONE, pp. 72 & 79.
56 MEMOIR OF W. A. B. JOHNSON; A. T. Pierson, pp. 85ff.
57 A. T. Pierson, SEVEN YEARS IN SIERRA LEONE, pp. 192-193.
58 William Johnson died at sea on 4 May 1823.
59 William Fox, A BRIEF HISTORY OF WESLEYAN MISSIONS ON THE WESTERN COAST OF AFRICA, London, 1851.
60 R. R. Gurley, LIFE OF JEHUDI ASHMUN, LATE COLONIAL AGENT IN LIBERIA, Washington, 1835.

Notes on Chapter 3: ORGANIZING FOR ADVANCE

1 K. S. Latourette, A HISTORY OF THE EXPANSION OF CHRIS-
   TIANITY, Volume IV, pp. 34-35.   2 Volume IV, pp. 65-66.
3 W. Jones, THE RELIGIOUS TRACT SOCIETY, pp. 12ff.
4 See American Tract Society, ANNUAL REPORT, 1826.
5 G. R. Balleine, A HISTORY OF THE EVANGELICAL PARTY
   IN THE CHURCH OF ENGLAND, p. 133.
6 W. Canton, A HISTORY OF THE BRITISH AND FOREIGN BIBLE
   SOCIETY, Volume I, pp. 1ff.
7 H. O. Dwight, CENTENNIAL HISTORY OF THE AMERICAN
   BIBLE SOCIETY, Volume I, pp. 7ff.
8 W. Roberts, MEMOIR OF THE LIFE OF HANNAH MORE.
9 W. CORSTON, THE LIFE OF JOSEPH LANCASTER, pp. 11 & 16.
10 See J. H. Harris, ROBERT RAIKES: THE MAN AND HIS WORK;
   E. W. Rice, THE SUNDAY SCHOOL MOVEMENT, 1780-1917.
11 E. A. Payne, 'The Evangelical Revival and the Beginning of the
   Modern Missionary Movement,' CONGREGATIONAL QUARTERLY,
   1943, XXI, pp. 223ff.
12 R. P. Beaver, 'The Concert of Prayer for Missions,' ECUMENICAL
   REVIEW, 1957-58, X, pp. 420ff.
13 E. A. Payne, THE CHURCH AWAKES, p. 31.
14 Eugene Stock, THE HISTORY OF THE CHURCH MISSIONARY
   SOCIETY, Volume I, p. 57.
15 See S. Pearce Carey, WILLIAM CAREY.
16 PROCEEDINGS OF THE WESLEY HISTORICAL SOCIETY, XXX,
   pp. 25-29.   17 S. Pearce Carey, WILLIAM CAREY, p. 83.
18 F. D. Walker, WILLIAM CAREY, MISSIONARY PIONEER.
19 William Carey, AN ENQUIRY INTO THE OBLIGATIONS OF
   CHRISTIANS TO USE MEANS FOR THE CONVERSION OF THE
   HEATHENS, Leicester, 1792.
20 R. Lovett, HISTORY OF THE LONDON MISSIONARY SOCIETY,
   Volume I, p. 5.
21 W. Carus, LIFE OF THE REV. CHARLES SIMEON, p. 229.
22 Findlay & Holdsworth, HISTORY OF THE WESLEYAN METHODIST
   MISSIONARY SOCIETY, Volume I, p. 72.
23 D. Mackichan, THE MISSIONARY IDEAL IN THE SCOTTISH
   CHURCHES, pp. 74, 112ff.
24 J. Edwin Orr, THE EAGER FEET, p. 91.
25 Peter Thacher, SOCIETY FOR PROPAGATING THE GOSPEL
   AMONG INDIANS AND OTHERS IN NORTH AMERICA.
26 J. W. Alexander, THE LIFE OF ARCHIBALD ALEXANDER,
   pp. 48-81.
27 C. G. Woodson, THE HISTORY OF THE NEGRO CHURCH,
   pp. 78ff.
28 C. H. Wesley, RICHARD ALLEN: APOSTLE OF FREEDOM.
29 See K. S. Latourette, A HISTORY OF THE EXPANSION OF
   CHRISTIANITY, Volume IV, pp. 335-336 for various sources.
30 This handicap is evidenced by statistics of births and marriages,
   regrettably even today, a century after emancipation.
31 Heman Humphrey, REVIVAL SKETCHES, pp. 286-287.
32 Ebenezer Mason, COMPLETE WORKS OF JOHN M. MASON,
   Volume III, pp. 270-271.
33 NEW YORK MISSIONARY MAGAZINE, January 1800, p. 9.
34 R. Pierce Beaver, PIONEERS IN MISSION, pp. 235ff.
35 John Blair Smith, THE ENLARGEMENT OF CHRIST'S KINGDOM.

36 ANNUAL BAPTIST REGISTER, III, pp. 535ff; CONNECTICUT EVANGELICAL MAGAZINE, Volume I, p. 14.
37 MASSACHUSETTS BAPTIST MISSIONARY SOCIETY, Volume I, pp. 5-12.
38 CONNECTICUT EVANGELICAL MAGAZINE, Volume I, p. 31.
39 S. B. Halliday, THE CHURCH IN AMERICA, pp. 515ff.
40 J. Tracy, HISTORY OF THE AMERICAN BOARD, pp. 24ff.
41 F. Wayland, MEMOIR OF ADONIRAM JUDSON.
42 J. M. Reid, MISSIONS AND MISSIONARY SOCIETY OF THE METHODIST EPISCOPAL CHURCH, Volume I, p. 17.
43 J. C. Emery, A CENTURY OF ENDEAVOR, pp. 29ff.
44 A. J. Brown, ONE HUNDRED YEARS, pp. 21ff.
45 George Drach, OUR CHURCH ABROAD, p. 23.
46 NEW YORK MISSIONARY MAGAZINE, Volume I, 1800, pp. 80-81.
47 THE PANOPLIST, Boston, Volume XI, January 1815, pp. 19-20.

Notes on Chapter 4: THE THIRD GENERAL AWAKENING

1   See J. Edwin Orr, THE EAGER FEET, Chapters 19-24, for an account of the Third General Awakening and fuller documentation.
2   C. G. Finney, MEMOIRS OF REV. CHARLES G. FINNEY.
3   W. E. Farndale, THE SECRET OF MOW COP, passim.
4   THE HOME MISSIONARY JOURNAL, 1831, p. 210.
5   AMERICAN BAPTIST MAGAZINE, 1831, p. 155.
6   See J. Edwin Orr, THE EAGER FEET, Chapter 19.
7   THE JOURNAL OF FRANCIS ASBURY, Volume III, pp. 210-211.
8   G. L. Curtiss, MANUAL OF METHODIST EPISCOPAL HISTORY, pp. 148-149.
9   H. C. Vedder, A SHORT HISTORY OF THE BAPTISTS, p. 327.
10 See J. Edwin Orr, THE EAGER FEET, Chapter 20.
11 R. W. Church, THE OXFORD MOVEMENT: 1833-45, pp. 82ff.
12 James Caughey, METHODISM IN EARNEST; and SHOWERS OF BLESSING, passim.
13 Thomas Rees, HISTORY OF PROTESTANT NONCONFORMITY IN WALES, passim.
14 W. J. Couper, SCOTTISH REVIVALS, passim.
15 See J. Edwin Orr, THE EAGER FEET, pp. 152ff.
16 H. A. Ironside, A HISTORICAL SKETCH OF THE BRETHREN MOVEMENT, pp. 10ff.
17 J. Edwin Orr, THE EAGER FEET, Chapter 21.
18 See A. R. Tippett, PEOPLE MOVEMENTS IN SOUTHERN POLYNESIA, passim.
19 O. H. Gulick, THE PILGRIMS OF HAWAII, pp. 315ff.
20 G. C. Henderson, FIJI AND THE FIJIANS, passim.
21 N. Grundemann, JOHANN FRIEDRICH REIDEL, passim.
22 See Chapter 2: 'Quickening at the Cape,' p. 10.
23 J. Edwin Orr, THE EAGER FEET, Chapter 24: 'Stirrings in the East.'
24 G. M. Thomssen, SAMUEL HEBICH OF INDIA, pp. 186ff.
25 See Francis Mason, THE KAREN APOSTLE: KO THAH-BYU.
26 W. W. Sweet, REVIVALISM IN AMERICA, p. 135.
27 C. G. Finney, LECTURES ON REVIVALS OF RELIGION, p. 5.
28 J. E. Hodder-Williams, LIFE OF SIR GEORGE WILLIAMS.
29 J. W. Ewing, GOODLY FELLOWSHIP: THE LIFE AND WORK OF THE WORLD'S EVANGELICAL ALLIANCE.
30 See Chapter 5: 'Social Impact of Revival,' following.

Notes on Chapter 5: SOCIAL IMPACT OF REVIVAL

1 JOHN WESLEY'S WORKS, (1872 Edition) Volume V, p. 296.
2 W. M. Gewehr, THE GREAT AWAKENING IN VIRGINIA, ch. 8.
3 W. W. Sweet, REVIVALISM IN AMERICA, p. 41.
4 T. Clarkson, ABOLITION OF THE AFRICAN SLAVE TRADE.
5 ENCYCLOPEDIA BRITANNICA, 1970, article on Slavery.
6 John Wesley, THOUGHTS UPON SLAVERY, 1774.
7 J. C. Colquhoun, WILBERFORCE: HIS FRIENDS AND TIMES.
8 G. M. Trevelyan, ENGLISH SOCIAL HISTORY, p. 495.
9 J. W. Bready, THIS FREEDOM—WHENCE? p. 44.
10 ENCYCLOPEDIA BRITANNICA, 1970, article on Slavery.
11 T. Clarkson, ABOLITION OF THE AFRICAN SLAVE TRADE.
12 J. Harris, A CENTURY OF EMANCIPATION, pp. 3ff.
13 G. H. Barnes, THE ANTI-SLAVERY IMPULSE, passim.
14 J. du Plessis, CHRISTIAN MISSIONS IN SOUTH AFRICA, p. 32.
15 G. M. Theal, RECORDS OF CAPE COLONY, 1821-22, p. 485.
16 C. G. Botha, COLLECTED WORKS, Volume I, p. 293.
17 Hansard, 25 July 1822.   18 G. M. Theal, RECORDS, p. 485..
19 J. Field, THE LIFE OF JOHN HOWARD, passim.
20 T. Taylor, MEMOIRS OF HOWARD, passim.
21 J. W. Bready, THIS FREEDOM—WHENCE? pp. 246ff.
22 A. R. C. Gardner, JOHN HOWARD IN PENAL REFORM.
23 J. W. Bready, THIS FREEDOM—WHENCE? pp. 251ff.
24 See J. Whitney, ELIZABETH FRY, QUAKER HEROINE.
25 Fliedner's Autobiography is found only in his native German.
26 A. B. Wentz, FLIEDNER, THE FAITHFUL, p. 13.
27 G. Fliedner, THEODOR FLIEDNER, (3rd Edition, 1892).
28 A. B. Wentz, FLIEDNER, p. 25.   29 A. B. Wentz, p. 29.
30 Sir Edward Cook, LIFE OF FLORENCE NIGHTINGALE, passim.
31 LIFE OF FLORENCE NIGHTINGALE, Volume I, p. 479.
32 J. W. Bready, LORD SHAFTESBURY AND SOCIAL-INDUSTRIAL
   PROGRESS.   33 THIS FREEDOM—WHENCE? pp. 261-262.
34 E. Hodder, THE LIFE AND WORK OF THE SEVENTH EARL
   OF SHAFTESBURY, Volume III, p. 3.
35 THIS FREEDOM—WHENCE? pp. 264ff.   36 pp. 264-268.
37 THE SEVENTH EARL OF SHAFTESBURY, Volume III, p. 3.
38 K. S. Latourette, A HISTORY OF THE EXPANSION OF CHRIS-
   TIANITY, Volume IV, p. 155.
39 J. W. Bready, THIS FREEDOM—WHENCE? p. 265.
40 J. W. Bready, THIS FREEDOM—WHENCE? p. 266.
41 Sidney & Beatrice Webb, HISTORY OF TRADE UNIONISM,
   affirms the significance of the Tolpuddle 'Martyrs' in British
   social history and trade unionists have long revered them.
42 J. W. Bready, THIS FREEDOM—WHENCE? p. 269.
43 He had later emigrated to Canada.
44 J. W. Bready, THIS FREEDOM—WHENCE? p. 275.
45 E. D. Branch, THE SENTIMENTAL YEARS, 1836-1860.
46 W. W. Sweet, REVIVALISM IN AMERICA, p. 159.
47 G. H. Barnes, THE ANTI-SLAVERY IMPULSE, pp. 18-28.
48 W. W. Sweet, REVIVALISM IN AMERICA, p. 159.
49 K. S. Latourette, A HISTORY OF THE EXPANSION OF CHRIS-
   TIANITY, Volume IV, p. 416.
50 Fairholme & Pain, CENTURY OF WORK FOR ANIMALS,
   passim.
51 G. M. Trevelyan, ENGLISH SOCIAL HISTORY, p. 504.

Notes on Chapter 6: ENCOUNTER WITH THE BANTU

1   See L. Fouche & P. J. Coertze, REPORTS ON THE EXCAVA-
    TIONS AT MAPUNGUBWE. Wilson & Thompson, THE OXFORD
    HISTORY OF SOUTH AFRICA, Volume I, have summarized the
    latest conclusions of investigators into Bantu origins in Chapters
    3 & 4; C. F. J. Muller, editor, FIVE HUNDRED YEARS: A
    HISTORY OF SOUTH AFRICA, has presented a much shorter
    account in Appendix I, pp. 434-450.
2   T. V. Bulpin, TO THE SHORES OF NATAL, passim.
3   See H. F. Fynn, DIARY, edited by Stuart & Malcolm.
4   Allen F. Gardiner, NARRATIVE OF A JOURNEY TO THE
    ZOOLO COUNTRY, 1836.
5   G. E. Cory, DIARY OF Rev. FRANCIS OWEN, MISSIONARY
    WITH DINGAAN in 1837-1838.
6   See Basil F. Holt, JOSEPH WILLIAMS AND THE PIONEER
    MISSION TO THE SOUTHEASTERN BANTU.
7   Methodist Conferences, London, 1832-1834, Vol. VII, pp. 6-7.
    MISSIONARY NOTICES.
8   Methodist Conferences, London, 1832-1834, Vol. VII, pp. 136,
    MISSIONARY NOTICES.
9   W. Eversleigh, THE SETTLERS AND METHODISM, p. 101.
10 J. S. Moffat, THE LIVES OF ROBERT AND MARY MOFFAT;
    see also Edwin W. Smith, ROBERT MOFFAT.
11 Robert Moffat, MISSIONARY LABOURS AND SCENES IN SOUTH
    AFRICA, 1842, p. 496.
12 J. duPlessis, A HISTORY OF CHRISTIAN MISSIONS IN SOUTH
    AFRICA, p. 163.
13 MINUTES of Methodist District Meeting of 1832, in Archives in
    Cory Library, Grahamstown.
14 Methodist Conferences, London, 1832-34, MISSIONARY NOTICES,
    Volume VII, p. 9.
15 Methodist Conference, January 1838, MISSIONARY NOTICES,
    p. 13; cf. William Shaw, THE STORY OF MY MISSION IN
    SOUTHEASTERN AFRICA, p. 186.
16 MINUTES of the Fourteenth Annual Methodist District Meeting,
    5 February 1838 at Butterworth; in the Archives of the Cory
    Library, Grahamstown.
17 See C. Northcott, G. Seaver, and others on Livingstone; also
    the extensive bibliography compiled by M. E. Appleyard in the
    University of Cape Town.
18 R. H. W. Shepherd, LOVEDALE, SOUTH AFRICA, 1841-1941,
    cf. G. E. Cory, THE RISE OF SOUTH AFRICA, Volume II,
    pp. 96ff.
19 See C. F. Pascoe, TWO HUNDRED YEARS OF THE S. P. G.,
    pp. 269-273.
20 W. E. Strong, THE STORY OF THE AMERICAN BOARD OF
    COMMISSIONERS FOR FOREIGN MISSIONS, pp. 132ff.
21 C. W. Mackintosh, COILLARD OF THE ZAMBESI, pp. 3ff.
22 J. duPlessis, A HISTORY OF CHRISTIAN MISSIONS IN SOUTH
    AFRICA, pp. 200ff.
23 J. duPlessis, A HISTORY OF CHRISTIAN MISSIONS IN SOUTH
    AFRICA, p. 373.
24 Andrew Burgess, UNKULUNKULU IN ZULULAND, pp. 104ff.
25 W. Claus, DR. LUDWIG KRAPF, weil Missioner in Ost-Africa.
    (See also J. L. Krapf, TRAVELS IN EAST AFRICA.)

Notes on Chapter 7: THE FOURTH GENERAL AWAKENING

1   See J. Edwin Orr, THE FERVENT PRAYER, Chapters 1-12, for an account of the Fourth General Awakening with more detailed documentation.
2   CHRISTIAN ADVOCATE, New York, 5 November 1857.
3   W. C. Conant, NARRATIVE OF REMARKABLE CONVERSIONS, & T. W. Chambers, THE NOON PRAYER MEETING.
4   W. C. Conant, NARRATIVE OF REMARKABLE CONVERSIONS, p. 394. (See J. Edwin Orr, THE FERVENT PRAYER, Ch. 6).
5   JOURNAL, XLI ANNUAL CONVENTION OF THE PROTESTANT EPISCOPAL CHURCH IN THE DIOCESE OF OHIO, 1858.
6   J. Edwin Orr, THE FERVENT PRAYER, p. 42.
7   Cf. MINUTES OF THE GENERAL ASSEMBLY OF THE PRESBYTERIAN CHURCH IN THE UNITED STATES OF AMERICA, 1863-1868; and W. W. Bennett, THE GREAT REVIVAL IN THE SOUTHERN ARMIES.
8   See J. Edwin Orr, THE FERVENT PRAYER, Chapters 24 & 25.
9   J. Edwin Orr, THE FERVENT PRAYER, Chapters 7-12.
10   'Christian Action,' see J. Edwin Orr, THE FERVENT PRAYER, Chapter 18.
11   Besides the standard biographies of D. L. Moody, see J. Edwin Orr, THE FERVENT PRAYER, 'The Evangelistic Extension.'
12   'Appreciation and Depreciation,' Chapter 12, J. Edwin Orr.
13   J. E. Hodder-Williams, THE LIFE OF SIR GEORGE WILLIAMS, pp. 187, 203.
14   See J. Edwin Orr, THE FERVENT PRAYER, pp. 132-133.
15   W. R. Moody, THE LIFE OF DWIGHT L. MOODY; J. F. Findlay, DWIGHT L. MOODY, and other biographies.
16   See G. M. Stephenson, THE RELIGIOUS ASPECTS OF SWEDISH IMMIGRATION; also J. Edwin Orr, THE FERVENT PRAYER, pp. 83ff.
17   See Paulus Scharpff, GESCHICHTE DER EVANGELISATION, pp. 249ff.
18   J. H. Lohrenz, THE MENNONITE BRETHREN CHURCH, pp. 27ff. and R. S. Latimer, LIBERTY OF CONSCIENCE UNDER THREE TSARS, pp. 71-76.
19   See C. P. Shedd, TWO CENTURIES OF STUDENT CHRISTIAN MOVEMENTS, pp. 110ff.
20   See J. Edwin Orr, THE FERVENT PRAYER, Chapter 20.
21   S. B. Halliday, THE CHURCH IN AMERICA, pp. 347ff.
22   'The Evangelization of Africa,' Chapter 11, following.
23   See J. Edwin Orr, THE FERVENT PRAYER, Chapter 19.
24   Chapter 24, J. Edwin Orr, THE FERVENT PRAYER.
25   T. L. Smith, REVIVALISM AND SOCIAL REFORM, p. 148.
26   Chapter 25, J. Edwin Orr, THE FERVENT PRAYER.
27   D. Carswell, BROTHER SCOTS, pp. 155ff; J. W. Bready, THIS FREEDOM—WHENCE ? pp. 277-282.
28   It was Dr. Max A. C. Warren, canon of Westminster Abbey, who drew the author's attention to the fact that his Oxford dissertation on the 1859 Revival in Britain demonstrated that a worldwide revival had occurred that caused no denominational cleavages.
29   Out of the 1859 Revival came the interdenominational missionary conference of 1860; then 1878, 1888, 1900 and 1910, for until 1910 the 'ecumenical movement' was directed by and supported by an Evangelical constituency.

Notes on Chapter 8: REVIVAL IN SOUTH AFRICA, I

1   J. du Plessis. THE LIFE OF ANDREW MURRAY, p. 27.
2   DE KERKBODE, 1859-60, indexed references.
3   DE KERKBODE, 27 August 1859, p. 294.
4   DE KERKBODE, 6 October 1859, pp. 327 & 334.
5   See DE KERKBODE, 30 July 1859.
6   S. I. Prime, THE POWER OF PRAYER, 1858.
7   SOUTH AFRICAN WATCHMAN, 1858, pp. 254-256, 324; 1859, 308-316; 1860, 353-360, etc.
8   James Cameron, Letter of 20 June 1860, Methodist Missionary Society Archives, London, the Cape of Good Hope Files, 1858-1860.
9   MINUTES, Methodist Conference, Cape Town, 1866.
10 James Cameron, Letter, Methodist Archives.
11 M. W. Retief, HERLEWINGS IN ONS GESKIEDENIS, Chapter 3, pp. 13ff.
12 DE KERKBODE, 27 August 1859, p. 294.
13 A. P. Smit, Archivist, GEDENKBOEK VAN DIE NEDERDUITS GEREFORMEERDE GEMEENTE, CALVINIA, and Address by Professor Nicholas Hofmeyr, 26 October 1860, reported in DE KERKBODE, 1860, pp. 392ff.
14 M. W. Retief, HERLEWINGS IN ONS GESKIEDENIS, Chapter 3, pp. 13ff.
15 Cf. M. de Villiers, BIOGRAPHY OF G. W. A. VAN DER LINGEN, p. 182; Van der Lingen, GODSDIENSVERSLAG, De Paarl, 1860, Archives, Dutch Reformed Church, Cape Town, file R. 1:9, p. 225.
16 Andrew Murray, GODSDIENSVERSLAG, Worcester, 1960, in the Archives, Dutch Reformed Church, Cape Town, file R. 4:4, p. 234.
17 DE KERKBODE, 1860, pp. 47, 92-94.
18 DE KERKBODE, 1860, pp. 141-144.
19 J. du Plessis, THE LIFE OF ANDREW MURRAY, p. 187; cf. DE KERKBODE, 1860, pp. 92-94, 141-144.
20 cf. DE KERKBODE, 1860, p. 141.
21 cf. DE KERKBODE, 1860, p. 142.
22 J. du Plessis, THE LIFE OF ANDREW MURRAY, p. 199.
23 DE KERKBODE, 1860, p. 174.
24 W. M. Douglas, biographer of Andrew Murray, had told the writer in 1936 that intimates of the veteran predikant used to tease him about his having tried to stop the Revival.
25 See James Cameron, Report in the WESLEYAN METHODIST MAGAZINE, November 1860.
26 Stefanus Hofmeyr, GODSDIENSVERSLAG, Montagu, 1860, in the Archives of the Dutch Reformed Church, Cape Town, file R. 2:6, pp. 290ff.
27 cf. DE KERKBODE, 1860, p. 32.
28 Prof. N. Hofmeyr, in Address to the South African Evangelical Alliance, 26 October 1860 (DE KERKBODE, 1860, pp. 392ff)
29 Stefanus Hofmeyr, cf. DE KERKBODE, 1860, pp. 253-254.
30 DE KERKBODE, 1860, p. 300, cf. Stefanus Hofmeyr.
31 Jan Christiaan de Vries was a cousin of General Jan Christiaan Smuts, son of Catharina de Vries.
32 J. du Plessis, THE LIFE OF ANDREW MURRAY, pp. 194ff.
33 Dr. A. T. Robertson, WORD PICTURES IN THE NEW TESTAMENT, Vol. III, p. 20; Dr. David Downie in Andhra 1906, in the Archives of the American Baptist Foreign Mission; Donald Fraser, WINNING A PRIMITIVE PEOPLE, p. 279.

34 J. du Plessis, THE LIFE OF ANDREW MURRAY, p. 194ff.
35 Andrew Murray, GODSDIENSVERSLAG, Worcester, 1860, in the Archives of the Dutch Reformed Church, Cape Town, file R. 4:4, p. 234.
36 See memoirs of Ds. J. C. de Vries, in J. du Plessis, THE LIFE OF ANDREW MURRAY, pp. 194ff.
37 Andrew Murray, GODSDIENSVERSLAG, Worcester, 1860, in the Archives of the Dutch Reformed Church, cf. biography by Prof. J. du Plessis.
38 J. du Plessis, THE LIFE OF ANDREW MURRAY, pp. 194ff.
39 Andrew Murray, GODSDIENSVERSLAG, Worcester, 1860.
40 See W. M. Douglas, ANDREW MURRAY AND HIS MESSAGE, pp. 88-89.
41 J. du Plessis, THE LIFE OF ANDREW MURRAY, p. 196.
42 Andrew Murray, GODSDIENSVERSLAG, Worcester, 1861, file R. 4:4, p. 339.
43 Prof. N. Hofmeyr, in Address to the South African Evangelical Alliance, 26 October 1860 (DE KERKBODE, 1860, pp. 392ff)
44 GODSDIENSVERSLAG, Wellington, 1861, in the Archives of the Dutch Reformed Church, Cape Town, file R. 1:9, p. 356.
45 GODSDIENSVERSLAG, Tulbagh, 1860, file R. 4:4, p. 231, cf. DE KERKBODE, 1860, p. 392, and Prof. Hofmeyr's Address.
46 See ACTA, Ring van Swellendam, 1860, file R. 2:6, p. 290; and GODSDIENSVERSLAG, Robertson, 1861, p. 365; in the Archives: Dutch Reformed Church, Cape Town.
47 G. W. A. van der Lingen, GODSDIENSVERSLAG, Paarl, 1860— Archives of the Dutch Reformed Church, file R. 1:9, p. 225.
48 G. W. A. van der Lingen, GODSDIENSVERSLAG, Paarl, 1860— Archives of the Dutch Reformed Church, file R. 1:9, p. 344.
49 Van der Lingen, GODSDIENSVERSLAG, Paarl, 1864, cf. DIE KWARTMILLENIUM GEDENKBOEK VAN DIE NEDERDUITS GEREFORMEERDE GEMEENTE VAN PAARL, pp. 135ff, 'De Opwekking, 1860.'
50 Prof. N. Hofmeyr, in Address to the South African Evangelical Alliance, 26 October 1860 (DE KERKBODE, 1860, pp. 392ff)
51 See GEDENKBOEK VAN DIE NEDERDUITS GEREFORMEERDE GEMEENTE, Beaufort-Wes, 1820-1945, p. 36 (A. P. Smit)
52 DE KERKBODE, 1861, p. 108.
53 DE KERKBODE, 1861, p. 128.
54 GODSDIENSVERSLAG, Prins Albert, 1861, R. 6:2, p. 89, in the Archives of the Dutch Reformed Church, Cape Town.
55 DE KERKBODE, 1861, pp. 206 & 123.
56 DE ZUID-AFRIKAAN VERENIGD, 17 August 1915.
57 DE KERKBODE, 1861-62, indexed notes.
58 A. C. Barnard, EEUFEES GEDENKBOEK VAN DIE NEDERDUITS GEREFORMEERDE GEMEENTE, Heidelberg, Kaapland, 1855-1955, pp. 49-50, 54-55, 60ff.
59 See H. C. Hopkins, DIE MOEDER VAN ONS ALMAL, 1963. (Die Groote Kerk, Kaapstad).
60 J. du Plessis, THE LIFE OF ANDREW MURRAY, p. 196.
61 M. W. Retief, HERLEWINGS IN ONS GESKIEDENIS, Chapter 7, 'Sending.'
62 A. C. Barnard, EEUFEES VAN DIE PINKSTERBIDURE, cf. HERINNERING AAN HET LEVEN EN DEN ARBEID VAN GOTTLIEB WILHELM ANTHONY VAN DER LINGEN, for a consideration of the Hour of Prayer movement.

Notes on Chapter 9: REVIVAL IN SOUTH AFRICA, II

1   See REPORT, Wesleyan Methodist Missionary Society, April 1868, p. 40.
2   G. M. Theal, RECORDS OF THE CAPE COLONY, 1964 edition, Volume VII, pp. 205ff.
3   MINUTES, Methodist District Meetings, 1854-58, in the Archives of the Cory Library, Grahamstown.
4   Report of John Ayliff, November 1857 & 1858, in the Archives of Cory Library, Grahamstown.
5   MINUTES, Methodist District Meetings, 1854-58, in the Archives of Cory Library, Grahamstown.
6   See REPORT, Wesleyan Methodist Missionary Society, April 1868, p. 40.
7   Josiah Tyler, forty years after landing in Natal on 17th July 1849, reported in CHRISTIAN EXPRESS, November 1889.
8   Josiah Tyler, CHRISTIAN EXPRESS, November 1889, forty years old report.
9   See REPORT, American Board of Commissioners for Foreign Missions, Boston, 1859, p. 45.
10 REPORT, American Board, Boston, 1859, p. 45.
11 Letter of Joshua Gaskin, 9 May 1860, in Methodist Missionary Society Archives, London.
12 REPORT, Wesleyan Methodist Missionary Society, p. 39.
13 Cf. Report of Joseph Jackson, in the WESLEYAN METHODIST MAGAZINE, London, January 1860.
14 REPORT, American Board, 1861, p. 30.
15 Archives, Cory Library, contain MS lists of 'newly awakened' in Botswana District, dated 29 June 1859.
16 REPORT, American Board, 1861, p. 30.
17 REPORT, American Board, 1862, p. 62.
18 REPORT, American Board, 1863, p. 48.
19 REPORT, American Board, 1867, pp. 53ff.
20 REPORT, American Board, 1868, pp. 9ff.
21 MISSIONARY HERALD, Boston, 1860, p. 4.
22 MISSIONARY HERALD, Boston, 1860, p. 357.
23 William Taylor, THE STORY OF MY LIFE, pp. 73-75; also pp. 218-229.
24 K. S. Latourette, A HISTORY OF THE EXPANSION OF CHRISTIANITY, cites William Taylor a dozen times in three volumes, an extraordinary tribute to his versatility.
25 William Taylor, THE STORY OF MY LIFE, pp. 255ff.
26 REPORT, Wesleyan Methodist Missionary Society, 1867, p. 36.
27 William Taylor, CHRISTIAN ADVENTURES IN SOUTH AFRICA (autobiographical), pp. 38ff., 62ff.
28 William Taylor, CHRISTIAN ADVENTURES, pp. 41ff.
29 Letter of Charles Pamla, 1 June 1866, in WESLEYAN METHODIST MAGAZINE.
30 William Taylor, CHRISTIAN ADVENTURES, pp. 120ff.
31 See REPORTS of the Wesleyan Methodist Missionary Society for 1866-68 indicating a membership increase from 614 in 1865 to 810 in 1866 to 927 in 1867, a 50% increase in two years, with additional hundreds on trial.
32 Report of William Impey, Grahamstown, and Letter of William Sargent, Healdtown, WESLEYAN METHODIST MAGAZINE, 1866, pp. 928 & 1036.

33 Wesleyan Methodist Missionary Reports, 1866-68, noted an increase of 180, with 245 on trial.
34 WESLEYAN MISSIONARY MAGAZINE, February 1867, p. 176, William Taylor, CHRISTIAN ADVENTURES, pp. 224ff.
35 Report, Kamastone Circuit, 1866, Archives, Cory Library, cf. Wesleyan Methodist Missionary Reports, 1866-68.
36 See Basil F. Holt, Article, 'Blazing Firebrand,' (William Taylor and his mission), p. 14.
37 Report of the Butterworth Circuit, 1866, Archives in Cory Library, Grahamstown.
38 Report of the Clarkebury Circuit, 1866, Archives in Cory Library, cf. Wesleyan Methodist Missionary Reports, 1866-68.
39 William Taylor, CHRISTIAN ADVENTURES, p. 316.
40 Report of the Shawbury Circuit, 1866, Cory Archives; see also William Taylor, CHRISTIAN ADVENTURES IN SOUTH AFRICA.
41 Report of the Osborn Circuit, 1866. Cory Archives; Wesleyan Methodist Missionary Reports, 1866- 68.
42 Letter of William J. Davis, 15 August 1866, in the WESLEYAN METHODIST MAGAZINE, November 1866.
43 Reports in WESLEYAN METHODIST MAGAZINE, November 1866 onward; cf. Wesleyan Missionary Reports, 1866-1868.
44 William Taylor, CHRISTIAN ADVENTURES IN SOUTH AFRICA, pp. 41ff; cf. Wesleyan Missionary Reports, 1866-68.
45 William Taylor, CHRISTIAN ADVENTURES IN SOUTH AFRICA, pp. 41ff; cf. Wesleyan Missionary Reports, 1866-68.
46 cf. Wesleyan Methodist MISSIONARY NOTICES, 1866-68, and Missiohary Reports.
47 William Taylor, CHRISTIAN ADVENTURES IN SOUTH AFRICA, pp. 41ff; cf. Wesleyan Missionary Reports, 1866-68.
48 MINUTES, Quarterly Meeting, at Fort Beaufort, 9 November 1866, in the Archives, Cory Library, Grahamstown.
49 William Taylor, CHRISTIAN ADVENTURES, pp. 41ff.
50 Rev. H. H. Dugmore, Sermon preached 15 July 1866, in Queenstown, cited by W. Taylor in CHRISTIAN ADVENTURES IN SOUTH AFRICA, not recorded elsewhere.
51 See MISSIONARY NOTICES; Wesleyan Missionary Reports, 1866 to 1868.
52 CHRISTIAN EXPRESS, 1 October 1876.
53 William Taylor, CHRISTIAN ADVENTURES IN SOUTH AFRICA, pp. 474ff; MISSIONARY NOTICES, Wesleyan Methodist Missionary Reports, 1866-68.
54 Letter of C. Harmon, WESLEYAN METHODIST MAGAZINE, November 1867, pp. 1038-1039.
55 MINUTES of the Methodist Conferences, London, 1865-69, pp. 318, 550; 121, 355, & 584.
56 Letter to Samuel Hardy, 24 January 1867, in MINUTES (MS) Cape Town Conference, 1866, and the Report of the Wesleyan Methodist Missionary Society, April 1867, pp. 38, 44.
57 E. W. Smith, THE MABILLES OF BASUTOLAND, passim.
58 W. C. Holden, THE STORY OF KAMA, pp. 24-25.
59 See J. Whiteside, HISTORY OF METHODISM IN SOUTH AFRICA; cf. Basil F. Holt, Article, 'Blazing Firebrand,' (William Taylor and his mission).
60 See THE EAST AND THE WEST, Volume XI, p. 389 (Gibson), cf. L. A. Hewson, AN INTRODUCTION TO SOUTH AFRICAN METHODISTS, passim.

Notes on Chapter 10:   CHRISTIAN ACTION

1   United States (1860) 30,000,000;   United Kingdom (1861) 27,000,000
    approximate population.
2   See Warren C. Candler, GREAT REVIVALS AND THE GREAT
    REPUBLIC, pp. 215-216, regarding the United States;   and
    J. Edwin Orr, THE SECOND EVANGELICAL AWAKENING IN
    BRITAIN, p. 207 & Appendices A-E regarding Britain.
3   W. A. Candler,   pp. 222-223.
4   F. G. Beardsley, A HISTORY OF AMERICAN REVIVALS,
    p. 230.
5   Everywhere, laymen initiated the first united prayer meetings.
6   Cf. G. E. Morgan, R. C. MORGAN: HIS LIFE AND TIMES,
    pp. 159-160.
7   See J. Edwin Orr, THE SECOND EVANGELICAL AWAKENING
    IN BRITAIN, p. 251.
8   See W. W. Sweet, REVIVALISM IN AMERICA, p. 160; cf.
    C. H. Hopkins, A HISTORY OF THE Y. M. C. A., passim.
9   R. C. Morgan, Editor, in THE REVIVAL, 6 August 1859.
10 J. E. Hodder-Williams, LIFE OF SIR GEORGE WILLIAMS,
    pp. 187, 203.
11 See J. Edwin Orr, THE SECOND EVANGELICAL AWAKENING
    IN BRITAIN,   pp. 215ff.
12 THE REVIVAL,   2 February 1861.
13 R. Sandall, HISTORY OF THE SALVATION ARMY, Volume I,
    pp. 22, 41-44.
14 Cf. THE CHRISTIAN, 11 February 1909; & P. C. Headley,
    E. PAYSON HAMMOND,   passim.
15 Cf. Edwin W. Rice, THE SUNDAY SCHOOL MOVEMENT,
    1780-1917; & Arlo A. Brown, A HISTORY OF RELIGIOUS
    EDUCATION IN RECENT TIMES,   passim.
16 THE REVIVAL, 27 August 1859 & Appendix D, J. Edwin Orr,
    THE SECOND EVANGELICAL AWAKENING IN BRITAIN.
17 See Basil F. Holt, THE CLEANSING STREAM, unpublished
    typescript, pp. 14-15. Cf. E. C. Millard, WHAT HATH GOD
    WROUGHT (George Grubb's Mission Tour of 1889-1890).
18 J. Edwin Orr, THE SECOND EVANGELICAL AWAKENING IN
    BRITAIN, pp. 208-209; cf. W. Canton, passim.
19 W. Canton, THE HISTORY OF THE BRITISH AND FOREIGN
    BIBLE SOCIETY, Volume III, pp. 33ff, 43ff, 74ff & passim.
20 F. W. Sass, 'The Influence of the Church of Scotland on the Dutch
    Reformed Church in South Africa,' unpublished Edinburgh thesis.
21 J. du Plessis, THE LIFE OF ANDREW MURRAY OF SOUTH
    AFRICA,   pp. 78ff.
22 See W. W. Sweet, THE STORY OF RELIGION IN AMERICA,
    Chapter XIV, describing the rise of lay ministry, westwards.
23 Note S. P. Engelbrecht, GESKIEDENIS VAN DIE NEDERDUITS
    HERVORMDE KERK VAN AFRIKA, Volume I, pp. 114ff.
24 Cf. J. McCarter, THE DUTCH REFORMED CHURCH IN SOUTH
    AFRICA,   passim.
25 See C. F. Pascoe, TWO HUNDRED YEARS OF THE S. P. G.,
    pp. 269ff; cf. E. H. Day, THE LIFE OF ROBERT GRAY.
26 J. Whiteside, HISTORY OF THE WESLEYAN METHODIST
    CHURCH IN SOUTH AFRICA, pp. 406ff.
27 N. C. Sargant, THE DISPERSION OF THE TAMIL CHURCH,
    pp. 60ff.

Notes on Chapter 11: THE EVANGELIZATION OF AFRICA

1   J. Edwin Orr, THE SECOND EVANGELICAL AWAKENING IN
    BRITAIN, pp. 189ff.
2   C.F.Pascoe, TWO HUNDRED YEARS OF THE S.P.G., p. 306.
3   G. W. Cox, THE LIFE OF JOHN WILLIAM COLENSO.
4   J. D. Taylor, editor, CHRISTIANITY AND THE NATIVES OF
    SOUTH AFRICA, pp. 264ff.
5   W. P. Livingstone, CHRISTINA FORSYTH OF FINGOLAND.
6   J. Wells, THE LIFE OF JAMES STEWART, p. 171.
7   W. C. Holden, THE STORY OF KAMA pp. 24-25.
8   J. Whiteside, HISTORY OF THE WESLEYAN METHODIST
    CHURCH IN SOUTH AFRICA, cf. Holt, 'Blazing Firebrand.'
9   L. A. Hewson, SOUTH AFRICAN METHODISTS, p. 74.
10 G. & N. Pamla, AMABALANA NGO BOMI BUKA (A Life of
    Charles Pamla—notes translated by Dr. Basil F. Holt).
11 William Taylor, CHRISTIAN ADVENTURES IN SOUTH AFRICA,
    p. 96.   12 William Taylor, CHRISTIAN ADVENTURES, p. 548.
13 G. & N. Pamla, AMABALANA NGO BOMI BUKA.
14 HET VOLKSBLAD, Cape Town, 15 September 1860.
15 J. du Plessis, THE LIFE OF ANDREW MURRAY, pp. 201ff.
16 J. McCarter, THE DUTCH REFORMED CHURCH IN SOUTH
    AFRICA, p. 42.
17 J. du Plessis, A HISTORY OF CHRISTIAN MISSIONS IN SOUTH
    AFRICA, p. 292.   18 J.W.L.Hofmeyr, STEFANUS HOFMEYR.
19 See Stefanus Hofmeyr, TWINTIG JAREN IN ZOUTPANSBERG,
    pp. 144ff.   20 Recorded interview, Martha (Dorothea).
21 J. du Plessis, MISSIONS IN SOUTH AFRICA, pp. 287ff.
22 Cf. Horton Davies, GREAT SOUTH AFRICAN CHRISTIANS,
    p. 150; & G. B. A. Gerdener, THE STORY OF CHRISTIAN
    MISSIONS IN SOUTH AFRICA, pp. 26 & 28.
23 E. Weeks, W. SPENCER WALTON, biography.
24 MISSIONARY REVIEW OF THE WORLD, 1905, pp. 363ff.
25 J. du Plessis, THE LIFE OF ANDREW MURRAY, pp. 384ff.
26 G. H. Wilson, UNIVERSITIES MISSION TO CENTRAL AFRICA.
27 C. W. Mackintosh, COILLARD OF THE ZAMBESI, p. 3.
28 C. W. Mackintosh, COILLARD OF THE ZAMBESI, passim.
29 F. Coillard, ON THE THRESHOLD OF CENTRAL AFRICA.
30 R. Laws, REMINISCENCES OF LIVINGSTONIA, passim.
31 A. Hetherwick, THE ROMANCE OF BLANTYRE, pp. 14ff.
32 C. W. Mackintosh, COILLARD OF THE ZAMBESI, p. 33.
33 E. Baker, LIFE OF FREDERICK STANLEY ARNOT.
34 Dan Crawford, THINKING BLACK (Central Africa).
35 Donald Fraser, LIVINGSTONIA, passim.
36 STUDENTS AND THE MODERN MISSIONARY CRUSADE, p. 302.
37 MISSIONARY REVIEW OF THE WORLD, 1899, pp. 98ff.
38 INTERNATIONAL REVIEW OF MISSIONS, 1912, p. 236.
39 MISSIONARY REVIEW OF THE WORLD, 1902, pp. 749ff.
40 Worcester Conference, S. C. A. of South Africa, 1904, p. 45.
41 J.S.Moffat, ROBERT AND MARY MOFFAT, pp. 161ff, 186ff.
42 J. Richter, GESCHICHTE DER EVANGELISCHEN MISSION IN
    AFRIKA, p. 485.
43 See E. W. Smith, THE WAY OF THE WHITE FIELDS IN
    RHODESIA, Appendix IV.
44 Findlay & Holdsworth, THE HISTORY OF THE WESLEYAN
    METHODIST MISSIONARY SOCIETY, Volume IV, pp. 378ff.

45 JUBILEUM VAN DIE N. G. K. Sending in Mashonaland, 1941.
46 See J. W. Springer, THE HEART OF CENTRAL AFRICA, pp. 19-53.
47 H. F. Davidson, SOUTH AND CENTRAL AFRICA, passim.
48 J. W. Springer, THE HEART OF CENTRAL AFRICA, p. 19.
49 G. Hawker, THE LIFE OF GEORGE GRENFELL, passim.
50 Mrs. H. Grattan Guinness, THE NEW WORLD OF CENTRAL AFRICA, pp. 175ff.
51 BAPTIST MISSIONARY MAGAZINE, 1887, cf. J. du Plessis, THE EVANGELIZATION OF PAGAN AFRICA, pp. 211-212.
52 MISSIONARY REVIEW OF THE WORLD, 1900, pp. 817ff.
53 BAPTIST MISSIONARY MAGAZINE, 1887, p. 70.
54 MISSIONARY REVIEW OF THE WORLD, 1901, pp. 40ff.
55 MISSIONARY REVIEW OF THE WORLD, 1902, p. 796.
56 J. du Plessis, EVANGELIZATION OF PAGAN AFRICA, pp. 211ff
57 Mrs. A. Macaw, THE CONGO: FIRST ALLIANCE MISSION, and Mrs. H. Grattan Guinness, THE NEW WORLD OF CENTRAL AFRICA, pp. 461ff.
58 J. E. Lundahl, NILS WESTLIND, Stockholm, 1915.
59 A. J. Brown, ONE HUNDRED YEARS, p. 217.
60 P. Steiner, KAMERUN ALS KOLONIE UND MISSIONFELD.
61 J. du Plessis, EVANGELIZATION OF PAGAN AFRICA, pp. 329ff.
62 J. Richter, GESCHICHTE DER EVANGELISCHEN MISSION IN AFRIKA, p. 485.
63 See J. H. Speke, WHAT LED TO THE DISCOVERY OF THE SOURCE OF THE NILE, p. 366.
64 DAILY TELEGRAPH, London, 7 November 1875.
65 See Eugene Stock, HISTORY OF THE CHURCH MISSIONARY SOCIETY, Volume III, pp. 98-102.
66 See S. G. Stock, THE STORY OF UGANDA, London, 1892.
67 Eugene Stock, Volume III, pp. 410-412, 441-448.
68 A. W. Tucker, EIGHTEEN YEARS IN UGANDA AND EAST AFRICA, autobiography, two volumes, London, 1908.
69 C. F. Harford-Battersby, PILKINGTON OF UGANDA, Ch. XII.
70 N. C. Sargant, THE DISPERSION OF THE TAMIL CHURCH, pp. 74ff.   71 Y. Samuel, TAMIL DAVID, biography.
72 PROCEEDINGS, Church Missionary Society, 1894, p. 9.
73 Cf. Annual Statistics of the Uganda Mission, 1892 & 1907, in the PROCEEDINGS of the Church Missionary Society.
74 Prof. du Plessis supplied C. M. S. figures without quoting sources.
75 PROCEEDINGS of the Church Missionary Society, 1893, p. 41.
76 PROCEEDINGS of the Church Missionary Society, 1894, p. 9.
77 Jesse Page, THE BLACK BISHOP: SAMUEL ADJAI CROWTHER, pp. 183ff; F. D. Walker, THE BLACK RIVER, p. 130ff.
78 W. P. Livingstone, MARY SLESSOR OF CALABAR.
79 R. L. McKeown, TWENTY-FIVE YEARS IN QUA IBOE.
80 The Lott Carey Baptist Foreign Mission Society, and the Foreign Mission Board of the National Baptist Convention.
81 See J. C. Hartzell, 'American Methodism in Africa,' MISSIONARY REVIEW OF THE WORLD, XXXII, pp. 565ff.
82 Maurice Whitlow, BISHOP J. TAYLOR SMITH, pp. 42ff.
83 William Fox, WESLEYAN MISSIONS ON THE WEST COAST OF AFRICA, passim.
84 S. M. E. P., NOS CHAMPS DE MISSION, pp. 23-28.
85 See C. F. Pascoe, TWO HUNDRED YEARS OF THE S. P. G., pp. 260ff.

215

Notes on Chapter 12: MOODY AND THE STUDENTS

1 W. R. Moody, THE LIFE OF DWIGHT L. MOODY, a standard
   text, and a recent work, J. F. Findlay, DWIGHT L. MOODY,
   provide the best earliest and latest findings on Moody, though a
   vast bibliography of volumes on the evangelist is available.
2 J. C. Pollock, MOODY: A BIBLIOGRAPHICAL PORTRAIT, p. 14.
3 Moody wrote home to tell of his involvement in the 1858 Revival in
   Chicago. Earlier authors, in spite of the fact that Moody had dated
   his letter January 6, 1857, assumed that he was referring to the
   Awakening in Chicago in the New Year of 1858, but later authors
   (a century afterward, such as Findlay, p. 63 & Pollock, p. 19) have
   suggested that he was referring to an earlier local excitement.
   The obvious explanation is that Moody (like many another) used the
   date 1857 inadvertently in early January 1858; no awakening in
   January 1857 was reported. Cf. W. R. Moody, THE LIFE OF
   DWIGHT L. MOODY, p. 47.
4 W. R. Moody, THE LIFE OF DWIGHT L. MOODY, pp. 55ff.
5 F. G. Beardsley, HISTORY OF AMERICAN REVIVALS, p. 237.
6 W. R. Moody, THE LIFE OF DWIGHT L. MOODY, pp. 131ff.
7 See J. McPherson, HENRY MOORHOUSE, pp. 48 & 66; cf.
   G. C. Needham, RECOLLECTIONS OF HENRY MOORHOUSE.
8 W. R. Moody, THE LIFE OF DWIGHT L. MOODY, p. 149.
9 See THE CHRISTIAN, 3 June 1909, on Henry Varley; and Henry
   Varley, Jr., HENRY VARLEY'S LIFE STORY; W. R. Moody,
   THE LIFE OF DWIGHT L. MOODY, p. 134ff.
10 R. Braithwaite, THE REV. WILLIAM PENNEFATHER: LIFE
   AND LETTERS.
11 W. R. Moody, THE LIFE OF DWIGHT L. MOODY, pp. 152ff.
12 EDINBURGH COURANT, December 1873; THE CHRISTIAN
   (January and February 1874 issues).
13 W. R. Moody, THE LIFE OF DWIGHT L. MOODY, pp. 197ff.
14 See DUBLIN EVENING NEWS, November 1874.
15 W. R. Moody, THE LIFE OF DWIGHT L. MOODY, pp. 215ff,
   pp. 223ff.
16 F. Engels, SOCIALISM, UTOPIAN & SCIENTIFIC, introduction.
17 See NEW YORK TIMES, 4 February 1876.
18 W. R. Moody, THE LIFE OF DWIGHT L. MOODY, pp. 291ff.
19 See THE CHRISTIAN, 6 July 1882.
20 J. C. Pollock, MOODY: A BIOGRAPHICAL PORTRAIT, p. 241.
21 W. R. Moody, THE LIFE OF DWIGHT L. MOODY, pp. 297ff.
22 MISSIONARY REVIEW OF THE WORLD, May 1895.
23 W. R. Moody, THE LIFE OF DWIGHT L. MOODY, pp. 409ff.
24 See KANSAS CITY STAR, 11 & 18 November 1899.
25 W. W. Sweet, REVIVALISM IN AMERICA, p. 169.
26 J. du Plessis, THE LIFE OF ANDREW MURRAY, p. 322.
27 See DE KERKBODE, Cape Town, issues of 1874 & 1875.
28 J. du Plessis, THE LIFE OF ANDREW MURRAY, passim.
29 Cf. DE KERKBODE, 1876; & J. du Plessis, THE LIFE OF
   ANDREW MURRAY, p. 322.
30 M. C. Dick, DAVID RUSSELL, p. 89.
31 W. E. Boardman, THE HIGHER CHRISTIAN LIFE, Boston, 1858;
   London, 1860; see M. M. Boardman, THE LIFE AND LABOURS
   OF THE REV. W. E. BOARDMAN, New York, 1887.
32 W. B. Sloan, THESE SIXTY YEARS, p. 10.
33 J. C. Pollock, THE KESWICK STORY, pp. 30ff.

34 W. B. Sloan, THESE SIXTY YEARS, p. 19.
35 J. H. Battersby, MEMOIR OF T. D. HARFORD-BATTERSBY, (Vicar of Keswick, a founder of the Keswick Convention).
36 W. B. Sloan, THESE SIXTY YEARS, indexed references on the visiting and regular speakers at Keswick.
37 J. du Plessis, THE LIFE OF ANDREW MURRAY, passim.
38 W. Y. Fullerton, THE LIFE OF F. B. MEYER, passim.
39 A. M. Hay, CHARLES INWOOD, HIS MINISTRY AND ITS SECRET, passim.
40 See C. F. Harford-Battersby, PILKINGTON OF UGANDA, chapter XII.
41 Donald Fraser, WINNING A PRIMITIVE PEOPLE, p. 279.
42 J. C. Pollock, MOODY, A BIOGRAPHICAL PORTRAIT, p. 228. & passim; cf. J. C. Pollock, A CAMBRIDGE MOVEMENT.
43 W. R. Moody, THE LIFE OF DWIGHT L. MOODY, pp. 350ff.
44 THE CHRISTIAN, 23 November 1882.
45 Wilfred Grenfell, A LABRADOR DOCTOR, (Autobiography).
46 J. C. Pollock, A CAMBRIDGE MOVEMENT, passim.
47 C. P. Shedd, TWO CENTURIES OF STUDENT CHRISTIAN MOVEMENTS, pp. 110-111.
48 L. D. Wishard, 'The Beginning of the Students' Era in Christian History,' pp. 52-53.
49 COLLEGE BULLETIN, New York, April 1880.
50 L. D. Wishard, 'The Beginning of the Students' Era in Christian History,' p. 129.
51 L. D. Wishard, 'The Beginning of the Students' Era in Christian History,' p. 138.
52 See Basil Mathews, JOHN R. MOTT: WORLD CITIZEN, & John R. Mott, HISTORY OF THE STUDENT VOLUNTEER MOVE-MENT, passim.
53 C. P. Shedd, TWO CENTURIES OF STUDENT CHRISTIAN MOVEMENTS, pp. 248ff.
54 REPORT OF THE FIRST INTERNATIONAL CONVENTION OF THE STUDENT VOLUNTEER MOVEMENT, pp. 161-163.
55 C. P. Shedd, TWO CENTURIES OF STUDENT CHRISTIAN MOVEMENTS, pp. 259ff, cf. SPRINGFIELD REPUBLICAN, 2nd August 1886; & J. R. Mott, HISTORY OF THE STUDENT VOLUNTEER MOVEMENT, p. 12.
56 C. P. Shedd, TWO CENTURIES OF STUDENT CHRISTIAN MOVEMENTS, p. 267; THE INTERCOLLEGIAN, May 1887; W. R. Moody, THE LIFE OF DWIGHT L. MOODY, p. 358.
57 G. A. Smith, THE LIFE OF HENRY DRUMMOND, pp. 370ff. C. P. Shedd, TWO CENTURIES OF STUDENT CHRISTIAN MOVEMENTS, p. 275; J. H. Oldham, STUDENT CHRISTIAN MOVEMENT OF GREAT BRITAIN AND IRELAND, p. 13.
58 C. K. Ober, LUTHER D. WISHARD, pp. 122ff.
59 Cf. THE INTERCOLLEGIAN, December 1889; SPRINGFIELD UNION, 7 July 1892; & J. H. Oldham, STUDENT CHRISTIAN MOVEMENT OF GREAT BRITAIN AND IRELAND, pp. 14ff.
60 J. H. Oldham, STUDENT CHRISTIAN MOVEMENT OF GREAT BRITAIN AND IRELAND, pp. 21ff.
61 K. S. Latourette, HISTORY OF THE EXPANSION OF CHRISTIANITY, Volume IV, pp. 97-98.
62 See S. B. Halliday, THE CHURCH IN AMERICA AND ITS BAPTISMS OF FIRE, pp. 347ff; cf. R. P. Anderson, THE STORY OF CHRISTIAN ENDEAVOR, passim.

Notes on Chapter 13: CONTINUED SOCIAL IMPACT

1 Gilbert Seldes, THE STAMMERING CENTURY, p. 141.
2 L. A. Weigle, AMERICAN IDEALISM, p. 188, & J. W. Jones, CHRIST IN THE CAMP, passim.
3 T. L. Smith, REVIVALISM & SOCIAL REFORM, Chaps. XII-XIII.
4 G. M. Trevelyan, ENGLISH SOCIAL HISTORY, pp. 492ff.
5 THE CHRISTIAN, 3 June 1909.
6 W. Canton, HISTORY OF THE BRITISH AND FOREIGN BIBLE SOCIETY, Volume III, pp. 1-2.
7 J. W. Bready, LORD SHAFTESBURY & SOCIAL-INDUSTRIAL PROGRESS, pp. 313, 318ff, 326, 333.
8 K. S. Latourette, THE NINETEENTH CENTURY IN EUROPE, Vol. II, p. 376; & J. W. Bready, LORD SHAFTESBURY, p. 402.
9 See THE REVIVAL, 27 August 1859, on education.
10 K. S. Latourette, NINETEENTH CENTURY IN EUROPE, Volume II, pp. 355ff.
11 J. W. Bready, DR. BARNARDO: PHYSICIAN, PIONEER AND PROPHET, p. 50.
12 THE CHRISTIAN, 22 April 1886, on Quarrier's Homes; & G. E. Morgan, R. C. MORGAN, pp. 144, 156, on Fegan's Homes.
13 Young and Ashton, BRITISH SOCIAL WORK, p. 41.
14 ENCYCLOPEDIA BRITANNICA, 1960, 'Probation.'
15 Young and Ashton, BRITISH SOCIAL WORK, pp. 159, 165, 174.
16 Josephine Butler, REMINISCENCES OF A GREAT CRUSADE.
17 Cf. J. Baillie, THE REVIVAL, p. 63; & W. Weir, ULSTER AWAKENING, pp. 151, 190, 196.
18 G. E. Morgan, R. C. MORGAN, p. 145; cf. THE REVIVAL, 1860 onwards, with many reports on 'The Midnight Movement.'
19 Young and Ashton, BRITISH SOCIAL WORK, pp. 205ff.
20 Josephine Butler, REMINISCENCES OF A GREAT CRUSADE; G. E. Morgan, R. C. MORGAN, pp. 298ff; Millicent Fawcett, JOSEPHINE BUTLER, passim.
21 Young and Ashton, BRITISH SOCIAL WORK, pp. 209ff, 221.
22 Charles Dickens, ALL THE YEAR ROUND, 5 November, 1859.
23 Cf. Registrar-General, QUARTERLY RETURNS OF BIRTHS, DEATHS AND MARRIAGES, 1858-65; MONTHLY RETURNS of Eight Principal Towns of Scotland.
24 See C. P. Shedd, HISTORY OF THE WORLD'S ALLIANCE OF YOUNG MEN'S CHRISTIAN ASSOCIATIONS, pp. 82ff.
25 M. T. Boardman, UNDER THE RED CROSS FLAG, p. 32.
26 See M. Gumpert, DUNANT: STORY OF THE RED CROSS.
27 B. & S. Epstein, HENRI DUNANT, p. 22.
28 T. L. Smith, REVIVALISM AND SOCIAL REFORM, p. 148.
29 A. F. C. Bourdillon, VOLUNTARY SOCIAL SERVICES, p. 45.
30 J. Whiteside, HISTORY OF THE WESLEYAN METHODIST CHURCH IN SOUTH AFRICA.
31 M. A. Sherring, THE INDIAN CHURCH, p. 218.
32 J. Richter, HISTORY OF MISSIONS IN INDIA, pp. 347ff.
33 W. C. Barclay, HISTORY OF METHODIST MISSIONS, p. 507; cf. C. Reynolds, PUNJAB PIONEER, Life of Dr. Edith Brown; W. Wanless, AN AMERICAN DOCTOR AT WORK IN INDIA; & M. P. Jeffrey, DR. IDA: INDIA, passim.
34 J. Spargo, KARL MARX: HIS LIFE AND WORK.
35 Friedrich Engels, SOCIALISM, UTOPIAN AND SCIENTIFIC; Introduction.

Notes on Chapter 14: THE FIFTH GENERAL AWAKENING

1 See J. Edwin Orr, THE FLAMING TONGUE, Chapters 1-25, for an account of the Fifth General Awakening and fuller documentation of the details.
2 On 1st July 1916, the Ulster Division was decimated in the battle of the Somme.
3 F. C. Ottman, J. Wilbur Chapman, p. 272.
4 MISSIONARY REVIEW OF THE WORLD, 1903, pp. 20ff.
5 For an account of the prisoner-of-war awakenings, see Chapter 15, 'The Mission of Peace,' pp. 121ff.
6 J. Edwin Orr, THE FLAMING TONGUE, Chapter 23, 'Taikyo Dendo in Japan.'
7 MISSIONARY REVIEW OF THE WORLD, 1903, pp. 20ff.
8 On the ministry of Gipsy Rodney Smith, see Chapter 15, 'The Mission of Peace' in South Africa, pp. 125-129.
9 J. Edwin Orr, THE FLAMING TONGUE, Chapters 1-3.
10 J. Vyrnwy Morgan, THE WELSH RELIGIOUS REVIVAL: A RETROSPECT AND A CRITICISM, pp. 248ff.
11 Keir Hardie, converted in the Fourth General Awakening, active as a Christian throughout his trade union career, died in 1915.
12 THE RECORD, 16 June 1905; THE WITNESS, 17 February 1905; and other British journals reported Anglican support.
13 J. Edwin Orr, THE FLAMING TONGUE, Chapter 4, 'Irish and Scottish Awakenings.'
14 'Awakening in Scandinavia,' THE FLAMING TONGUE, Chapter 7.
15 J. Edwin Orr, THE FLAMING TONGUE, Chapter 8, European continental reports.
16 STATESMAN'S YEARBOOK, 1905 & 1909 figures.
17 J. Edwin Orr, THE FLAMING TONGUE, Chapters 9-12, giving North American accounts.
18 'The 1905 American Awakening,' pp. 74-75; 'Impact on Church and State,' pp. 93-94; in THE FLAMING TONGUE.
19 THE FLAMING TONGUE, pp. 76-79; and passim.
20 'The 1905 American Awakening,' pp. 79-80.
21 J. Edwin Orr, THE FLAMING TONGUE, p. 80.
22 STATESMAN'S YEARBOOK, 1905 & 1911 data.
23 'The Mission of Peace,' p. 133, following.
24 J. Edwin Orr, THE FLAMING TONGUE, Chapters 17-20, giving an account of Awakenings in India.
25 92nd ANNUAL REPORT, American Baptist Missionary Union, pp. 99 & 119; cf. 93rd ANNUAL REPORT.
26 'The Korean Pentecost,' Chapter 22, THE FLAMING TONGUE.
27 CHINA MISSION YEAR BOOK, 1915.
28 ATLAS OF PROTESTANT MISSIONS, 1903; and WORLD ATLAS OF CHRISTIAN MISSIONS, 1911.
29 J. Edwin Orr, THE FLAMING TONGUE, Chapter 13, 'Latin American Quickening.'
30 'The African Awakenings,' Chapter 16, following.
31 J. Edwin Orr, THE FLAMING TONGUE, Chapter 24, 'The Pentecostal Aftermath.'
32 WESLEYAN METHODIST MAGAZINE, 1905, p. 65; CHRISTIAN ADVOCATE, 6 January 1906.
33 J. Edwin Orr, THE FLAMING TONGUE, pp. 97ff.
34 K. S. Latourette, A HISTORY OF THE EXPANSION OF CHRISTIANITY, Volume IV, Chapter 11.

Notes on Chapter 15: THE MISSION OF PEACE

1 DE KERKBODE, 1901, pp. 315, 398 & 510.
2 Rev. William Meara, DIARY (MS) in the Cory Library.
3 Louis Hofmeyr, Letter of April 1902, Cape Town; see also MISSIONARY REVIEW OF THE WORLD, 1903, pp. 616ff.
4 DE KERKBODE, 1901, indexed references.
5 See W. Canton, A HISTORY OF THE BRITISH AND FOREIGN BIBLE SOCIETY, Volume III, pp. 294-295.
6 DE KERKBODE, 1901-1902, passim.
7 DE KERKBODE, 1901, pp. 501, 526, 612 and 623ff.
8 DE KERKBODE, 1901, pp. 35, 84, 329, 286ff.
9 CHRISTIAN STUDENT, Cape Town, September 1901.
10 CHRISTIAN STUDENT, Cape Town, March 1902.
11 Recollections of A. J. A. Rowland, centenarian.
12 DE KERKBODE, 11 April 1901, p. 221.
13 4 July 1901, p. 388.   14 13 June 1901, p. 345.
15 22 August 1901, p. 478.   16 19 September 1901, p. 536.
17 DE KERKBODE, 14 November 1901, p. 622.
18 MISSIONARY REVIEW OF THE WORLD, 1906, p. 552.
19 Cf. p. 169 & Nicol MacNichol, PANDITA RAMABAI, p. 118.
20 DE KERKBODE, 24 April 1902, p. 182.
21 DE KERKBODE, 1902, pp. 41, 377 & 385ff.
22 CHRISTIAN STUDENT, Cape Town, March 1903.
23 DE KERKBODE, 1901, pp. 46, 54, 85, 147, 254, 465 & 573ff.
24 DE KERKBODE, 1902, pp. 445, 449.
25 CHRISTIAN STUDENT, Cape Town, March 1903.
26 DE KERKBODE, 26 May 1902.
27 DE KERKBODE, 1901, pp. 315, 475 & 510.
28 Ds. W. Robertson, Letter of 11 July 1901, DE KERKBODE.
29 CHRISTIAN EXPRESS, 1 June 1902, p. 81.
30 DE KONINGSBODE, July 1903, 'De Opwekking.'
31 CHRISTIAN STUDENT, Cape Town, November 1903.
32 DE KONINGSBODE, February 1904, p. 184.
33 DE KONINGSBODE, June 1904; also DE KERKBODE, 1904, pp. 161-162.
34 DE KERKBODE, 1904, pp. 191ff & later issues.
35 CHRISTIAN EXPRESS, 1 November 1902.
36 MISSIONARY REVIEW OF THE WORLD, 1908, p. 271.
37 1904, p. 557.   38 DE KERKBODE, 1906, p. 270.
39 MISSIONARY REVIEW OF THE WORLD, 1908, p. 471.
40 Cf. DE KERKBODE, 1905, pp. 35, 46ff; METHODIST CHURCH- MAN, 11 January & 8 March 1905; & CHRISTIAN EXPRESS, 1 July 1905, p. 107.
41 METHODIST CHURCHMAN, 8 June 1904, p. 887.
42 Gipsy Smith, A MISSION OF PEACE, passim.
43 DE KERKBODE, 5 May 1904, p. 206.
44 Gipsy Smith, A MISSION OF PEACE, p. 22.
45 Autobiography of Gipsy Smith, 1912, p. 287.
46 CAPE ARGUS, 18 April 1904.   47. A.J.A. Rowland, notes.
48 Gipsy Smith, A MISSION OF PEACE, p. 23.
49 CAPE ARGUS, 27 April 1904.   50. A. J. A. Rowland, notes.
51 DE KERKBODE, 1904, p. 71.
52 Gipsy Smith, A MISSION OF PEACE, pp. 25ff.
53 Gipsy Smith, pp. 34ff.   54 Gipsy Smith, pp. 38ff.
55 KIMBERLEY FREE PRESS, 14 & 21 May 1904.

56 METHODIST CHURCHMAN, 8 June 1904, p. 887.
57 METHODIST CHURCHMAN, 22 June 1904, p. 821.
58 THE FRIEND, Bloemfontein, 30 May 1904 & following.
59 METHODIST CHURCHMAN, 21 September 1904.
60 THE FRIEND, 11 & 15 June 1904.
61 THE STAR, Johannesburg, 11 June 1904.   62 13 June 1904.
63 DE KERKBODE, 30 June 1904, p. 315.
64 METHODIST CHURCHMAN, 13 July 1904.
65 Gipsy Smith, A MISSION OF PEACE, pp. 85ff.
66 METHODIST CHURCHMAN, 24 August 1904.
67 NATAL MERCURY, Durban, 25 July 1904.
68 26 July 1904.   69 1 August 1904.   70 2 August 1904.
71 Gipsy Smith, A MISSION OF PEACE, pp. 100ff.
72 NATAL TIMES & NATAL WITNESS, Pietermaritzburg.
73 METHODIST CHURCHMAN, 31 August 1904.
74 MISSIONARY HERALD, Boston, 1904, p. 493.
75 DAILY DESPATCH, East London, 20 August 1904.
76 DAILY DESPATCH, 22 & 29 August 1904.
77 Gipsy Smith, A MISSION OF PEACE, pp. 129-130.
78 DAILY TELEGRAPH, Port Elizabeth, 5 September 1904.
79 DAILY TELEGRAPH, 12 & 13 September 1904.
80 METHODIST CHURCHMAN, 14 & 21 September 1904.
81 14 September 1904.   82 7 September 1904.
83 Address of the South African Conference, MINUTES OF THE
   BRITISH METHODIST CONFERENCE, 1905, p. 459.
84 MINUTES, SOUTH AFRICAN METHODIST CONFERENCE, 1901-
   1910; (note 1905, p. 43).
85 Cf. DE KERKBODE & DE KONINGSBODE, May-July 1905;
   METHODIST CHURCHMAN, 11 January & 8 March 1905; &
   CHRISTIAN EXPRESS, 1 July 1905.   86 Same issues.
87 DE KONINGSBODE, June 1905, pp. 46-47.
88 METHODIST CHURCHMAN, 4 July & 8 August 1905.
89 DE KERKBODE, 3 August 1905.
90 DE CHRISTELIJKE STREVER, September 1905.
91 DE KERKBODE, 24 August 1905, p. 400.
92 DE KERKBODE, 12 October 1905, p. 493.
93 DE CHRISTELIJKE STREVER, September 1905, p. 12.
94 DE CHRISTELIJKE STREVER, September 1905, p. 13.
95 GODSDIENSVERSLAG, Fransch Hoek.
96 See H. C. Hopkins, EEUFEES GEDENKBOEK, NEDERDUITS
   GEREFORMEERDE GEMEENTE, HEIDELBERG, Kaap, p. 74.
97 METHODIST CHURCHMAN, 29 August 1905, pp. 2-9.
98 19 September 1905, p. 13.   99 17 October 1905, p. 14.
100 Cf. THE CHRISTIAN, London, 10 August 1905.
101 METHODIST CHURCHMAN, 7 November 1905, p. 13.
102 12 December 1905, pp. 2-3.   103 31 October; 7 November.
104 21 & 28 November 1905.   105 19 December 1905.
106 personal knowledge.
107 MINUTES, Grahamstown District Methodist Synod, Graaff-
    Reinet, 7-13 February 1906, in the Archives, Cory Library.
108 J. Edwin Orr, THE SECOND EVANGELICAL AWAKENING.
109 MINUTES, South African Methodist Conference, 1901-1910.
110 MINUTES, Methodist Synod Meeting, Rhodesia, 1900-1902.
111 MINUTES, 1903-1904, Rhodesia District (Archives, Salisbury).
112 WESLEYAN METHODIST MISSIONARY SOCIETY, 1906, p. 108.

Notes on Chapter 16: THE AFRICAN AWAKENINGS

1 CHRISTIAN EXPRESS, 1877, p. 1.   2 1903, p. 2.
3 G. B. A. Gerdener, RECENT DEVELOPMENTS IN THE SOUTH
   AFRICAN MISSION FIELD, p. 15.
4 M. W. Retief, HERLEWINGS IN ONS GESKIEDENIS, pp. 84ff,
   & J. F. Naude, VECHTEN EN VLUCHTEN, (Fight and Flight)
5 MISSIONARY REVIEW OF THE WORLD, 1903, pp. 616ff.
6 Cf. G. B. A. Gerdener, RECENT DEVELOPMENTS, p. 15; &
   MISSIONARY REVIEW OF THE WORLD, 1903, pp. 616ff.
7 DE KERKBODE, 1904, p. 75, cf. RECENT DEVELOPMENTS.
8 MISSIONARY REVIEW OF THE WORLD, 1903, p. 317.
9 MISSIONARY REVIEW OF THE WORLD, 1903, p. 79.
10 INTERNATIONAL REVIEW OF MISSIONS, October 1912, p. 37.
11 MISSIONARY REVIEW OF THE WORLD, 1906, pp. 645ff.
12 G. & N. Pamla, AMABALANA NGO BOMI BUKA, Ch. XI-XIV.
13 MINUTES of Methodist Conference, Cape Town, 1913.
14 W. Searle, REVIVAL AT LUTUBENI (Pondoland).
15 SOUTH AFRICAN PIONEER, January 1914.
16 SOUTH AFRICAN PIONEER, August-September 1916.
17 N. P. Grubb, REES HOWELLS, INTERCESSOR.
18 SOUTH AFRICAN PIONEER, October 1916.
19 SOUTH AFRICAN PIONEER, December 1917.   20 July 1918.
21 See Letters of Evelyn Richardson, 25 May, 6 & 13 June 1918, in
   Archives of the South Africa General Mission, Roodepoort.
22 Letter, 25 May 1918.   23 Letter, 13 June 1918.
24 SOUTH AFRICAN PIONEER, January and March 1919.
25 See B. P. Head, RETROSPECT AND REVIVAL IN GAZALAND,
   & ADVANCE IN GAZALAND: Continued Story of Revival; &
   SOUTH AFRICAN PIONEER, August-September 1919.
26 A. F. Calvert, SOUTH-WEST AFRICA DURING THE GERMAN
   OCCUPATION, 1889-1919, passim.
27 MISSIONARY REVIEW OF THE WORLD, 1910, p. 883.
28 Cf. Charles Inwood, AN AFRICAN PENTECOST, passim.
29 MISSIONARY REVIEW OF THE WORLD, 1910, p. 465, & 1911,
   p. 81; cf. Donald Fraser, THE WINNING OF A PRIMITIVE
   PEOPLE, pp. 279-288.
30 Cf. Charles Inwood, AN AFRICAN PENTECOST, passim.
31 Donald Fraser, THE WINNING OF A PRIMITIVE PEOPLE,
   pp. 279-288.
32 Dan Crawford, THINKING BLACK: TWENTY-TWO YEARS
   WITHOUT A BREAK IN THE LONG GRASS OF CENTRAL
   AFRICA, pp. 354ff.
33 C. P. Groves, THE PLANTING OF CHRISTIANITY IN AFRICA,
   Volume III, p. 234; cf. A. L. Hofmeyr, HET LAND LANGS
   HET MEER (N. G. K. Mission in Nyasaland).
34 S. C. Neill, A HISTORY OF CHRISTIAN MISSIONS, p. 380.
35 MISSIONARY REVIEW OF THE WORLD, 1901, pp. 556ff; cf.
   W. H. Sheppard, PRESBYTERIAN PIONEERS IN THE CONGO.
36 MISSIONARY REVIEW OF THE WORLD, 1902, p. 715.
37 Cf. R. D. Bedinger, TRIUMPHS OF THE GOSPEL IN THE
   BELGIAN Congo, passim.
38 MISSIONARY REVIEW OF THE WORLD, 1906, p. 308;   also
   1914, p. 628.
39 MISSIONARY REVIEW OF THE WORLD, 1907, p. 952.
40 MISSIONARY REVIEW OF THE WORLD, 1906, p. 325.

41 See Mrs. A. Macaw, THE CONGO: FIRST ALLIANCE MISSION, & ALLIANCE WEEKLY, 1907, p. 211.
42 ALLIANCE WEEKLY, 1908, p. 177.
43 BAPTIST MISSIONARY MAGAZINE, Boston, 1910.
44 MISSIONARY REVIEW OF THE WORLD, 1913, p. 953.
45 N. P. Grubb, C. T. STUDD; CRICKETER AND PIONEER.
46 J. T. Tucker, ANGOLA: THE LAND OF THE BLACKSMITH PRINCE, p. 67, & p. 70.
47 F. S. Arnot, MISSIONARY TRAVELS IN CENTRAL AFRICA.
48 MISSIONARY REVIEW OF THE WORLD, 1911, p. 954.
49 ASSEMBLY HERALD, 1907, p. 119.
50 Cf. A. J. Brown, THE TESTING OF A MISSION, 1904-1913; & ASSEMBLY HERALD, 1909, p. 5.
51 ASSEMBLY HERALD, 1909, p. 105; 1910, p. 121.
52 G. von Götzen, DEUTSCH-OSTAFRIKA IM AUFSTAND, 1905-1906; cf. J. Richter, GESCHICHTE DER EVANGELISCHEN MISSION IN AFRIKA.
53 PROCEEDINGS of the Church Missionary Society, 1905-1906, p. 57. 54 H. R. A. Philp, A NEW DAY IN KENYA, p. 20.
55 CHURCH MISSIONARY INTELLIGENCER, 1906, p. 50.
56 PROCEEDINGS of the Church Missionary Society, 1905-1906, p. 89; 1906-1907, p. 95; cf. MISSIONARY REVIEW OF THE WORLD, 1907, p. 405.
57 CHURCH MISSIONARY INTELLIGENCER, 1906, pp. 371ff.
58 Cf. CHURCH MISSIONARY INTELLIGENCER, 1906, p. 615; PROCEEDINGS of the Church Missionary Society, 1906-1907.
59 MISSIONARY REVIEW OF THE WORLD, 1905, pp. 590-596.
60 See J. H. Maxwell, NIGERIA: THE LAND, THE PEOPLE, AND CHRISTIAN PROGRESS, for the life of Karl Kumm.
61 J. H. Hunter, A FLAME OF FIRE: THE LIFE AND WORK OF ROWLAND V. BINGHAM.
62 PROCEEDINGS of the Church Missionary Society, 1902-1903.
63 PROCEEDINGS, 1902-1903, p. 77.
64 MISSIONARY REVIEW OF THE WORLD, 1906, p. 463.
65 PROCEEDINGS of the Church Missionary Society, 1905-1906, and 1915-1916, Niger Mission Reports.
66 MISSIONARY REVIEW OF THE WORLD, 1914, pp. 805-806.
67 MISSIONARY REVIEW OF THE WORLD, 1914, pp. 805-806.
68 See Findlay & Holdsworth, HISTORY OF THE WESLEYAN METHODIST MISSIONARY SOCIETY, Volume IV, p. 205.
69 MISSIONARY REVIEW OF THE WORLD, 1902, p. 317; also C. H. Robinson, HISTORY OF THE CHRISTIAN MISSIONS, p. 293.
70 W. J. Platt, AN AFRICAN PROPHET——Biography of William Wade Harris.
71 T. S. Johnston, THE STORY OF A MISSION, p. 21.
72 MISSIONARY REVIEW OF THE WORLD, 1909, p. 871.
73 MISSIONARY REVIEW, 1917, p. 542; 1918, p. 236.
74 MISSIONARY REVIEW, 1905, p. 638.
75 MISSIONARY REVIEW, 1914, p. 874.
76 MISSIONARY REVIEW, 1919, p. 150; 1924, pp. 922-923.
77 MISSIONARY REVIEW,   903, pp. 795ff.
78 MISSIONARY REVIEW, 1906, p. 458.
79 MISSIONARY REVIEW, 1906, pp. 308, 405.
80 WORLD MISSIONARY CONFERENCE, 1910, Volume I, p. 40.
81 David B. Barrett, CHURCH GROWTH BULLETIN, May 1969.
82 S. C. Neill, A HISTORY OF CHRISTIAN MISSIONS, pp. 568-569.

Notes on Chapter 17: EXTENDED SOCIAL IMPACT

1 GEOGRAPHICAL JOURNAL, May 1902, pp. 541-560.
2 Robert Moffat, MISSIONARY LABOURS IN SOUTH AFRICA.
3 C. W. Mackintosh, COILLARD OF THE ZAMBESI.
4 Ernest Baker, THE LIFE OF FREDERICK STANLEY ARNOT.
5 J. W. Jack, DAYBREAK IN LIVINGSTONIA, pp. 105, 111.
6 J. S. Dennis, CHRISTIAN MISSIONS AND SOCIAL PROGRESS, Volume II, p. 425.
7 Eugene Stock, A HISTORY OF THE C.M.S., Volume II, p. 137.
8 See Lord Hailey, AN AFRICAN SURVEY, passim.
9 Cf. J. du Plessis, CHRISTIAN MISSIONS IN SOUTH AFRICA, pp. 243-244, & J. E. Hutton, MORAVIAN MISSIONS, p. 266.
10 David Livingstone, MISSIONARY TRAVELS, pp. 647-650.
11 Eugene Stock, A HISTORY OF THE C.M.S., Volume III, p. 76.
12 Hansard, 1903, House of Commons debate.
13 J. S. Dennis, SOCIAL PROGRESS, Volume II, pp. 290ff.
14 See J. C. Warner, KAFFIR LAWS & CUSTOMS; W. Taylor, CHRISTIAN ADVENTURES, pp. 325ff; G. M. Theal, THE BEGINNING OF SOUTH AFRICAN HISTORY, pp. 57-58; & J. A. Chalmers, TIYO SOGA, pp. 349ff; for substantiation.
15 Cf. C. G. Seligman, THE RACES OF AFRICA, passim.
16 See Sir Philip Mitchell, Essay upon 'Africa and the West in Historical Perspective,' TROPICAL AFRICA.
17 MISSIONARY RECORD, May 1903, p. 202 (B. J. Ross).
18 Cf. J. S. Dennis, SOCIAL PROGRESS, Volume II, p. 74.
19 South African Native Races Committee, THE NATIVES OF SOUTH AFRICA: Their Economic and Social Condition, p. 188.
20 J. S. Dennis, SOCIAL PROGRESS, Volume II, p. 73.
21 J. S. Dennis, SOCIAL PROGRESS, Volume II, p. 74.
22 J. S. Dennis, SOCIAL PROGRESS, Volume II, p. 71.
23 See MISSIONARY REVIEW OF THE WORLD, March 1900, p. 212; cf. September 1903, p. 719.
24 NATIVES OF SOUTH AFRICA, pp. 182-184; cf. C. T. Loram, THE EDUCATION OF THE SOUTH AFRICAN NATIVE.
25 J. S. Dennis, SOCIAL PROGRESS, Volume II, p. 69.
26 J. S. Dennis, SOCIAL PROGRESS, Volume II, p. 100.
27 ZAMBESI INDUSTRIAL MISSION MONTHLY, November 1903.
28 J. S. Dennis, SOCIAL PROGRESS, Volume II, p. 101.
29 J. S. Dennis, SOCIAL PROGRESS, Volume II, p. 75.
30 J. S. Dennis, SOCIAL PROGRESS, Volume II, pp. 68-69.
31 George Pilkington, THE GOSPEL IN UGANDA, p. 20.
32 SCRIBNER'S MAGAZINE, August 1910.
33 Institute of International Education, New York, 1961, 'Survey of the African Student,' p. 7.
34 See Meyer, Fortes & Evans-Pritchard, AFRICAN POLITICAL SYSTEMS, New York, 1950.
35 See Philip Meyer, TOWNSMEN OR TRIBESMEN.
36 Cowan, O'Connell & Scanlon, EDUCATION AND NATION BUILDING IN AFRICA, p. 144.
37 P. F. Bohannon, AFRICA AND THE AFRICANS, p. 235.
38 Lord Hailey, AN AFRICAN SURVEY, revised 1956, p. 1066.
39 Librairie Evangelique du Congo, ATLAS OF PROTESTANT MISSIONS, Leopoldville, 1946.
40 S. C. Neill, A HISTORY OF CHRISTIAN MISSIONS, p. 385; cf. K. S. Latourette, Volume V, p. 414.

Notes on Chapter 18: BETWEEN WARS AWAKENINGS

1 See A. C. Stanley Smith, ROAD TO REVIVAL, the Story of the Ruanda Mission, pp. 26ff; Patricia St. John, BREATH OF LIFE, the Story of the Ruanda Mission, pp. 53ff.
2 A. C. Stanley Smith, ROAD TO REVIVAL, pp. 41-43.
3 Patricia St. John, BREATH OF LIFE, p. 55.
4 See J. Church, AWAKE UGANDA: the Story of Blasio Kigozi, second edition in English of BUGANDA ZUKUKA, Kampala.
5 The foregoing treatises refer to deeper life experiences of Stanley Smith, Joe Church, Blasio Kigozi, and Simeoni Nsibambi.
6 See D. B. Barrett, SCHISM AND RENEWAL IN AFRICA, p. 26; and Catherine Mabie, in American Baptist Foreign Mission Society, ANNUAL REPORT, 1923, pp. 177-178; cf. H. Fehderau, 'Kimbanguism: Prophetic Christianity in the Congo,' PRACTICAL ANTHROPOLOGY, 1962, IX, pp. 157ff.
7 American Baptist Foreign Mission Society, ANNUAL REPORTS, 1923, pp. 177-178; 1925, pp. 185ff; 1926, p. 153, 1927, p. 159; 1928, pp. 150-151; 1966, pp. 130-131.
8 See ANNUAL REPORT, 1930, p. 183.
9 See also J. W. Westgarth, THE HOLY SPIRIT AND THE PRIMITIVE MIND, London, 1946.
10 I. U. Nsasak, 'Report on a Spiritual Movement which Started in 1927 during the Universal Spiritual Revival,' typescript dated 1967, Inter-Church Commission of Inquiry, Lagos.
11 Eva Stuart-Watt, THE QUEST FOR SOULS IN QUA IBOE, pp. 100-112; cf. QUA IBOE MISSION QUARTERLY, 1927-28.
12 H. W. Turner, HISTORY OF AN AFRICAN INDEPENDENT CHURCH: I, THE CHURCH OF THE LORD (Aladura), pp. 16ff.
13 D. B. Barrett, SCHISM AND RENEWAL IN AFRICA, p. 118.
14 MISSIONARY REVIEW OF THE WORLD, July 1931.
15 MISSIONARY REVIEW OF THE WORLD, October 1931.
16 A. E. Southon, GOLD COAST METHODISM, pp. 149-154.
17 D. B. Barrett, SCHISM AND RENEWAL IN AFRICA, p. 18.
18 Cf. W. J. Platt, AN AFRICAN PROPHET, & A. E. Southon, GOLD COAST METHODISM, passim; F.D. Walker, THE STORY OF THE IVORY COAST, passim.
19 D. B. Barrett, SCHISM AND RENEWAL IN AFRICA, p. 20.
20 J. C. Thiessen, A SURVEY OF WORLD MISSIONS, p. 192.
21 MISSIONARY REVIEW OF THE WORLD, September 1931.
22 W. R. Wheeler, 'One Hundred Years in West Africa,' article in MISSIONARY REVIEW OF THE WORLD, June 1932.
23 MISSIONARY REVIEW OF THE WORLD, May 1939.
24 Andrew MacBeath, 'Revival in Central Africa,' MISSIONARY REVIEW OF THE WORLD, October 1936.
25 MacBeath described the movement to the writer in Africa.
26 Beach & Fahs, WORLD MISSIONARY ATLAS, pp. 76-77.
27 A. R. Stonelake, CONGO, PAST AND PRESENT, p. 158.
28 American Baptist ANNUAL REPORT, 1933, p. 109.
29 Taped Report, 1966, Lewis Brown; & Viola Smith, DIATUNGWA VA TADI; & American Baptist ANNUAL REPORTS, 1938-39.
30 Report, J. M. Springer, Umtali, Rhodesia, January 1939.
31 See Beach & Fahs, WORLD MISSIONARY ATLAS, p. 77; & J. I. Parker, INTERPRETATIVE SURVEY OF THE WORLD MISSION OF THE CHRISTIAN CHURCH, p. 19.
32 Patricia St. John, BREATH OF LIFE, p. 65.

33 A. C. Stanley Smith, ROAD TO REVIVAL, p. 55; cf. I. V. F. Graduates' News-Letter, Number 20, 'Present-day Revival in Africa,' and I. V. F. CHRISTIAN GRADUATE, November-December 1971, 'Power behind the Scenes,' A. C. Stanley Smith; Patricia St. John, BREATH OF LIFE, p. 72.

34 Cf. Max Warren, REVIVAL—AN ENQUIRY, p. 45; John V. Taylor, GROWTH OF THE CHURCH IN BUGANDA, p. 100; N. Landford-Smith, 'Revival in East Africa,' INTERNATIONAL REVIEW OF MISSIONS, XLIII, pp. 77-78; See C. P. Groves, THE PLANTING OF CHRISTIANITY IN AFRICA, Volume IV, p. 312; L. A. Newton, 'A Revival in East Africa,' MISSIONARY REVIEW OF THE WORLD, 1938, p. 44; & D. B. Barrett SCHISM AND RENEWAL IN AFRICA, p. 11.

35 See F. B. Welbourn, EAST AFRICAN CHRISTIANS, passim.

36 Andrew Gih, CHINA'S WONDERFUL REVIVING, passim; Marie Monsen, THE AWAKENING; Gustav Carlberg, CHINA IN REVIVAL; L. T. Lyall, BIOGRAPHY OF JOHN SUNG.

37 Advocates, on various continents, were inclined to ask about a new acquaintance, 'Is he broken?' interpreted 'Is he one of us?'

38 See Max Warren, REVIVAL—AN ENQUIRY, pp. 68-71; & J. V. Taylor, GROWTH OF THE CHURCH IN BUGANDA, p. 101; & J. Edwin Orr, EVANGELICAL AWAKENINGS IN INDIA, Chapter XVI, 'Confession in Revival,' (p. 143).

39 D. B. Barrett, SCHISM AND RENEWAL IN AFRICA, p. 11-12, describes the secession of sixteen thousand Luo opposed to the East African Revival, themselves claiming Anglican loyalty.

40 The writer visited Kenya during the Mau Mau Uprising and met with a group of Kikuyu Christians of the Revival party on the edge of the Aberdare Forest, where troops were shooting to kill.

41 Thus William Nagenda and Festo Kivengere, Baganda Anglicans, ministered in many parts of Great Britain, United States, and other parts of the English-speaking world. A Uganda team visited India in the 1950s.

42 Individual Roman Catholics and Anglo-Catholics professed to be helped by the revival, but neither church fellowship in any way countenanced the movement.

43 See WORLD DOMINION, January-February 1951, 'The Revival Movement in Kenya'; July-August 1951, 'The Revival Movement in Central Tanganyika'; September-October 1951, 'Revival in East Africa.'

44 In ten months of travel in South Africa in 1953, the writer heard neither sermon, lecture nor conversation regarding the East Africa Revival, in Afrikaans or English-speaking circles. Dr. Church—without his African colleagues—ministered in the South.

45 Rees Howells, whom the writer met at the Bible College of Wales, offered hospitality to Emperor Haile Selassie in distress there.

46 R. J. Davis, FIRE ON THE MOUNTAINS, pp. 109ff.

47 F. P. Cotterell, in BULLETIN of the Society for African Church History, 1969-1970, pp. 68ff.

48 Lectures by Dr. F. P. Cotterell at School of World Mission, 1972.

49 Persecution of Evangelicals by the Orthodox Church of Ethiopia has been documented and reported to Ecumenical authorities.

50 See 'Statistical Summary,' F. P. Cotterell, BULLETIN of the Society for African Church History, 1969-1970, p. 97.

51 Lectures by Dr. F. P. Cotterell.

52 J. C. Thiessen, A SURVEY OF WORLD MISSIONS, p. 300.

Notes on Chapter 19: EVANGELISM IN TENSION

1   STATESMAN'S YEARBOOK, 1919, p. 210; 1943, p. 437.
2   See YEARBOOK OF THE COMMONWEALTH OF AUSTRALIA, 1939, p. 381.
3   STATESMAN'S YEARBOOK, 1919, p. 210; 1943, p. 437.
4   Cf. A. C. Barnard, EEUFEES VAN DIE PINKSTERBIDURE.
5   The writer was acquainted with Dutch Reformed evangelists of at least three generations, seniors, contemporaries, and juniors.
6   This was true of Gipsy Smith before World War I, Lionel B. Fletcher before World War II, and several known to the writer since World War II, such as Oswald J. Smith and Paul B. Smith.
7   See G. B. A. Gerdener, RECENT DEVELOPMENTS IN THE SOUTH AFRICAN MISSION FIELD, pp. 71-73. The C. E. S. A. lost its property to the Church of the Province in Natal in 1909; but was supported by the Supreme Court in litigation in 1932. Its Bishop, Stephen Bradley, was born in Australia.
8   The Most Rev. Geoffrey Clayton chaired the writer's meetings in Cape Town, the Right Rev. Ambrose Reeves in Johannesburg.
9   Statistics of various evangelistic campaigns confirm this.
10 This is the conclusion of W. G. Hollenweger, ENTHUSIASTICHES CHRISTENTUM, pp. 124ff, 162ff, but it is contested.
11 C. W. Malcolm, TWELVE HOURS IN THE DAY: The Life and Work of Rev. Lionel B. Fletcher, p. 115.
12 Comment of Dr. H. A. Ironside, of the Moody Church, Chicago.
13 See L. B. Fletcher, MIGHTY MOMENTS, 1932.
14 L. B. Fletcher, SOUTH AFRICAN JEWELS, 1937.
15 C. W. Malcolm, TWELVE HOURS IN THE DAY, pp. 150ff.
16 Fletcher discouraged the use of counsellors in the inquiry room, preferring to give follow-up talks himself to inquirers.
17 C. W. Malcolm, TWELVE HOURS IN THE DAY, pp. 155ff.
18 See Issues of THE CHRISTIAN, London, June-August 1938.
19 C. W. Malcolm, TWELVE HOURS IN THE DAY, p. 150.
20 See J. Edwin Orr, IF YE ABIDE, London, 1936.
21 The Rt. Rev. A. J. Appasamy, graduate of Harvard, doctor of Oxford, Marburg and Serampore Universities.
22 A. J. Appasamy, WRITE THE VISION, pp. 91ff. See also THE CHRISTIAN RECORDER, Standerton, Transvaal, 27 November 1953, 'The Test of Time in Evangelism,' by John R. M. Gibson.
23 John Alexander Dowie's story is found in the DICTIONARY OF AMERICAN BIOGRAPHY, Volume V, pp. 413-414; cf. G. C. Loud, EVANGELIZED AMERICA, pp. 290-294. 'Isonto lika Mahon,' Mahon's Mission, broke away from the Dowie group and affiliated with Grace Missionary Church in Zion, Illinois. See W. F. P. Burton, WHEN GOD MAKES A MISSIONARY.
24 Bengt Sundkler, BANTU PROPHETS IN SOUTH AFRICA, p. 48. Relationship of the various groups is not at all clear.
25 This point is stressed by both Sundkler and Hollenweger, but no mention of it is found in texts by Pentecostal writers.
26 Personal friendship with Dr. David du Plessis since the 1930s.
27 Bengt Sundkler, BANTU PROPHETS IN SOUTH AFRICA; Donald Gee, THE PENTECOSTAL MOVEMENT, depreciated the idea of a connection between Pentecostalism and Zionism in South Africa.
28 D. B. Barrett, SCHISM AND RENEWAL IN AFRICA, p. 23.
29 Contacts with Burke through the School of World Mission.
30 See E. G. Wilson, MAKING MANY RICH, passim.

31 Nicholas Bhengu published an autobiography, REVIVAL FIRE IN SOUTH AFRICA. The writer has drawn on conversations.
32 Bhengu, in personal conversation in East London, surprised the writer with his ready espousal of parallel development.
33 K. Schlosser, EINGEBORENENKIRCHEN IN SUD-AFRIKA, p. 65. Manilal Gandhi resented Bantu attitudes to Indians.
34 See also DAILY DESPATCH, East London, 15 April 1952.
35 Personal knowledge.
36 W. A. Theron, OP DIE HORISON, Pretoria, 1944.
37 G. B. A. Gerdener, RECENT DEVELOPMENTS IN THE SOUTH AFRICAN MISSION FIELD, p. 48.
38 Dorothea Mission News Letters.
39 Ingrid Otto, DAS HAT GOTT GETAN.
40 Dorothea Mission News Letters.
41 Ingrid Otto, DAS HAT GOTT GETAN.
42 Dorothea Mission News Letters.
43 In 1967, the writer ministered for the Dorothea Mission from Cape Town to Salisbury, and gained an insight into a remarkable work.
44 G. B. A. Gerdener, pp. 30ff.
45 G. B. A. Gerdener, pp. 64ff.
46 Baptist Union of South Africa, Johannesburg; personal contact.
47 G. B. A. Gerdener, pp. 51ff.
48 G. B. A. Gerdener, pp. 71ff & 67ff.
49 This has been a popular opinion among those so opposed to South African politics that they credit no good thing there.
50 G. B. A. Gerdener, pp. 42ff.
51 CHRISTIAN RECORDER, Standerton, 27 November 1953.
52 A. J. Appasamy, WRITE THE VISION, p. 143.
53 C. M. Albertyn, MESSENGER OF REVIVAL, p. 47.
54 See CHRISTIAN RECORDER, 27 November 1953, and also A. J. Appasamy, WRITE THE VISION, p. 143.
55 Denis Clark to Bishop Appasamy, see WRITE THE VISION, pp. 211-212.
56 Personal knowledge of Ds. Wilhelm Marais.
57 Project Evangelism News Letters, Port Shepstone.
58 See THE OUTLOOK, African Enterprise, Pasadena, California.
59 CHRISTIANITY TODAY, Washington, D.C.
60 Issues of April 1973.

Notes on Chapter 20:   THE WINDS OF CHANGE

1 Patricia St. John, BREATH OF LIFE, p. 162.
2 WORLD CHRISTIAN HANDBOOK, 1957, pp. 82-83.
3 WORLD DOMINION, January-February 1951, p. 29.
4 Archbishop Beecher discussed the movement with the writer.
5 Patricia St. John, BREATH OF LIFE, p. 162.
6 Harry Campbell, C. M. S., drove the writer out from Nairobi. The writer hitch-hiked back again through Mau Mau territory!
7 WORLD DOMINION, May-June 1954, pp. 175ff. Canon Max Warren made a sympathetic but objective study of the Revival Movement in East Africa in REVIVAL, AN ENQUIRY.
8 Bishop Stanway, of Central Tanganyika, discussed the revival with the writer in Melbourne in 1957. See WORLD DOMINION, July-August 1951, pp. 227ff.
9 WORLD CHRISTIAN HANDBOOK, 1957, p. 106.
10 There were quickenings in other missions, without secessions.

11 See M. W. Randall, PROFILE FOR VICTORY, pp. 49, 52. The Anglo-Catholic constituency is slightly larger.
12 WORLD CHRISTIAN HANDBOOK, 1957, p. 91.
13 Tillman Houser, 'Graph of Total Membership, Free Methodist & Methodist Churches, Mozambique, 1900 to 1970.'
14 D. B. Barrett, SCHISM AND RENEWAL IN AFRICA, pp. 27 & 72; cf. J. T. Tucker, ANGLOA, pp. 76-81.
15 British Baptists in the nearby Congo protested publicly.
16 See Eva Stuart-Watt, FLOODS ON DRY GROUND.
17 Worldwide Evangelization Crusade, THIS IS THAT, pp. 7-8.
18 'A Tornado of Blessing,' Chapter II, THIS IS THAT.
19 Chapter III, pp. 22-24.
20 'Overwhelming Floods,' Chapter IV.
21 Chapter V, pp. 43-49.
22 ALONG KINGDOM HIGHWAYS, 1961, pp. 30-31; 1962, p. 33; 1965, p. 37.
23 Cf. WORLD CHRISTIAN HANDBOOK, 1957, pp. 68-70.
24 Tshombe was a practising Evangelical Christian.
25 Dr. E. Stanley Jones described the movement to the writer.
26 The writer visited all parts of Rwanda in 1967, making notes.
27 The Danish missionaries attended the Kumbya Convention, on the shores of Lake Kivu, when the writer ministered there in 1967.
28 See INTERNATIONAL REVIEW OF MISSIONS, January 1961.
29 Cf. Appendices, D. B. Barrett, SCHISM AND RENEWAL IN AFRICA, tribes indexed.
30 WORLD CHRISTIAN HANDBOOK, 1957, pp. 88-89.
31 (Source) Harold Germaine, cited in G. W. Peters, SATURATION EVANGELISM, p. 102.
32 CHURCH GROWTH BULLETIN, Volumes I-V, pp. 309-311.
33 7th July 1967, en route Addis Ababa from Abidjan.
34 WORLD CHRISTIAN HANDBOOK, 1957, p. 81.
35 D. B. Barrett, SCHISM AND RENEWAL IN AFRICA, p. 182.
36 ALLIANCE WITNESS, formerly ALLIANCE WEEKLY, has catalogued many local revivals, awakenings and folk movements.
37 The writer visited Ouagoudougou in mid-summer 1967.
38 See T. McMahan, SAFARI FOR SOULS, With Billy Graham in Africa, passim.
39 The writer conducted evangelistic meetings in 1940 for Harry Strachan, founder of the Mission, and renewed association with Kenneth Strachan in 1951 in Costa Rica.
40 Issues of JAPAN EVANGELIST, Tokyo, 1901ff. Taikyo Dendo (Aggressive Evangelism) is described in J. Edwin Orr, THE FLAMING TONGUE, Chapter 23.
41 Literature is available from New Life for All Headquarters, Sudan Interior Mission, P. O. Box 77, Jos, Nigeria.
42 See Dorothy Swank, MARVELOUS IN OUR EYES, passim.
43 Report of the West African Congress on Evangelism, Ibadan, 1968.
44 The writer has drawn upon conversations with Michael Cassidy, and issues of AFRICAN ENTERPRISE OUTLOOK.
45 The report written by Odhiambo Okite for CHRISTIANITY TODAY noted that Nairobi ministers reported greatly increased church attendance, and transformation of church life.
46 Personal friends attended the Johannesburg meetings.
47 RELIGIOUS NEWS SERVICE, London.
48 WORLD VISION, Report of Pastors' Conference at Kampala.
49 Information received from Burundi missionaries.

50 The popular fallacy, that Christianity is losing Africa to Islam—recently propounded by the late Bishop James Pike—is utterly contradicted by statistics, which show the growth of the Muslim faith south of the Sahara to be little more that family growth. The Christian constituency—Evangelical, Independent, and Catholic—appears to be multiplying much faster than the population. The vitality of Evangelical Christianity in Africa was evident in the Congress on World Evangelization held at Lausanne.

SELECT BIBLIOGRAPHY

In the Archives of the Methodist Church of South Africa, in the Cory Library, Rhodes University, Grahamstown: JOURNAL OF THE REV. WILLIAM SHAW, 1830; JOURNAL OF THE REV. WILLIAM MEARA, 1902; LETTERS OF J. KENDRICK, 20 November 1810, G. MIDDLEMISS, 1 November 1809—all in MS; MINUTES OF THE METHODIST DISTRICT MEETINGS, GRAHAMSTOWN, 1830-1832, 1845-1858, and 1906; MINUTES OF THE METHODIST QUARTERLY MEETING, FORT BEAUFORT, & REPORTS OF BUTTERWORTH, CLARKEBURY, KAMASTONE, OSBORN & SHAWBURY, 1866.

In the Archives of the Methodist Conference of Rhodesia, Salisbury; MINUTES OF THE METHODIST DISTRICT MEETINGS OF THE RHODESIA DISTRICT (in Salisbury or Bulawayo) 1900-1905.

In the Archives of the Methodist Conference of South Africa, Cape Town: MINUTES OF SOUTH AFRICAN METHODIST CONFERENCES, 1866, 1901-1912.

In the Archives of the Methodist Missionary Society, Marylebone, London; LETTERS OF J. CAMERON, 20 June 1860; J. GASKIN, 9 May 1860; W. SHAW, 19 December 1831, S. Young, 24 July & 10 October 1831; MINUTES OF WESLEYAN METHODIST CON-FERENCES, Great Britain, 1869, 1905, etc; also MISSIONARY NOTICES, 1832-1834; and REPORTS OF WESLEYAN METHODIST MISSIONARY SOCIETY, 1866-1868.

In the archives of the Nederduits Gereformeerde Kerk, Cape Town; ACTA, RING VAN SWELLENDAM, 1860; GODSDIENSVERSLAG (or State of Religion Report) Montagu, De Paarl, Tulbagh and Worcester, 1860; De Paarl, Prins Albert, Robertson, Villiersdorp, Wellington and Worcester, 1861; De Paarl, 1864.

ADDRESS TO THE SOUTH AFRICAN EVANGELICAL ALLIANCE, by Professor Nicholas J. Hofmeyr, 26 October 1860.

ADDRESSES DELIVERED IN ST. GEORGE'S CATHEDRAL, CAPE TOWN, by the Rev. George Grubb, Cape Town, 1890.

DIARY OF HENRY FRANCIS FYNN, edited by Stuart and Malcolm, Pietermaritzburg, 1950.

DIARY OF THE REVEREND FRANCIS OWEN, MISSIONARY WITH DINGAAN IN 1837-1838, edited by G. E. Cory, Cape Town, 1926.

LETTERS OF THE AMERICAN MISSIONARIES, 1832-1834, edited by D. J. Kotze, Cape Town, 1950.

LETTERS OF EVELYN RICHARDSON, May & June 1918, unedited (MS), South Africa General Mission, Roodepoort, Transvaal.

PROCEEDINGS OF THE CHURCH MISSIONARY SOCIETY, 1893-1894, 1905-1906, 1906-1907, etc., London.

QUARTERLY CHRONICLE OF THE LONDON MISSIONARY SOCIETY, Volume I, 1815-1819, London, 1821.

REPORTS OF THE ANNUAL MEETINGS OF THE BRITISH SOUTH AFRICA COMPANY, London, 1889-1895.

REPORT OF A SPIRITUAL MOVEMENT WHICH STARTED IN 1927 DURING THE UNIVERSAL SPIRITUAL REVIVAL, Typescript, Inter-Church Commission of Inquiry, Lagos, 1967.

REPORTS OF THE AMERICAN BAPTIST FOREIGN MISSION SOCIETY, (ALONG KINGDOM HIGHWAYS), 1923—.

REPORTS OF THE AMERICAN BOARD OF COMMISSIONERS FOR FOREIGN MISSIONS, 1859 & 1860, Boston, 1859 & 1860.

Newspapers & Periodicals
alphabetically arranged, newspapers by location,
periodicals by title

THE FRIEND, Bloemfontein, 30 May, 11 & 15 June 1904.
CAPE ARGUS, Cape Town, 19 November 1890; 18 & 27 April 1904.
HET VOLKSBLAD, Cape Town, 15 September & 25 October 1860,
  23 & 30 October 1862.
NATAL MERCURY, Durban, 25, 26 July, 1 & 2 August 1904.
DAILY DESPATCH, East London, 20, 22 & 29 August 1904; & 15
  April 1952.
GRAHAMSTOWN JOURNAL, Grahamstown, 4 & 27 July; 8, 13 & 22
  August; and 5 & 7 September 1866.
THE STAR, Johannesburg, 11 & 13 June 1904.
KIMBERLEY FREE PRESS, Kimberley, 14 May 1904.
DAILY TELEGRAPH, London, 15 November 1875, & 22 July 1910.
NATAL TIMES, Pietermaritzburg, issues of August 1904.
NATAL WITNESS, Pietermaritzburg, issues of August 1904.
DAILY TELEGRAPH, Port Elizabeth, 5, 12 & 13 September 1904.

AFRICAN ENTERPRISE OUTLOOK, Pasadena, California, 1965—
ALLIANCE WITNESS, New York, 1965—
American Baptist Foreign Mission Society, ALONG KINGDOM HIGH-
  WAYS, Valley Forge, Pennsylvania, 1960—
ASSEMBLY HERALD, Philadelphia, 1900-1910.
BAPTIST MISSIONARY MAGAZINE, Boston, 1887 & 1910.
CHRISTIAN AND MISSIONARY ALLIANCE WEEKLY, New York.
CHRISTELIJKE STREVER, Christian Endeavourer, Cape Town, 1905.
THE CHRISTIAN, London, 1860—, 1905—, 1938.
CHRISTIAN EXPRESS, Lovedale, 1876-77, 1902-05.
CHRISTIAN RECORDER, Standerton, Transvaal, 1953.
CHRISTIAN STUDENT, Cape Town, 1901-1903.
CHURCH GROWTH BULLETIN, Pasadena, California, 1964—
CHURCH MAGAZINE FOR SOUTH AFRICA, Cape Town, 1890-91.
DE KERKBODE, Cape Town, 1858-61, 1874-75, 1901-06. (indexed)
DE KONINGSBODE, Cape Town, 1903-1906.
DOROTHEA MISSION NEWS LETTERS, Pretoria, 1960—
INTERNATIONAL REVIEW OF MISSIONS, London, 1912—
INTER-VARSITY CHRISTIAN GRADUATE, London, 1971.
INTER-VARSITY GRADUATES' NEWS LETTER, London, 1971.
JAPAN EVANGELIST, Tokyo, 1901—
METHODIST CHURCHMAN, Cape Town, 1904-1905.
MISSIONARY HERALD, Boston, 1904.
MISSIONARY REVIEW OF THE WORLD, London, 1900-1911.
NEW LIFE FOR ALL, Jos, Nigeria, 1967—
SCRIBNER'S MAGAZINE, New York, 1910.
SOUTH AFRICAN METHODIST, Cape Town, 1888.
SOUTH AFRICAN PIONEER, Cape Town, 1914-1919.
SOUTH AFRICAN WATCHMAN, Grahamstown, 1858-1860.
STATESMAN'S YEARBOOK, London, 1919.
WESLEYAN METHODIST MAGAZINE, London, 1810ff, & 1860-1867.
WORLD CHRISTIAN HANDBOOK, London, 1957.
WORLD DOMINION, London, 1951.
YEARBOOK OF THE COMMONWEALTH OF AUSTRALIA, 1939.
ZAMBESI INDUSTRIAL MISSION MAGAZINE, London, 1903.

Biographical:

Anshelm, Carl, BISKOP HANS PETER HALLBECK, den Förste Svenska Missionären i Afrika, Lund, 1927.
Appasamy, A. J., WRITE THE VISION, Madras, 1964.
Baker, Ernest, THE LIFE AND EXPLORATIONS OF FREDERICK STANLEY ARNOT, London, 1921.
Becker, P., PATH OF BLOOD: Rise and Conquests of Mzilikazi, Founder of the Matabele Tribe, London, 1962.
Becker, P., RULE OF FEAR: Life and Times of Dingane, King of the Zulus, London, 1964.
Bond, G., CHAKA THE TERRIBLE, London, 1961.
Boyce, W. B., MEMOIR OF THE REV. WILLIAM SHAW, London, 1874.
Brooke, A., ROBERT GRAY, FIRST BISHOP OF CAPE TOWN, Cape Town, 1947.
Burton, W. F. P., WHEN GOD MAKES A MISSIONARY: the Life Story of Edgar Mahon, London, 1936.
Chalmers, J. A., TIYO SOGA: a biography, Edinburgh, 1877.
Church, J. E., AWAKE UGANDA: the Story of Blasio Kigozi and His Vision of Revival, (Second Edition), Kampala, 1957.
Claus, Wilhelm, Dr. LUDWIG KRAPF, weil Missionar, Basel, n.d.
Cousins, H. T., FROM KAFIR KRAAL TO PULPIT, the story of Tiyo Soga, London, 1897.
Cowper, William, THE POWER OF GRACE ILLUSTRATED, (the biography of an unnamed minister: H. R. van Lier) Edinburgh, 1792.
Cox, G. W., THE LIFE OF JOHN WILLIAM COLENSO, BISHOP OF NATAL, two volumes, London, 1888.
Crawford, Dan, THINKING BLACK: TWENTY-TWO YEARS IN THE LONG GRASS OF CENTRAL AFRICA, London, 1912.
Crouch, E. H., THE LIFE OF THE REV. H. H. DUGMORE, Poet, Preacher, 1810-1897, Cape Town, 1920.
Davies, Horton, GREAT SOUTH AFRICAN CHRISTIANS, Cape Town, 1951.
Day, E. H., ROBERT GRAY, FIRST BISHOP OF CAPE TOWN, London, 1930.
De Villiers, M., HERINNERING AAN HET LEVEN EN DEN ARBEID VAN GOTTLIEB WILHELM ANTHONY VAN DER LINGEN, Utrecht, 1875.
Dick, M. C., DAVID RUSSELL: A SKETCH FOR A PORTRAIT, Durban, 1939.
Douglas, W. M., ANDREW MURRAY AND HIS MESSAGE, London, 1926.
Du Plessis, J., THE LIFE OF ANDREW MURRAY OF SOUTH AFRICA, London, 1919.
Grauer, O. C., FREDRIK FRANSON, Chicago, 1940.
Grubb, N. P., C. T. STUDD, CRICKETER AND PIONEER, London, 1952.
Grubb, N. P., REES HOWELLS, INTERCESSOR, London, 1952.
Hanekom, T. N., HELPERUS RITZEMA VAN LIER, DIE LEBENS-BEELD VAN 'N KAAPSE PREDIKANT UIT DIE 18de EEU, Cape Town, 1959.
Harford-Battersby, C. F., PILKINGTON OF UGANDA, London.
Hawker, George, THE LIFE OF GEORGE GRENFELL, CONGO MISSIONARY AND EXPLORER, London, 1909.

Hofmeyr, M. N., HET LEVEN VAN STEPHANUS HOFMEYR—
ZENDELING TE ZOUTPANSBERG, Wellington, 1907.
Holt, B. F., JOSEPH WILLIAMS AND THE PIONEER MISSION TO
THE SOUTHEASTERN BANTU, Lovedale, 1954.
Holden, W. C., BRITISH RULE IN SOUTH AFRICA: THE STORY
OF KAMA AND HIS TRIBE, London, undated.
Holden, W. C., REMINISCENCES OF THE REV. JOHN EDWARDS,
Second edition, London, 1886.
Hunter, J. H., A FLAME OF FIRE: THE LIFE AND WORK OF
R. V. BINGHAM, Toronto, 1961.
Kestell, J. D., HET LEVEN VAN PROF. N. J. HOFMEYR, Cape
Town, 1911.
Kruger, S. J. P., THE MEMOIRS OF PAUL KRUGER, Four times
President of the South African Republic, London, 1902.
Livingstone, W. P., CHRISTINA FORSYTH OF FINGOLAND, London,
1919.
Livingstone, W. P., LAWS OF LIVINGSTONIA, London, 1921.
Louw, A. F., MY EERSTE NEENTIG JAAR, Cape Town, 1958.
Lundahl, J. E., NILS WESTLIND, Stockholm, 1915.
Mackenzie, W. D., JOHN MACKENZIE . . . SOUTH AFRICAN MIS-
SIONARY, London, 1902.
Mackintosh, C. W., COILLARD OF THE ZAMBESI, 1858-1904,
London, 1907.
Malcolm, C. W., TWELVE HOURS IN THE DAY: the Life and
Work of the Rev. Lionel B. Fletcher, London, 1956.
Marsh, J. W., A MEMOIR OF ALLEN F. GARDINER, R. N.,
London, 1857.
Martin, A. D., DOCTOR VAN DER KEMP, London, undated.
Moffat, J. S., THE LIVES OF ROBERT AND MARY MOFFAT,
London, 1886.
Murray, Harold, SIXTY YEARS AN EVANGELIST, (the Life of Gipsy
Rodney Smith), London, 1936.
Pamla, G. & N., AMABALANA NGO BOMI BUKA: (the Life of the
Rev. Charles Pamla, in Xhosa), Palmerton, C. P., 1934.
Paul, John, THE SOUL DIGGER: THE LIFE AND TIMES OF
WILLIAM TAYLOR, Upland, Indiana, 1928.
Philip, John, MEMOIR OF MRS. MATHILDA SMITH, LATE OF
CAPE TOWN, London, 1824.
Philip, Robert, THE ELIJAH OF SOUTH AFRICA: OR THE
CHARACTER AND SPIRIT OF THE LATE REV. JOHN PHILIP,
UNVEILED AND VINDICATED, London, 1851.
Platt, W. J., AN AFRICAN PROPHET (The Biography of William
Wade Harris), London, 1934.
Retief, M. W., WILLIAM MURRAY OF NYASALAND, Lovedale, 1958.
Seaver, George, DAVID LIVINGSTONE: HIS LIFE AND LETTERS,
London, 1957.
Shaw, William, THE STORY OF MY MISSION IN SOUTHEASTERN
AFRICA, London, 1860.
Smith, E. W., THE MABILLES OF BASUTOLAND, London, 1939.
Smith, Rodney, GIPSY SMITH: his Life and Work, London, 1926.
Taylor, William, THE STORY OF MY LIFE, New York, 1895.
Taylor, William, CHRISTIAN ADVENTURES IN SOUTH AFRICA,
New York, 1877.
Vos, M. C., MERKWAARDIG VERHAAL, Amsterdam, 1824.
Weeks, E., W. SPENCER WALTON, London, 1907.
Wells, J., THE LIFE OF JAMES STEWART, London, 1909.

Missionary:

Allen, W. O. B., & Edmund McClure, TWO HUNDRED YEARS: THE
    HISTORY OF THE SOCIETY FOR PROMOTING CHRISTIAN
    KNOWLEDGE, 1698-1898, London, 1898.
Arnot, F. S., MISSIONARY TRAVELS IN CENTRAL AFRICA,
    London, 1914.
Barnard, A. C., EEUFEES GEDENKBOEK VAN DIE NEDERDUITS
    GEREFORMEERDE GEMEENTE, HEIDELBERG, KAAPLAND,
    1885-1955, Cape Town, 1955.
Barnard, A. C., EEUFEES VAN DIE PINKSTERBIDURE, 1861-1961,
    Cape Town, 1961.
Barrett, D. B., SCHISM AND RENEWAL IN AFRICA, Nairobi,
    1968 (Oxford University Press).
Batts, H. J., THE STORY OF A HUNDRED YEARS, 1820-1920;
    History of the Baptist Church in South Africa, Cape Town, undated.
Bedinger, R. D., TRIUMPHS OF THE GOSPEL IN BELGIAN
    CONGO, Richmond, undated.
Bhengu, Nicholas, REVIVAL FIRE IN SOUTH AFRICA, Philadelphia,
    1949.
Brown, A. J., THE TESTING OF A MISSION: 1904-1913 IN THE
    WEST AFRICAN MISSION, New York, 1913.
Brown, A. J., ONE HUNDRED YEARS: A History of the Foreign
    Missionary Work of the Presbyterian Church in the United States
    of America, New York, 1937.
Burgess, Andrew, UNKULUNKULU IN ZULULAND, Minneapolis,
    1934.
Callaway, G., PIONEERS IN PONDOLAND, Lovedale, undated.
Campbell, John, TRAVELS IN SOUTH AFRICA, London, 1815.
Coillard, Francois, ON THE THRESHOLD OF CENTRAL AFRICA,
    translated into English by C. W. Mackintosh, New York, 1903.
Cook, Thomas, MISSION TOUR IN SOUTH AFRICA, London, 1893.
Davis, R. J., FIRE ON THE MOUNTAINS, Grand Rapids, 1966.
Davidson, H. F., SOUTH AND CENTRAL AFRICA, Elgin, 1915.
Du Plessis, J., THE EVANGELIZATION OF PAGAN AFRICA,
    Cape Town, 1930.
Du Plessis, J., A HISTORY OF CHRISTIAN MISSIONS IN SOUTH
    AFRICA, London, 1911.
Ellenberger, V., A CENTURY OF WORK IN BASUTOLAND, (a
    translation from the French by E. M. Ellenberger), Morija, 1938.
Engelbrecht, S. P., GESKIEDENIS VAN DIE NEDERDUITS HER-
    VORMDE KERK VAN AFRIKA, Pretoria, 1920.
Eversleigh, William, THE SETTLERS AND METHODISM, Cape
    Town, 1920.
Fletcher, Lionel B., MIGHTY MOMENTS, London, 1932.
Fletcher, Lionel B., SOUTH AFRICAN JEWELS, London, 1936.
Findlay, G. G., & W. W. Holdsworth, THE HISTORY OF THE
    WESLEYAN METHODIST MISSIONARY SOCIETY, London, 1922.
Fox, William, A BRIEF HISTORY OF THE WESLEYAN MISSIONS
    ON THE WESTERN COAST OF AFRICA, London, 1851.
Fraser, Donald, WINNING A PRIMITIVE PEOPLE, New York, 1916.
Gardiner, A. F., NARRATIVE OF A JOURNEY TO THE ZOOLU
    COUNTRY, London, 1836.
Gerdener, G. B. A., RECENT DEVELOPMENTS IN THE SOUTH
    AFRICAN MISSION FIELD, London, 1958.

Gerdener, G. B. A., THE STORY OF CHRISTIAN MISSIONS IN SOUTH AFRICA, Johannesburg, 1950.
Green & Eldridge, A PONDOLAND HILLTOP, London, undated.
Groves, C. P., THE PLANTING OF CHRISTIANITY IN AFRICA, four volumes, London, 1948-1958.
Guinness, Mrs. H. Grattan, THE NEW WORLD OF CENTRAL AFRICA, New York, 1890.
Head, Bessie P., RETROSPECT AND REVIVAL IN GAZALAND, London, 1916.
Head, Bessie P., ADVANCE IN GAZALAND: THE CONTINUED STORY OF REVIVAL, London, 1918.
Hetherwick, Alexander, THE ROMANCE OF BLANTYRE, London, undated.
Hewson, Leslie A., AN INTRODUCTION TO SOUTH AFRICAN METHODISTS, Cape Town, 1950.
Hinchliff, P. B., THE ANGLICAN CHURCH IN SOUTH AFRICA, (the Church of the Province), London, 1963.
Hofmeyr, A. L., HET LAND LANGS HET MEER, Stellenbosch, 1917.
Hofmeyr, Stefanus, TWINTIG JAREN IN ZOUTPANSBERG, Cape Town, 1890.
Hollenweger, Walter G., ENTHUSIASTISCHES CHRISTENTUM, Die Pfingstbewegung in Geschichte und Gegenwart, Zurich, 1969.
Hopkins, H. C., DIE MOEDER VAN ONS ALMAL, GESKIEDENIS VAN DIE GEMEENTE KAAPSTAD, 1665-1965, Cape Town, 1965.
Hylander, Nils, MORGONLJUS, (Ethiopia), 1865-1916, Stockholm.
Inwood, Charles, AN AFRICAN PENTECOST: A MISSIONARY TOUR IN CENTRAL AFRICA, London, 1912.
JUBILEUM VAN DIE NEDERDUITS GEREFORMEERDE KERK SENDING IN MASHONALAND, Cape Town, 1941.
Kotze, D. A., DIE GEMEENTE FRASERBURG, (Kaap Provinsie), 1851-1951, Stellenbosch, 1951.
Latourette, K. S., A HISTORY OF THE EXPANSION OF CHRISTIANITY, seven volumes, London, 1943-1945.
Laws, Robert, REMINISCENCES OF LIVINGSTONIA, Edinburgh, 1934.
Livingstone, David, MISSIONARY TRAVELS AND RESEARCHES IN SOUTH AFRICA, London, 1857.
Lovett, Richard, HISTORY OF THE LONDON MISSIONARY SOCIETY, 1795-1895, two volumes, London, 1899.
Macaw, Mrs. A., THE CONGO: THE FIRST ALLIANCE MISSION FIELD, Harrisburg, Pennsylvania, undated.
McCarter, John, THE DUTCH REFORMED CHURCH IN SOUTH AFRICA, Edinburgh, 1867.
McKeown, R. L., TWENTY-FIVE YEARS IN QUA IBOE, THE STORY OF A MISSIONARY EFFORT IN NIGERIA, London, 1912.
McMahan, T., SAFARI FOR SOULS, With Billy Graham in Africa, Columbia, S. C., 1960.
Maree, W. L., LIG IN SOUTPANSBERG: SENDINGWERK VAN DIE NEDERDUITS GEREFORMEERDE KERK, Pretoria, 1962.
Moffat, Robert, MISSIONARY LABOURS AND SCENES IN SOUTH AFRICA, London, 1842.
Neill, S. C., A HISTORY OF CHRISTIAN MISSIONS, London, 1964.
Oberholster, G. J., KWAARTMILLENIUM GEDENKBOEK VAN DIE NEDERDUITS GEREFORMEERDE GEMEENTE, PAARL, 1941.
Orr, J. Edwin, THE EAGER FEET, (Evangelical Awakenings 1792— and 1830— Worldwide), Chicago, 1975.

Orr, J. Edwin, THE FERVENT PRAYER, (Evangelical Awakenings 1858-1899 Worldwide), Chicago, 1974.

Orr, J. Edwin, THE FLAMING TONGUE, (Evangelical Awakenings 1900— Worldwide), Chicago, 1973.

Orr, J. Edwin, THE LIGHT OF THE NATIONS, Evangelical Renewal and Advance in the Nineteenth Century, Exeter, 1965, & Grand Rapids, 1965.

Otto, Ingrid, DAS HAT GOTT GETAN, Wuppertal, 1971.

Parker, Joseph I., INTERPRETATIVE SURVEY OF THE WORLD MISSION OF THE CHRISTIAN CHURCH, New York, 1928.

Pascoe, C. F., TWO HUNDRED YEARS OF THE SOCIETY FOR THE PROPAGATION OF THE GOSPEL IN FOREIGN PARTS, 1701-1900, London, 1901.

Philp, H. R. A., A NEW DAY IN KENYA, London, 1936.

Pilkington, George, THE GOSPEL IN UGANDA, London, 1890.

Randall, M. W., PROFILE FOR VICTORY: NEW PROPOSALS FOR MISSIONS IN ZAMBIA, South Pasadena, 1970.

Retief, M. W., HERLEWINGS IN ONS GESKIEDENIS, Cape Town, 1951.

Richter, Julius, GESCHICHTE DER EVANGELISCHEN MISSION IN AFRICA, Gutersloh, 1922.

Robinson, C. H., HAUSALAND: or, FIFTEEN HUNDRED MILES THROUGH THE CENTRAL SUDAN, London, 1896.

Sargant, N. C., THE DISPERSION OF THE TAMIL CHURCH, Madras, 1940.

Sass, F.W., 'The Influence of the Church of Scotland on the Dutch Reformed Church in South Africa,' thesis, Edinburgh, 1956.

St. John, Patricia, BREATH OF LIFE, London, 1971.

Schlosser, Katesa, EINGEBORENENKIRCHEN IN SUD- & SUDWEST-AFRIKA, Muhlau, 1953.

Searle, W., REVIVAL AT LUTUBENI, (Pondoland), London, 1911.

Shaw, Barnabas, MEMORIALS OF SOUTH AFRICA, London, 1840.

Shepherd, R. H. W., LOVEDALE, SOUTH AFRICA, THE STORY OF A CENTURY, 1841-1941, Lovedale, 1941.

Sheppard, William H., PRESBYTERIAN PIONEERS IN CONGO, Richmond, undated.

Smit, A. P., GEDENKBOEK VAN DIE NEDERDUITS GEREFOR-MEERDE KERK GEMEENTE VAN BEAUFORT WES, 1820-1945, Cape Town, 1945.

Smit, A. P., GEDENKBOEK VAN DIE NEDERDUITS GEREFOR-MEERDE KERK GEMEENTE VAN CALVINIA, 1847-1947, Cape Town, 1947.

Smith, A. C. Stanley, ROAD TO REVIVAL, London, 1947.

Smith, E. W., THE WAY OF THE WHITE FIELDS IN RHODESIA, London, 1928.

Smith, Rodney (Gipsy), A MISSION OF PEACE, London, 1904.

Smith, Viola, DIATUNGWA VA TADI, Kinshasa, 1966.

Societe des Missions Evangeliques, NOS CHAMPS DE MISSION, Paris, 1908.

Southon, A. E., GOLD COAST METHODISM, THE FIRST HUNDRED YEARS, 1835-1935, London, 1935

Spoelstra, C., HET KERKELIJK EN GODSDIENSTIG LEVEN DER BOEREN NA DEN GROOTEN TREK, Kampen, 1918.

Springer, J. W., HEART OF CENTRAL AFRICA, Cincinnati, 1909.

Steiner, P., KAMERUN ALS KOLONIE UND MISSIONFELD, Basel, 1909.

Stewart, James, DAWN IN THE DARK CONTINENT, or AFRICA AND ITS MISSIONS, London, 1903.

Stock, Eugene, HISTORY OF THE CHURCH MISSIONARY SOCIETY, four volumes, London, 1899-1916.

Stonelake, A. R., CONGO PAST AND PRESENT, London, 1937.

Strong, William E., THE STORY OF THE AMERICAN BOARD: AN ACCOUNT OF THE FIRST HUNDRED YEARS OF THE AMERICAN BOARD OF COMMISSIONERS FOR FOREIGN MISSIONS, Boston, 1910.

Stuart-Watt, Eva, FLOODS ON DRY GROUND, London, 1936.

Stuart-Watt, Eva, THE QUEST FOR SOULS IN QUA IBOE, London, 1951.

Sundkler, B.engt G. M., BANTU PROPHETS IN SOUTH AFRICA, London, 1948.

Swank, Dorothy, MARVELOUS IN OUR EYES, Jos, Nigeria.

Taylor, J. D., editor: CHRISTIANITY AND THE NATIVES OF SOUTH AFRICA, Lovedale, 1928.

Taylor, J. D., A HUNDRED YEARS OF THE AMERICAN BOARD MISSION IN SOUTH AFRICA, Durban, 1935.

Taylor, J. V., THE GROWTH OF THE CHURCH IN BUGANDA, London, 1958.

Theron, W. A., OP DIE HORISON, Pretoria, 1944.

Thiessen, J. C., A SURVEY OF WORLD MISSIONS, Chicago, Revised Edition, 1961.

Tucker, A. W., EIGHTEEN YEARS IN UGANDA AND EAST AFRICA, two volumes, London, 1908.

Tucker, J. T., ANGOLA: THE LAND OF THE BLACKSMITH PRINCE, London, 1933.

Turner, H. T., HISTORY OF AN AFRICAN INDEPENDENT CHURCH: I, THE CHURCH OF THE LORD (ALADURA), Oxford, 1967.

Van der Merwe, W. J., THE DEVELOPMENT OF MISSIONARY ATTITUDES IN THE DUTCH REFORMED CHURCH IN SOUTH AFRICA, Cape Town, 1936.

Victor, O., THE SALIENT OF SOUTH AFRICA, London, 1931.

Warren, M. A. C., REVIVAL, AN ENQUIRY, London, 1954.

Welbourn, F. B., EAST AFRICAN CHRISTIAN, London, 1965.

Westgarth, J. W., THE HOLY SPIRIT AND THE PRIMITIVE MIND, London, 1946.

Whiteside, J., HISTORY OF THE WESLEYAN METHODIST CHURCH IN SOUTH AFRICA, London, 1906.

Whitlow, Maurice, J. TAYLOR SMITH, London, 1938.

Wilson, E. G., MAKING MANY RICH, Springfield, Mo., 1955.

Wilson, G. H., THE HISTORY OF THE UNIVERSITIES' MISSION TO CENTRAL AFRICA, London, 1936.

Worldwide Evangelistic Crusade, THIS IS THAT, London, 1954.

GENERAL BIBLIOGRAPHY

Bennett, W. W., THE GREAT REVIVAL IN THE SOUTHERN ARMIES,
  Philadelphia, 1877.
Bloch-Hoell, N., THE PENTECOSTAL MOVEMENT, Oslo, 1964.
Boardman, M. M., THE LIFE AND LABOURS OF THE REV. W. E.
  BOARDMAN, New York, 1887.
Boardman, M. T., UNDER THE RED CROSS FLAG, Philadelphia, 1915.
Boardman, W. E., THE HIGHER CHRISTIAN LIFE, Boston, 1858.
Bois, Henri, LE REVEIL AU PAYS DE GALLES, Toulouse, 1905.
Bourdillon, A. F. C., VOLUNTARY SOCIAL SERVICES, London, 1945.
Braithwaite, R., THE REV. WILLIAM PENNEFATHER: LIFE AND
  LETTERS, London, 1878.
Branch, E. D., THE SENTIMENTAL YEARS, 1836-1860, New York,
  1934.
Bready, J. Wesley, THIS FREEDOM—WHENCE? London, 1942.
Brown, Arthur Judson, ONE HUNDRED YEARS: A HISTORY OF
  THE FOREIGN MISSIONARY WORK OF THE PRESBYTERIAN
  CHURCH IN THE U. S. A., New York, 1937.
Butler, J., PERSONAL REMINISCENCES OF A GREAT CRUSADE,
  London, 1913.
Candler, W. A., GREAT REVIVALS AND THE GREAT REPUBLIC,
  Nashville, 1904.
Canton, William, A HISTORY OF THE BRITISH AND FOREIGN
  BIBLE SOCIETY, London, 5 Volumes, 1904-1910.
Carey, S. Pearce, WILLIAM CAREY, FELLOW OF THE LINNAEAN
  SOCIETY, New York, 1923.
Carey, William, AN ENQUIRY INTO THE OBLIGATION OF
  CHRISTIANS TO USE MEANS FOR THE CONVERSION OF THE
  HEATHENS, Leicester, 1792.
Carus, William, MEMOIRS OF THE LIFE OF THE REV. CHARLES
  SIMEON, London, 1847.
Caughey, James, METHODISM IN EARNEST, Richmond, 1852.
Caughey, James, SHOWERS OF BLESSING, Boston, 1857.
Chambers, T. W., THE NOON PRAYER MEETING, New York, 1858.
Church, R. W., THE OXFORD MOVEMENT, 1833-1845, London,
  1891.
Clark, Elmer T., editor, JOURNAL AND LETTERS OF FRANCIS
  ASBURY, Nashville, 3 Volumes, 1958.
Clarkson, Thomas, THE RISE, PROGRESS AND ACCOMPLISHMENT
  OF THE ABOLITION OF THE AFRICAN SLAVE TRADE BY
  THE BRITISH PARLIAMENT. London, 1808.

239

Colquhoun, John Campbell, WILBERFORCE: HIS FRIENDS AND HIS TIMES, London, 1867.
Conant, W. C., NARRATIVE OF REMARKABLE CONVERSIONS, New York, 1858.
Cook, Sir Edward, THE LIFE OF FLORENCE NIGHTINGALE, London, 2 Volumes, 1913.
Couper, W. J., SCOTTISH REVIVALS, Dundee, 1918.
Craig, J. A., FORTY YEARS AMONG THE TELUGUS, Toronto, 1912.
Crookshank, C. H., HISTORY OF METHODISM IN IRELAND, London, 3 Volumes, 1888.
Davis, G. T. B., TORREY AND ALEXANDER, New York, 1905.
Dickens, Charles, ALL THE YEAR ROUND, London, 1859.
Drach, George, editor, OUR CHURCH ABROAD: THE FOREIGN MISSIONS OF THE LUTHERAN CHURCH IN AMERICA, Philadelphia, 1926.
Dwight, H. O., CENTENNIAL HISTORY OF THE AMERICAN BIBLE SOCIETY, New York, 1916.
Dyer, H. S., REVIVAL IN INDIA, London, 1907.
Ellis, W. T., BILLY SUNDAY, New York, 1936.
Emery, Julia C., A CENTURY OF ENDEAVOR, 1821-1921: A RECORD OF THE MISSIONARY SOCIETY OF THE PROTESTANT EPISCOPAL CHURCH, New York, 1921.
Fairholme, E. G., & Wellesley Pain, A CENTURY OF WORK FOR ANIMALS: THE R. S. P. C. A., 1824-1924, London, 1924.
Farndale, W. E., THE SECRET OF MOW COP, London, 1950.
Fawcett, Millicent, JOSEPHINE BUTLER, London, 1927.
Findlay, J. F., DWIGHT L. MOODY, Chicago, 1969.
Findlay, G. G., & Holdsworth, W. W., THE HISTORY OF THE WESLEYAN METHODIST MISSIONARY SOCIETY, London, 5 Volumes, 1921-1924.
Finney, Charles G., LECTURES ON REVIVALS OF RELIGION, New York, 1835, (Edinburgh, 1928).
Finney, Charles G., MEMOIRS OF REV. CHARLES G. FINNEY, New York, 1876.
Frodsham, S. H., WITH SIGNS FOLLOWING, Springfield, Mo., 1946.
Fullerton, W. Y., THE LIFE OF F. B. MEYER, London, 1929.
Gardner, A. R. C., THE PLACE OF JOHN HOWARD IN PENAL REFORM, London, 1926.
Garrard, M. N., MRS. PENN-LEWIS, London, undated.
Gee, Donald, THE PENTECOSTAL MOVEMENT, London, 1949.
Goforth, Jonathan, "BY MY SPIRIT," London, undated.
Gulick, O. H., THE PILGRIMS OF HAWAII, New York, 1918.
Haldane, Alexander, THE LIVES OF ROBERT HALDANE OF AIRTHREY AND OF HIS BROTHER, JAMES ALEXANDER HALDANE, Edinburgh, 1852 (5th edition, 1855.)
Halliday, S. B. & D. S. Gregory, THE CHURCH IN AMERICA AND ITS BAPTISMS OF FIRE, New York, 1896.
Harford-Battersby, J., MEMOIR OF T. D. HARFORD-BATTERSBY, London, 1890.
Harris, John, A CENTURY OF EMANCIPATION, London, 1933.
Headley, P. C., E. PAYSON HAMMOND, London, 1885.
Henderson, G. C., FIJI AND THE FIJIANS, 1835-1856, Sydney, 1931.
Hodder, Edwin, THE LIFE AND WORK OF THE SEVENTH EARL OF SHAFTESBURY, London, 1887.
Hodder-Williams, J. E., THE LIFE OF SIR GEORGE WILLIAMS, London, 1906.

Humphrey, Heman, REVIVAL SKETCHES, New York, 1859.
Ironside, H. A., A HISTORICAL SKETCH OF THE BRETHREN MOVEMENT, Grand Rapids, 1942.
Jeffrey, M. P., DR. IDA: INDIA, New York, 1938.
Jenkins, D. E., THE LIFE OF THOMAS CHARLES OF BALA, Denbigh, 1908.
Jones, J. W., CHRIST IN THE CAMP, Richmond, 1887.
Jones, R. B., RENT HEAVENS, London, 1909.
Jonzon, Bengt, STUDIER I PAAVO RUOTSULAINENS FROMHET, Stockholm, 1935.
Kemp, Winifred, JOSEPH W. KEMP, London, 1934.
Kennedy, John, THE APOSTLE OF THE NORTH, LIFE AND LABOURS OF THE REV. DR. MACDONALD, London, 1867.
Latimer, R. S., UNDER THREE TSARS: LIBERTY OF CONSCIENCE IN RUSSIA, 1856-1909, London, 1909.
Lloyd, J. Meirion, ON EVERY HIGH HILL, London, 1950.
Lyall, James, THE RECENT GREAT REVIVAL IN AUSTRALIA AND NEW ZEALAND, Edinburgh, 1905.
Mackichan, D., THE MISSIONARY IDEAL IN THE SCOTTISH CHURCHES, London, 1927.
MacPherson, J., HARRY MOORHOUSE: THE ENGLISH EVANGELIST, London, 1920.
Mason, Ebenezer, THE COMPLETE WORKS OF JOHN M. MASON, New York, 4 Volumes, 1849.
Mason, Francis, KAREN APOSTLE: KO THAH-BYU, Boston, 1843.
Mathews, Basil, JOHN R. MOTT, World Citizen, New York, 1934.
Miller, Basil, PRAYING HYDE, Grand Rapids, 1943.
Moody, W. R., THE LIFE OF DWIGHT L. MOODY, New York, 1900.
Morgan, G. E., R. C. MORGAN, HIS LIFE AND TIMES, London, 1909.
Morgan, J. V., THE WELSH RELIGIOUS REVIVAL, London, 1909.
Norborg, Sverre, HANS NIELSEN HAUGE, 1771-1804, Oslo, 1966.
Orr, J. Edwin, THE EAGER FEET, (Evangelical Awakenings 1792— & 1830— Worldwide), Chicago, 1975.
Orr, J. Edwin, THE FERVENT PRAYER, (Evangelical Awakenings 1858-1899 Worldwide), Chicago, 1974.
Orr, J. Edwin, THE FLAMING TONGUE, (Evangelical Awakenings 1900— Worldwide), Chicago, 1973.
Orr, J. Edwin, THE LIGHT OF THE NATIONS, Evangelical Renewal and Advance in the Nineteenth Century, Exeter, 1965.
Orr, J. Edwin, THE SECOND EVANGELICAL AWAKENING IN BRITAIN, (the 1859 Revival), London, 1949.
Ottman, F. C., J. WILBUR CHAPMAN, New York, 1920.
Phillips, D. M., EVAN ROBERTS, Welsh Revivalist, London, 1923.
Pollock, J. C., MOODY: A BIOGRAPHICAL PORTRAIT, London, 1963.
Ramsay, J. C., JOHN WILBUR CHAPMAN, New York, 1962.
Rees, Thomas, HISTORY OF PROTESTANT NONCONFORMITY IN WALES, London, 1861.
Reid, J. M., MISSIONS AND MISSIONARY SOCIETY: METHODIST EPISCOPAL CHURCH, New York, 3 Volumes, 1895-1896.
Reynolds, Charles, PUNJAB PIONEER, the Life of Dr. Edith Brown; New York, 1969.
Rice, Edwin Wilbur, THE SUNDAY SCHOOL MOVEMENT AND AMERICAN SUNDAY SCHOOL UNION, Philadelphia, 1927.
Richter, Julius, INDISCHE MISSIONSGESCHICHTE, Gütersloh, 1924.
Sandall, Robert, THE HISTORY OF THE SALVATION ARMY, Volume I, London, 1947.

Scharpff, Paulus, GESCHICHTE DER EVANGELISATION, Giessen, 1964.

Seldes, Gilbert, THE STAMMERING CENTURY, New York, 1928.

Shedd, C. P., HISTORY OF THE WORLD'S ALLIANCE OF YOUNG MEN'S CHRISTIAN ASSOCIATIONS, London, 1955.

Shedd, Clarence P., TWO CENTURIES OF STUDENT CHRISTIAN MOVEMENTS, New York, 1934.

Sherring, M. A., THE INDIAN CHURCH DURING THE GREAT REBELLION, London, 1859.

Sigston, James, A MEMOIR OF THE LIFE AND MINISTRY OF WILLIAM BRAMWELL, London, 1820.

Sloan, W. B., THESE SIXTY YEARS: THE KESWICK CONVENTION, London, 1935.

Smith, G. A., THE LIFE OF HENRY DRUMMOND, New York, 1898.

Smith, T. L., REVIVALISM AND SOCIAL REFORM, New York, 1957.

Speer, William, THE GREAT REVIVAL OF 1800, Philadelphia, 1872.

Sprague, William B., LECTURES ON REVIVALS OF RELIGION, New York, 1833.

Stephenson, George M., THE RELIGIOUS ASPECTS OF SWEDISH IMMIGRATION, Minneapolis, 1932.

Stewart, I. R., A SPLENDID OPTIMIST, Edinburgh, 1952.

Strickland, A. B., THE GREAT AMERICAN REVIVAL, Cincinnati, 1934.

Sweet, William Warren, REVIVALISM IN AMERICA: ITS RISE, PROGRESS, AND DECLINE, New York, 1945.

Thacher, Peter, A BRIEF ACCOUNT OF THE SOCIETY FOR PROPAGATING THE GOSPEL AMONG INDIANS AND OTHERS IN NORTH AMERICA, Boston, 1790.

Thomssen, G. M., SAMUEL HEBICH OF INDIA, Mangalore, 1915.

Tippet, Alan R., PEOPLE MOVEMENTS IN SOUTHERN POLYNESIA, Chicago, 1971.

Tracy, J., HISTORY OF THE AMERICAN BOARD OF COMMIS- SIONERS FOR FOREIGN MISSIONS, New York, 1842.

Trevelyan, George M., ENGLISH SOCIAL HISTORY, London, 1944.

Vedder, Henry C., A SHORT HISTORY OF THE BAPTISTS, Philadelphia, 1907.

Watt, Hugh, THOMAS CHALMERS AND THE DISRUPTION, Edin- burgh, 1943.

Wanless, William, AN AMERICAN DOCTOR AT WORK IN INDIA, New York, 1932.

Wayland, Francis, MEMOIR OF THE LIFE OF ADONIRAM JUDSON, Boston, 1853.

Webb, Sidney & Beatrice, A HISTORY OF TRADE UNIONISM, London, 1894.

Webster, James, THE REVIVAL IN MANCHURIA, London, 1910.

Weigle, Luther A., AMERICAN IDEALISM, New Haven, 1928.

Wesley, Charles H., RICHARD ALLEN: APOSTLE OF FREEDOM, Washington, 1935.

Westin, Gunnar, GEORGE SCOTT OCH HANS VERKSAMHET I SVERIGE, Stockholm, 2 Volumes, 1928-1929.

Whitney, Janet, ELIZABETH FRY, QUAKER HEROINE, Boston, 1936.

Woodson, Carter G., THE HISTORY OF THE NEGRO CHURCH, Washington, 2nd edition, 1921.

Young and Ashton, BRITISH SOCIAL WORK IN THE NINETEENTH CENTURY, London, 1936.